CHARTER SCHOOLS

Palgrave Studies in Urban Education

Series Editors: Alan R. Sadovnik and Susan F. Semel

CHARTER SCHOOLS

FROM REFORM IMAGERY TO REFORM REALITY

JEANNE M. POWERS

First published in 2009 by
PALGRAVE MACMILLAN®
in the United States—a division of St. Martin's Press LLC,
175 Fifth Avenue, New York, NY 10010.

Where this book is distributed in the UK, Europe and the rest of the world,
this is by Palgrave Macmillan, a division of Macmillan Publishers Limited,
registered in England, company number 785998, of Houndmills, Basing-
stoke, Hampshire RG21 6XS.

Palgrave Macmillan is the global academic imprint of the above companies and has companies and representatives throughout the world.

Palgrave® and Macmillan® are registered trademarks in the United States,
the United Kingdom, Europe and other countries.

ISBN: 978–0–230–60627–2

Library of Congress Cataloging-in-Publication Data

Powers, Jeanne M.
    Charter schools : from reform imagery to reform reality / by Jeanne
M. Powers.
        p. cm.—(Palgrave studies in urban education)
    Includes bibliographical references and index.
    ISBN 978–0–230–60627–2
    1. Charter schools—United States. I. Title.

LB2806.36.P69 2009
371.01—dc22   2008050341

A catalogue record of the book is available from the British Library.

Design by Newgen Imaging Systems (P) Ltd., Chennai, India.

First edition: June 2009

10 9 8 7 6 5 4 3 2 1

Printed in the United States of America.

To the teachers, parents, and
students at Hilltop Charter School,
Hearts and Hands Community School, and
Inspiration School.

CONTENTS

TABLES AND FIGURE

Tables

Figure

Series Editors' Foreword

Jeanne M. Powers's book *Charter Schools: From Reform Imagery to Reform Reality* is an important addition to research on charter schools, which for the most part has been ideological and often simplistic. The charter school debate, exemplified by the controversies surrounding the American Federation of Teachers study, which argued that traditional district schools outperform charter schools, revolved around methodological issues concerning research design, selection bias, and other empirical questions. Although these methodological debates are crucial to understanding differences between charter schools and district schools, too often these discussions have been driven by ideological rather than social scientific criteria. Moreover, these discussions usually define success by student and school achievement data, without analyzing the historical, sociological, and organizational contexts of different types of schools.

Powers has provided a corrective to much of this literature through a detailed analysis of the ways in which organizational context, school processes, philosophy, and mission affect the ways in which charter schools function. More importantly, she demonstrates how tensions between mission, capacity, and implementation provide keys to understanding the ways in which charter schools develop and to what degree they are able to implement their goals.

Through detailed and theoretically and methodologically rigorous case studies of three different types of charter schools, Powers demonstrates the complexities of charter school reform. She reminds us that school reform is locally situated and that charter schools, like district public schools, are not monolithic, but rather must be understood in relation to their specific organizational contexts. Nonetheless, drawing upon her rich ethnographic insights, she teases out a number of important themes that these schools have in common.

Powers uses a variety of existing data on charter schools to provide a larger context for her case studies. Her book supports previous research that shows charter schools are similar to district public schools, as there are excellent ones, good ones, mediocre ones, and truly abysmal ones. Her conclusions indicate that the simplistic arguments on both sides of the charter school debate—for advocates that charter schools, freed from the bureaucratic constraints of the district bureaucracy, are more effective in improving student achievement, especially for low-income children—for critics, that charter schools drain necessary resources from district schools, "cream" their best students and most involved families, and are part of a larger school choice movement to privatize education and weaken the power of teacher unions—are just that, inadequate analyses of far more complicated processes.

We are at a crossroads in educational reform, particularly in urban districts. We write this on the morning of the Presidential election. In the coming year, No Child Left Behind will be reauthorized in some form. Race- and social class-based achievement gaps that characterize urban schools and whose elimination has been an important goal of NCLB continue to be difficult to reduce. Numerous reforms, including standards-based reforms, school finance reforms, and continuing attempts to expand charter schools and voucher programs will continue to be points of contention about how to most effectively solve problems of educational inequality. As critics of school-based reform, such as Jean Anyon and David Berliner, correctly point out, such reforms will be limited in the absence of larger political and economic reforms. Nonetheless, as numerous studies demonstrate, teachers and schools can and do make a difference, and school level policy must also be a part of improving urban schools. This book reminds us of the complexities of school-based reforms and the differences between rhetoric and success. It is an important addition to the Palgrave Series on Urban Education, the literature on charter schools in particular and urban school reform in general.

ALAN R. SADOVNIK AND SUSAN F. SEMEL

ACKNOWLEDGMENTS

Writing a book is a long process, and I have many people to thank who have supported me on this journey. Joseph G. Jorgensen at the University of California, Irvine, was my first mentor in graduate school and I will always be grateful to him for introducing me to the promise and possibilities of social science research. Bud Mehan, Maria Charles, and Stephen Cornell deserve special recognition as mentors who have gone above and beyond the course of duty. Alan Sadovnik and Susan Semel have been important sources of advice as well as fine company. Early financial support for this project was provided by the AERA/Spencer Fellowship, a UC Presidents Dissertation Year Fellowship, a Mentoring Grant awarded to Hugh B. Mehan by the Spencer Foundation, and the Department of Sociology at the University of California, San Diego.

I have also been incredibly fortunate to have an amazing group of friends from graduate school: Karen Buerkle, Susan Dimock, Joshua Dunsby, Rod Ferguson, Shannon McMullen, Maria Martinez-Cosio, and Marisa Smith. I met Becky Fino and Jayne Henn along the way and I am grateful that they welcomed me into their circle of friends. My colleagues at Arizona State University also deserve special recognition for their friendship and intellectual support: David Berliner, Ursula Casanova, Arnold Danzig, Gustavo Fischman, David Garcia, Gene Glass, Michele Moses, Kimberly Scott, and Terrence Wiley. Gina Pazzaglia and Emily Ackman provided able research assistance.

Deep thanks also go to my family. My parents, James and Jeanne Powers, have kept me grounded and provided indispensable encouragement and support over the years. My brother Jim and his wife Marcia can always be counted on for their fine sense of humor and the occasional pun. Their daughter, my niece Sarah, is a joy. Although my grandfather, William J. Powers, Sr., passed away sixteen years ago, I know that he would have been proud to see this book in print, and so I also dedicate this book to his memory. My uncle, William J. Powers, Jr., deserves special thanks for being an important part of my life. I also thank Pat Cronin for her friendship and hospitality. Finally, the last word goes to my partner, Carl Hermanns, whose patience, love, and support keep me going, and whose commitment to social justice continues to inspire me. I look forward to the next adventure.

INTRODUCTION: CHARTER SCHOOLS IN THE REFORM IMAGINATION

Charter schools are not only diverse in type and mission but also appeal to proponents across the political spectrum with divergent—and often competing—agendas for reforming public education. Yet there is another interesting feature of the charter school movement worth exploring in. Charter schools are schools of choice organized around a theory of deregulation. In the policy talk about charter school reform, charter school organizers will be empowered to create "innovative" schools based on the principles defined in their charters because they are freed from the stifling regulations that conventional public schools are required to follow. A key assumption of the policy arguments for charter schools is that the relaxation of formal external controls on schools—that is, reducing the regulations schools must comply with—will foster education reform that will be driven primarily by forces within schools. In more elaborated versions of charter school policy talk, this groundswell of activity on the part of individual schools will have a broader and more systemic impact on student achievement and education reform. Some charter school policy talk links the themes outlined above by drawing on the discourses of business: Expanding school choice through charter schools will foster school improvement because schools will have to compete for students, thus creating an education "market."

Because they are being implemented within the highly decentralized system of public education in the United States, in practice charter schools are an odd hybrid. On one hand, charter schools are enabled by state level legislation that empowers agencies such as school districts or postsecondary educational institutions to approve individual charter schools. On the other, the ultimate initiative for charter school reform is highly local because it depends on the energy and political capital of charter school organizers (see, for example, Slayton, 2002; Stambach and Becker, 2006). To capture this dynamic, as an organizing frame for the analyses presented throughout this book, I draw on David Tyack and Larry Cuban's (1995) distinction among the three phases of policymaking: policy talk, policy action, and implementation. *Policy talk* is the "diagnosis of problems and the advocacy of solutions" (40). *Policy action* is the second stage of education reform that occurs when reforms are adopted. Finally, *implementation* refers to reforms that are enacted. These three phases of the policymaking process are important to distinguish, because proposals for education reform may remain of policy talk and never be implemented. In this book, I begin with the policy talk of charter school reform to frame my analysis of the different dimensions of charter school implementation. How do features of the policy context shape: (1) how policy talk becomes policy action; and (2) implementation. Is there a match between the goals driving charter school reform and charter schools in practice?

What Are Charter Schools?

Charter schools are *public schools* established by a contract between charter school organizers and a public agency, usually a local school district or a state agency such as a state board of education or a state charter school board. In some states, public colleges and universities are also authorized to grant charters. In exchange for being exempt from some of the state regulations conventional public schools are required to comply with (the extent varies by state), school organizers agree to be held accountable for the set of educational outcomes outlined in the school's charter. The charter functions as a mission statement and outlines how the school is to operate. There are two main types of charter schools, conversion charter schools and start-up charter schools. Conversion charter schools are existing public schools that have elected to convert to charter school status. In some states, private schools have been allowed to convert to public charter schools. Start-up charter schools are new schools created under the auspices of charter school legislation.

Charter schools are also a form of school choice. In general, students can enroll in charter schools regardless of where they live. Other forms of public school choice include magnet schools and open enrollment policies. Developed in the 1970s as a voluntary integration strategy in an attempt to avoid forced busing, magnet schools offer specialized education programs meant to attract students outside a school's attendance area. In doing so, magnet schools were intended to foster racial balance across schools. Some states and districts have open enrollment policies that allow students to enroll in public schools other than the schools they are assigned based on the neighborhood they reside in. Another form of school choice is school voucher programs. Students participating in a voucher program are provided with funds that they can use to pay tuition at a private school. While many voucher programs are privately funded, seven states and the District of Columbia provide vouchers funded with public dollars (National Conference of State Legislators, 2008).[1]

The charter school concept has been widely attributed to educator Ray Budde, who initially conceived of charter schools as a "school within a school" model based on an educational charter between a group of teachers and their local school board (Mulholland and Amsler, 1992). Budde's idea was taken to a national audience in 1988 by Albert Shanker, President of the American Federation of Teachers, who endorsed and elaborated the idea in a variety of speeches and newspaper columns. According to Joe Nathan's (1996) history of the charter school movement, Minnesota State Senator Ember Reichgott heard Shanker speak at a conference on reforming public schools. After the conference, Reichgott and four other conference attendees worked together to create charter school legislation for the state of Minnesota, which became law in 1991. Since then, charter school legislation has spread across the country. As of September 2006, forty states and the District of Columbia have charter school laws. Two of Reichgott's coauthors, Nathan and Ted Kolderie, have since become nationally prominent proponents of charter schools.

Charter Schools as Policy Talk

Charter school reform has become one of the most visible education reform proposals of the past two decades. An important backdrop for charter school reform is the long and sustained sense that public education was in crisis, which began roughly around the time that *A Nation at Risk* was released in 1983.[2] Arguably, public education has been one of the pressing political concerns of the past twenty-five years. Gusfield's (1981) distinction between social problems and public problems is useful here: "All social problems do not become public ones. They do not become matters of conflict or controversy in the arenas of public action. They do not eventuate in agencies to secure or in movements to work for their resolution" (5). Most charter school policy talk frames charter schools as a solution to the public problem of a failing K-12 public school system. The examples below illustrate this phenomenon.

From 1995 to 1998, a subcommittee of the House Committee on Education and the Workforce sponsored a series of twenty-two hearings structured around the theme, "what works and what is wasted in education." The overarching goal of the hearings, entitled "Education at a Crossroads," was to examine the federal role in education. The subcommittee visited twenty-six educational institutions and heard from 237 witnesses in the process, many of whom were associated with charter schools and organizations advocating charter schools or other market-driven choice programs, such as publicly and privately funded voucher programs. A large section of the final report is entitled "The Federal Role in Education: Bureaucracy vs. Children"(Education at a Crossroads, 1998). Subsections of this section evoke similar themes: "It Takes a Village to Complete the Paperwork" and "Baywatch and Jerry Springer: Your Tax Dollars at Work." In the testimony provided by participants, charter schools were framed as a beacon of light in an inefficient and overly bureaucratic system.

In *Redesigning American Education*, prominent education researcher James Coleman and his colleagues (1997) used the results of their analyses of the National Education Longitudinal Survey to make the case for "output-driven" schools, as opposed to "administratively-driven" schools. Administratively driven schools are hierarchically organized. Most of the decision-making occurs at the school district, and the school principal has some, albeit highly constrained, authority. In contrast, output-driven schools are evaluated by how well they met specific academic standards that were determined by an external organization. Coleman and his colleagues (1997) argued that these external standards will generate strong achievement-oriented norms that will have a positive effect on student achievement if they are coupled to (1) procedures for evaluating how well participants meet the standards; and (2) a system of rewards and sanctions linked to the results of the evaluations. Coleman and his colleagues were writing at a time when charter school legislation was spreading across the country—fifteen states passed charter school legislation between 1995 and 1996 (Dale and DeSchryver, 1997). At the time, Coleman (1997) identified charter schools as one of three education reforms that had the potential to create the type of output-driven school he envisioned on a large scale.[3]

In 1999, both the Education Commission of the States and Hugh Price, the president of the Urban League, advocated widespread conversion of public schools to charter schools (the latter focused specifically on inner city schools). Price's proposal, which appeared in *Education Week*, argued for both strong state power and strong school power (Price, 1999). According to Price, once the state imposes high standards for all children and equalizes educational resources across the state, schools should be "charterized" and as such given wide discretion to meet those standards. In this system, the school district's role is accreditation via the power to award and revoke charters. A *Wall Street Journal* editorial strongly endorsed both proposals as examples of the growing popularity of choice and competition, which were framed as solutions now being embraced by "establishment entities" for the country's "failing" system of public education ("Moment of Choice," 2000, A22).

More recently, the initial version of President George W. Bush's (2001) education plan, *No Child Left Behind* (NCLB), proposed a new "charter option" for states and districts, which would have extended the charter school principle beyond individual schools. In return for meeting the standards outlined in a performance agreement with the U.S. Department of Education, which included accountability for academic achievement, states and districts would be freed from categorical program requirements. In the final version of the NCLB legislation that was passed by Congress in 2002, charter schools were positioned as an option for students in underperforming schools. Students whose schools are identified as underperforming based on the standards outlined in their state's accountability program must be provided with the option to transfer to other schools within their districts, including to charter schools. In addition, the law outlines a timetable for interventions within schools identified as underperforming, which could ultimately entail reorganizing these schools as charter schools. Charter schools are also the centerpiece of the school choice provisions of NCLB. School districts are required to use federal funding to expand the options for choice within their boundaries (e.g., charter schools and magnet schools).

Finally, in October 2005, in the wake of Hurricane Katrina, the New Orleans school board voted to allow its first public schools to reopen after the storm as charter schools (Gewertz, 2005). One of the factors driving this decision was an impending state takeover of New Orleans public schools. The New Orleans School District had been struggling with academic failure and financial mismanagement long before the storm. Reopening its schools as charter schools allowed the district to retain some control of its schools when the state legislature voted to allow the state to take over the district's schools a month later (Robelen, 2005). A year later, thirty-two of the fifty-six schools that had reopened since Hurricane Katrina were charter schools (Abramson, 2006). What this brief discussion suggests is that policymakers of all stripes and political persuasions believe that reorganizing schools as charter schools will result in sweeping changes in education practice. This belief persists even though research on charter schools suggests a much more mixed picture of the efficacy of charter school reform (Lubienski, 2003). I address this issue in more detail in chapter 6.

Data and Methods

In this book, I bring together multiple sources of data and research methods as a way to analyze charter school reform. Quantitative analysis of large-scale survey data, policy analysis, and ethnographic case studies of three charter schools in an urban school district in California are combined to create a nuanced picture of charter school reform. I use these different sources of data to address: (1) how policy dynamics shape charter schools as organizations; and (2) the extent to which charter schools differ from conventional public schools.

The Quantitative Data

An important source of data on public schools in the United States is the Common Core of Data (CCD) collected yearly by the National Center for Education Statistics. The CCD includes basic enrollment, staffing, and student demographic information. Starting in 1998–1999, the CCD provided a variable indicating whether or not a school is a charter school. I use the most recent years of the CCD to provide an overview of the charter school movement nationally.

Another NCES-sponsored survey, the Schools and Staffing Survey (SASS), provides much more detailed data about schools. Although the Schools and Staffing Survey has been collected in multiple administrations starting in 1987, I use the 1999–2000 data here because it has combined a nationally representative sample of conventional public schools with almost the full population of charter schools operating in 1998–1999. In both cases, surveys of principals, teachers, and schools offer researchers a wealth of information about the two types of schools. Some of the topics covered by the SASS include: teachers' and principals' experience, training and professional development, school climate, leadership and decision-making, and accountability. As a result, the SASS provides a unique opportunity to compare charter schools and conventional public schools. The dataset includes all available charter schools (N = 890) and all conventional public schools in the sample located in the twenty-eight states with operating charter schools in 1998–1999 (N = 4726). The sample weights included in the SASS dataset were used to appropriately weight the data to produce estimates for the full populations of both types of schools, utilizing the balanced repeated replication (BRR bootstrap) method in the AM statistical software package. The Ns for the weighted samples are 1,010 charter schools and 54,266 conventional public schools.

The Ethnographic Case Studies

I also draw from three ethnographic case studies conducted in an urban school district in California in 1999 and 2000 using a purposive sampling strategy. First, I created a typology of charter schools by analyzing California charters available through October 1998. Because they outlined the philosophical and organizational rationales for their respective charter schools, the school charters were an important starting point.[4] While clearly there is a considerable amount of diversity within the population of charter schools, as I compared the statements of mission and intent in the charters, there were two broad types of schools related to the types of students attending the school: (1) schools that serve a traditional student population; and (2) schools that serve a nontraditional student population.

Schools that serve a traditional student population target students who would otherwise attend a conventional "brick and mortar" public or private school. There were three distinct types of schools in this first category: restructuring schools, community-based charters, and corporate model schools. These three types varied along the following characteristics: the primary actors identified as spearheading the reform; the degree of decentralization; and the degree to which the schools were reorganizing around the implementation of a specific curricular model. While in practice there is a great deal of overlap across the three types, these categories provided an initial analytical frame for sorting out possible similarities and differences in the three case study schools, which were enacting different ideological strands of education reform.

In *Restructuring schools*, teachers were the primary agents of organizational change. For the majority of these schools, converting to charter status was framed as a component of implementing site-based management, a form of decentralization. The term "restructuring" was used in the schools' charters to describe a range of practices that reorganizing as charter schools would enable: changes in curriculum and instructional practices; student assessment; staff selection, evaluation and professional development; increased control over budgetary decisions; school scheduling (team-teaching, looping, and shared planning time); governance (site-based decision-making and increased parent and community involvement); arrangements for student groupings (multiage and/or heterogeneous groups) and class sizes; and expanding school services to include health and social service provision.

Community-based charter schools were initiated by a group of community members, often parents with the support of teachers or other educators and/or a community organization, who came together to create a school in response to local conditions. Proponents tended to view the charter school as a way to implement a particular educational model (e.g., Waldorf education, Montessori) and to structure the curriculum around a thematic area such as arts education or, in the case of a community organization, to extend its model into an educational setting. Thus, the argument for local control or decentralization was more tightly focused around implementing the particular type of education program described in the charter.

Corporate model schools were charter schools organized by either non-profit or for-profit organizations that were structured around a business model. A parent company or organization served as the "corporate head-quarters" for multiple charter school sites, which implemented a standard curriculum and organizational structure at all of the sites. The parent companies also tended to draw upon the discourse of business in framing their goals.

Schools that served nontraditional student populations attracted students that left the education system in one of two ways: (1) students and parents who have affirmatively opted out of the public school system, such as home schoolers; and (2) students disenfranchised from the education system (i.e., "drop-outs"). The two schools in this category corresponded to their respective student populations: home school charters and charter schools for at-risk students. Both types tended to be organized around an independent study model, although some combined independent study with classroom-based activities.

Each of these "ideal-types" presented distinct rationales for either con-verting to charter school status, in the case of existing public schools, or creating new schools, in the case of "start-up" charter schools. Because my main interest was to understand charter schools as a reform aimed at changing the conventional model of schooling, I selected three charter schools located in a single urban school district, Geary Unified School District, to represent the three types of schools that served traditional student populations for the in-depth case studies. The three case study schools were all elementary schools and were similar in size (ranging from 300 to 500 students). All three served predominantly minority or low-income student populations. Holding these factors relatively constant allowed me to explore the similarities and differences across the three schools. Table I.1 summarizes the school types and the case study schools chosen to represent them. In the section that follows, I provide more detailed descriptions of the schools and the district context.

The data gathered for the case studies of Hilltop Charter School and Inspiration School took place in the winter and spring of 1999; at Hilltop Charter School I followed a change in leadership at the school through December of 1999. The fieldwork at Hearts and Hands Community School took place during the winter and spring of 2000. I spent approxi-mately two to three days per week at each school, observing classes, attend-ing meetings and other school events, and observing the informal spaces of school life. I also attended local and state charter school events over the course of the study. Fieldnotes from these events were created and analyzed. In addition, I conducted 58 formal interviews with a range of participants: 8 activists, 38 teachers and staff members at charter schools, 6 administrators,

Table I.1 Summary of School Types

	Restructuring	Community-based	Corporate Model
Case study school	Hilltop Charter School	Hearts and Hands Community School	Inspiration School
Primary actors	Teachers	Parents and community members	Corporation (nonprofit or for-profit)
Degree of decentralization	Low	Low	High
Degree of organizing around specific curricular model	None; change in technology of teaching	Specific educational model	Standardized by corporate headquarters

3 district employees, and 3 parents. I also drew on contemporaneous newspaper articles and school documents, particularly in the analyses of Hilltop Charter School and Hearts and Hands Community School. The names of the schools, the district, and the identities of the participants in this study have been masked. In addition, I masked the names of other organizations discussed in the analysis when necessary to preserve the confidentiality of the schools and/or district.

The Schools and the District Context

Hilltop Charter School
Hilltop Charter School was located a few blocks south of one of the main streets traversing the city, which begins about sixty blocks to the west in a more upscale area of town populated by eclectic boutiques, coffeehouses, and restaurants. Closer to the school, these retail establishments gave way to small ethnic niche businesses that catered to the immigrant populations living nearby. The school sat on a hill in a quiet residential area. Most of the houses and yards in the area immediately surrounding the school were well-maintained. The campus consisted of portable classrooms, a series of trailer-like buildings that, despite the misleading name, were permanent structures. Like the surrounding neighborhood, the grounds of the school were well-kept. Carefully manicured lawns and ornamental flowers and shrubs separated rows of buildings at the center of the school, although some of the classrooms at the school's perimeter were surrounded by either concrete or dirt pathways. A large marquee at the front of the school announced the week's events, and most of the windows were

decorated with colorful posters, student artwork, and/or signs welcoming parents. In front of the main office, a display case displayed pictures of popular school events: a literacy slumber party held at a major downtown hotel; the yearly Halloween Carnival organized by parents, teachers, and community members; and the annual Multicultural Fair. The school was surrounded by three playground areas: one small fenced in area outside the kindergarten and early primary classrooms, and two others outside the primary and elementary classrooms.

Hilltop Charter School had a long history in the neighborhood. The physical plant was more than forty years old. The school operated as a comprehensive K-6 school until it was converted to a school that served students with special needs. In the mid-1980s the school was closed, until it reopened in its current incarnation in September 1992, the same month California's charter school legislation became law. Two factors sparked an interest in reopening the school at the district level. The first was the rising student population in the surrounding attendance areas. The second was the need to create a model for school reform; the school received one of the first charters granted by the Geary Unified School District in 1993. Since reopening, the school served as an overflow school for students bused to the school from a central city neighborhood with high concentrations of poverty, underemployment, and high rates of residential mobility. Over the years, close to 90 percent of the school's students qualified for reduced or free lunch, which made the school eligible to participate in the school-wide Title I program. More than half of the students served by the school were English language learners (ELLs), the majority of whom were Spanish speakers who were taught in bilingual classrooms. About one-third of the school's students were ELL students taught in sheltered classrooms, which provided additional instructional support for English learners.

Hearts and Hands Community School
Located to the north and slightly east of Hilltop Charter School, Hearts and Hands Community School was a relatively small school comprised of a permanent structure and a series of portable classrooms located near a college campus and a block north of one of the main streets running west to east across the city, known locally as the "Strip." Thirty blocks to the west, the Strip had a reputation as one of the least desirable areas of town. However, in the ten-block radius surrounding the school, there were markers of development associated with a college town. A newly opened branch of a major supermarket and a Starbucks Coffee were located a few blocks away.

One-third of the school's lot was set apart from the rest by a fence and a hill; three classrooms in this area housed the sixth grade and the "junior high."

At the rear of these buildings the second through fifth grade portable classrooms formed an "L" around a playground area in the middle of the lot that contained a jungle gym and basketball hoops. At the far corner of the lot, the main building formed another "L" shape, which completed the rectangular configuration of the buildings. This building housed two each of kindergarten and first grade classrooms, the main office, the support team (the counseling center, nurse's office, the motor lab, and the resource room), the auditorium/cafeteria, and the library. Outside the library was the newly refurbished kindergarten play yard, a fenced-in area that boasted a new awning, which shaded a sandbox, a picnic area, climbing equipment, and a small man-made "pond," which was a small hole rimmed with stones. A number of gardens designated by grade were maintained around the perimeter of the school.

Approved by the Board of Education at the end of 1993 to begin operation the following academic year, Hearts and Hands Community School was the third charter school and the first "start-up" charter school approved by the Geary Unified School District. Hearts and Hands Community School was also one of a small but steady number of public schools—many of which were charter schools—based on the Waldorf school pedagogy and philosophy. Like Hilltop Charter School, Hearts and Hands Community School was also an overflow school for the central city area. In 1999–2000, 71 percent of the school's population qualified for reduced or free lunch, which was higher than the district average of 63 percent. However, unlike Hilltop Charter School, Hearts and Hands Community School served a much smaller—and declining—population of English language learners (ELLs). By 1999–2000, 18 percent of the students at the school were ELLs. The ELL students were integrated into regular classrooms and taught English as a Second Language as pullout groups by their classroom teachers, a few of whom are bilingual. A floating Spanish teacher provided additional instructional support for Spanish speakers and also Spanish instruction for English speakers. In addition to the music and physical education teachers one might expect to find at most other public elementary schools, because the school was a "Waldorf-inspired" school, there were also teachers on the staff who provided instruction in gardening and handwork.

Inspiration School

Inspiration School was housed on the grounds of a faith-based organization located south of Parkway Boulevard in a neighborhood about six miles southwest of the redeveloped downtown. Parkway Boulevard begins slightly southwest of the main downtown area. Most sections of Parkway Boulevard—even those closest to the downtown—were largely excluded from redevelopment efforts. Traveling west from downtown Parkway Boulevard, one passed through a number of working class and poor communities crowded into mobile homes and small bungalow style houses. Although small, many of these houses were well kept and neatly landscaped, although in some areas less so than in others. Small businesses in storefronts or older strip malls dotted the landscape, although some newer businesses were emerging in recently refurbished buildings.

In this setting, the residential area that surrounded the faith-based organization and the school it housed was an oasis of middle-class prosperity. In addition to the neatly landscaped bungalow homes, there was also a newer complex of townhouses located on the side streets off of Parkway Boulevard. The only detail that betrayed the neighborhood's age was the power lines that buzzed loudly overhead. The physical plant of the faith-based organization housing the school suggested long-term institutional stability. Located a few blocks south of Parkway Boulevard and perched at the top of a large hill, the grounds offered an expansive view of the area and, in the distance to the west, the downtown skyscrapers. A sign etched in stone in the front of the main building proclaimed: "Reaching the lost and teaching the saved to serve." Two plaques on the building's foundation told the organization's history. Founded in the 1960s, the building was renovated in the 1980s under the direction of Pastor Martin. Fifteen years later, Pastor Martin was one of the people who helped found the charter school. The faith-based organization's mission, described on its web site, was: "educational empowerment, economic development, social improvement, and political involvement." The school's other partner, Educational Enterprise Corporation, a not-for-profit educational management organization (EMO), was less visible on campus but was also an important presence in school life.

The kindergarten and first grade classrooms were housed in the basement of the main building on the compound. Another two-story building was located across a small playground with a brightly colored play structure and a paved area with a few basketball hoops. The second through sixth grade classrooms occupied the top floor; the lower floor housed the school's administrative office, the administrative offices for the faith-based organization, an auditorium, and a print shop. The school was heavily weighted toward the lower grades. There were three classrooms each for the kindergarten through third grades—a result of the way the school was expanding and also state-mandated class-size reduction, which limited K-3 classrooms to twenty students. There was one classroom each for the fourth, fifth, and sixth grades. In the school's first year of operation, the 1997–1998 school year, it served just over 150 students. Of these, 97 percent were drawn from a single "disadvantaged" minority group.[5] Thirty-eight percent of the students were eligible for reduced/free lunch.

None of the students were classified as ELLs. In its second year, Inspiration School expanded to serve 300 students. However, the demographics of the student population remained largely the same, with the exception that the percentage of low-income students attending the school increased to approximately 50 percent of the student population. Thus, compared to the two other schools in this study, Inspiration School served a relatively advantaged population of students.[6]

The District Context

Finally, turning to the district context, the Geary Unified School District is a large urban school district located in California. The district's demographics reflected trends that urban school districts have been experiencing across the country: a growing school-age population, declining numbers of white students, a rising immigrant population, and increasing numbers of white voters without children (for a discussion of some of the political implications of these changes see Glass, 2008). For example, 1982–1983— the year *A Nation at Risk* was released—was the last year that the district's schools served more white students than nonwhite students. The Geary Unified School District serves a broad range of communities, ranging from the largely white and middle to upper-middle class communities in the northern section of the district to the predominately minority and low-income communities in the south. The district is bisected by a major freeway, which has become a powerful physical and symbolic boundary between these areas.

Geary Unified has long had a reputation for being a reform-oriented district. John Tower, the superintendent hired in 1998, cemented this reputation. While I will discuss the district context in more detail in chapter 4, the reform effort underway in the district at the time of the fieldwork is of particular note. A noneducator, Tower hired a Chief Instructional Officer and together they embarked on a large scale systemic reform initiative that to some degree influenced all schools in the district, including the charter schools described here. The entire district was reoriented around teaching and learning. The central administration was reorganized, pared down, and charged with a massive professional development campaign. All of the schools in the district were divided into geographically and economically diverse "learning communities" headed by an instructional leader who provided professional support and development for principals. In turn, principals were expected to provide instructional leadership to the teachers at their school sites.

In the first phase of the reform, a district-wide focus on literacy was instituted. Based on research conducted in New Zealand schools, the

Balanced Literacy approach combines a variety of teaching techniques that acts as a scaffold to the reading process for students. Schools were expected to implement a three-hour literacy block in the mornings, during which teachers were to focus on literacy using four main techniques: Read Alouds, Shared Reading, Guided Reading, and Independent Reading. Read Alouds and Shared Reading are whole-class activities. While Read Alouds are self-explanatory, in Shared Reading all students must be able to see the text being read and participate in reading out loud. In both of these activities the teacher's role is to model reading strategies for students. In Guided Reading and Independent Reading, the teacher works with students in small groups and one-on-one, respectively, to assist students as they practice the strategies they learned in Read Alouds and Shared Reading. Taken as a whole, the goal of the Balanced Literacy techniques is to transfer the responsibility for the reading task from the teacher to the students.

In December 1999, a new initiative to end social promotion was unveiled, which codified and expanded many of the reforms already under-way and established a variety of programs across the district that increased the instructional time for the lowest performing students in literacy and math during the regular instructional day, and in before-school, after-school, and intersession programs. This comprehensive effort at reform, entitled *The Plan for Student Learning*, was significant because it aimed to get all of the district's schools to use a common conceptual language and set of practices around the teaching and learning of literacy. As the reform unfolded, the district leadership added math and science initiatives. In contrast, in the policy talk around charter schools, the hallmark of char-ter school reform is the individuality of the schools that are created under its auspices. I explore the impact of this systemic reform initiative on the charter schools in this study in chapter 4.

The Plan of the Book

Chapter 1 expands upon the discussion of policy talk, policy action, and implementation to provide an overview of the current state of charter school reform nationally. One of the main goals of the chapter is to illus-trate the wide variation in charter school reform across states. I begin by looking at variation in charter school policy talk in the states with the largest percentage share of charter school students by analyzing the state-ments of legislative intent as an indicator of the different aims of charter school reform. Next I narrow the focus to the top three chartering states, California, Arizona, and Michigan, and analyze key aspects of each state's charter school law to show the similarities and differences in policy action.

The remainder of the chapter uses data from the CCD and SASS to provide an overview of charter school reform nationally, and also within specific state contexts.

In chapter 2 I expand on the theme of state level variation through case studies of the policy dynamics that culminated in charter school legislation in three states: California, Arizona, and Missouri. I use these case studies to show how the different policy contexts in each state shaped policy action, in this case charter school legislation. In chapter 3 I look at the variation in charter school implementation at the school level through case studies of three charter schools focused around the concepts of organizational structure and school culture. These case studies provide important background for the analyses that follow in chapters 4 and 5, where I examine how aspects of the state and local policy contexts shaped the three school's trajectories. In chapter 4 I focus on school foundings while chapter 5 examines how shifts in the state policy context around assessment and accountability affected Hilltop Charter School and Inspiration School. I also focus on implementation in chapter 6, but here I am interested in understanding the relationship between policy talk and implementation. I use data from the 1999–2000 SASS to compare accountability and decision-making in charter schools and in conventional public schools.

A Brief Note on Terminology

In some sections of the analysis I compare charter schools with their other public school counterparts, which I refer to here and throughout the book as conventional public schools. I prefer the term "conventional public schools" to the term "traditional public schools" because, as the above discussion of charter school policy talk suggests, the descriptor "traditional" maps onto the dominant discourse about charter schools and thus implies that charter schools are different than conventional public schools. While some charter schools are indeed very different than conventional public schools, many are also very similar to conventional public schools. The ways and also the extent to which charter schools are different from conventional public schools are empirical questions, which I discuss in chapter 1 and address in greater detail in chapter 6. In these chapters, I often refer to the two types of schools as sectors, in the sense that they are parts or subdivisions of a larger entity—the American system of public education. Public education is, in turn, part of the public sector, or a set of goods and services that are provided by local, state, and federal governments.

CHAPTER ONE

MAPPING THE TERRAIN OF
CHARTER SCHOOL REFORM

In this chapter I provide an overview of charter school reform, drawing on the data from the CCD and the SASS described in the Introduction. During the 2005–2006 academic year, 3690 charter schools were operating in 40 states and the District of Columbia, and enrolled just over 1 million students, or 2 percent of all public school students.[1] Not surprisingly, as the state with the most public school students, California had the highest share of these 1 million charter school students in 2005–2006 (19 percent), followed by Arizona, Michigan, and Florida (all approximately 9 percent). Charter school enrollment as a percentage of all public school enrollment also varies considerably across states. For example, the District of Columbia had the highest percentage of its public school students enrolled in charter schools in 2005–2006 (22 percent), followed by Arizona (8 percent) and Colorado (6 percent). With only three schools enrolling 210 students, which amounted to a fraction of the state's 1.8 million public school students, Virginia had the lowest enrollment of students in charter schools.

One of the key features of charter school reform that often gets lost in the policy talk about charter schools is an outcome of the highly decentralized structure of American public education. As I pointed out in the Introduction, charter school legislation must be passed by states. Most often this entails legislation that is created and vetted through state legislative processes, that is, a bill is passed by a state legislature that is approved by the governor. Yet this is only the first stage of charter school reform. Ultimately, how charter school reform evolves in each state depends on how charter school organizers use charter school legislation to create new schools or convert existing public (or in some cases private) schools to charter school status. The vast majority of charter schools are start-up charter schools.[2]

Charter school operators are a diverse group, ranging from grassroots community members (e.g., teachers, parents, and/or local activists) who organize around the project of creating a new school, community-based nonprofit organizations that see operating a charter school as an extension of their missions, and educational management organizations (EMOs), or companies that contract with charter holders to manage charter schools or submit charters directly to charter school sponsors for approval. Most EMOs are for-profit corporations, although there are some nonprofit EMOs, as was the case with Educational Enterprise Corporation, the EMO that ran Inspiration School.[3] State departments of education are often charged with facilitating the creation and opening of new charter schools. Likewise, the federal government has supported charter schools since 1994 through the Public Charter Schools Program. The Public Charter Schools Program provides funding for charter schools that is channeled through state departments of education. Federal funds are also used to support research on charter schools and to provide informational resources for constituents ranging from parents to education researchers. As a result, charter school reform is a coherent policy in name only and is best understood as a patchwork of policies that vary widely across states. I take up the issue of variation in state charter school laws in the two sections that follow.

The Goals of Charter School Reform

I begin by revisiting charter school policy talk, but this time with an eye toward understanding the wide range of policy goals pursued under the banner of charter school reform. To assess the different aims of charter school reform and how these vary across the states, I compare the statements of legislative intent incorporated into charter school legislation, or the introduction to a statute that describes the purpose the new law is intended to fulfill. Of the forty states with operational charter schools in 2005–2006, I chose to look more closely at the seven states that enrolled the highest percentage of the total population of students attending charter schools. Together, these seven states enrolled 70 percent of all charter school students. Of these, only Michigan's charter school legislation does not contain a statement of legislative intent.[4] In addition, because it was the first state to pass charter school legislation, and as a result its legislation became a model for other states' charter school laws, I also included the statement of legislative intent from Minnesota's charter school law. The statements of legislative intent vary widely. Some consist of one or two sentences (Arizona and Ohio) while others (Colorado, Florida) contain long lists of goals for charter school reform.

To facilitate comparison across states, I extracted the main goals for charter school reform from the statements of legislative intents, which are listed on the left hand side of table 1.1. Most of the goals could be

Table 1.1 Main Goals for Charter School Reform

	MN (1991)	CA (1992)	CO (1993)	AZ (1994)	TX (1995)	FL¹ (1996)	OH (1997)	PA (1997)
Teaching and Learning								
Improve pupil learning	√	√			√	√ (shall)		√
Improve pupil learning by creating schools with high, rigorous standards			√					
Meet high standards of student achievement						√ (g.p.)		
Improve student achievement				√		√ (shall)		
Increase learning opportunities	√	√	√		√	√ (shall)		√
Expanded learning opportunities for low-achieving students		√	√			√ (shall)		
Different/innovative teaching methods	√	√	√					√
Research-based/proven teaching methods		√						
Innovative learning methods			√		√	√ (shall)		
Establish limited experimental education programs in a deregulated setting							√	
Assessment								
Require the measurement of learning outcomes	√					√ (shall)		
Create innovative forms of measuring outcomes	√					√ (may)		
Promote the development of longitudinal analysis of student achievement				√				
Inform parents if their child is reading at grade level/gains at least a year's worth of learning for each year of charter school attendance						√ (g.p.)		

Continued

Table 1.1 Continued

	MN (1991)	CA (1992)	CO (1993)	AZ (1994)	TX (1995)	FL¹ (1996)	OH (1997)	PA (1997)
Accountability								
Establish new forms of accountability	√				√			
Change from rule-based accountability to performance-based accountability		√						
Accountable for measurable pupil outcomes		√						
Accountable for meeting state content standards or academic standards			√					√
Accountable through state assessments, longitudinal analysis of student progress, and adequate yearly progress.			√					
Promote enhanced academic success and financial efficiency by aligning responsibility with accountability						√ (g.p.)		
Provide a method to establish accountability systems								√
Professional Opportunities								
For teachers	√	√	√		√	√ (may)		√
For principals			√					
Responsibility for learning program at the school site	√	√				√ (may)		√
New employment options			√					
Responsible for the achievement results at the school site			√					
Attract new teachers to the school system					√			
Other								
Expanded choice		√	√	√	√	√ (g.p.)	√	√
Competition to stimulate improvement		√			(may)	√		
Provide an avenue for citizen participation in education			√					

Continued

Table 1.1   Continued

	MN (1991)	CA (1992)	CO (1993)	AZ (1994)	TX (1995)	FL[1] (1996)	OH (1997)	PA (1997)
Other, cont.								
Promote parent and community involvement			√					
Expand the capacity of the existing public school system						√ (may)		
Mitigate the impact of new residential dwelling units						√ (may)		

Note: [1] The parentheses distinguish whether a goal is a guiding principle (g.p.), and the purposes that the charter schools "shall" fulfill and "may" fulfill in the Florida legislation.

grouped into one of four broader categories: (1) goals related to teaching and learning; (2) goals related to assessment; (3) goals related to accountability; and (4) goals related to professional opportunities for teachers and other staff members. A final category contains a handful of goals that did not fit in the categories above and, with the exception of two (expanded choice and competition to stimulate improvement), were unique to a particular state. The eight states are listed across the top of the table in chronological order by the year their charter school legislation became law.

The columns underneath each state indicate if its statement of legislative intent contained a particular goal. Florida's charter school law is slightly different from the seven other states' charter school laws because it begins with a set of guiding principles and then differentiates between the purposes charter schools "shall" fulfill and the purposes charter schools "may" fulfill, which I also noted in table 1.1 (Florida Statutes of 2006, Title XLVII §1002.33). When relevant, a separate category indicates elaborations on a goal. For example, while six of the nine states' charter school laws note that charter schools are intended to increase learning opportunities for all students, three of these contain an additional clause stating that charter schools are specifically intended to increase learning opportunities for low-achieving students. Similarly, while five states' laws frame charter schools as a means to improve student learning, the statement of legislative intent in Colorado's charter school law makes the more forceful assertion that charter schools will "improve student learning by creating schools with high, rigorous standards for pupil performance" (Colorado Rev. Stat. of 2006, §22–30. 5–101).

I also noted variation within the categories when relevant. For example, I distinguished between student learning and student achievement. While the former seemed to reference broader learning processes, the latter seemed to focus on a specific type of learning, that is, learning that is measured on a standardized test. Only two states, Florida and Arizona, described charter schools as a method to improve student achievement; in Florida's statement of legislative intent, charter schools are intended to improve student achievement *and* student learning. Grouping the goals into broad categories allows us to see the similarities across the eight states as well as the nuances within each category.

The analysis in table 1.1 suggests that while there is a good deal of variation in the goals for charter schools across states, there is also a fair amount of consistency. Not surprisingly, seven of the eight states saw charter schools as a way to expand school choice for parents and students. After school choice, the three most widely shared goals for charter school reform were: (1) improve pupil learning; (2) increase learning opportunities for all students; and (3) expand professional opportunities for teachers. All of these goals were mentioned in six states' statements of legislative intent. Comparing across the four categories of goals, there is the most consistency in state lawmakers' views of the effects of charter schools on teaching and learning. All of the states had at least one goal for charter school reform related to teaching and learning. Colorado and Florida's statements of legislative intent had the most nuanced discussions of how charter schools will change teaching and learning. Goals related to assessment were the least common across the nine states. Only three of the nine states' statements of legislative intent outlined goals for charter schools related to assessment, and of these, Florida's was the most elaborate. One of the guiding principles of Florida's charter school law is that charter schools will "provide parents with sufficient information on whether their child is reading at grade level and whether the child gains at least a year's worth of learning for every year spent in the charter school" (Florida Statutes of 2006, Title XLVII §1002.33). In addition, charter schools are required to assess learning outcomes, and ideally charter schools will also "create innovative measuring tools" (Florida Statutes of 2006, Title XLVII §1002.33).

Six of the eight states' statements of legislative intent outlined goals for charter school reform related to accountability. However, there was a considerable amount of variation (and vagueness) in how state legislators conceptualized accountability. Only three of the states outlined what charter schools should be accountable for: measurable student outcomes (California), state content standards (Colorado), and academic standards (Pennsylvania). Most of the goals for charter schools related to accountability describe—with varying degrees of precision—the type of accountability charter school reform will foster. For example, Minnesota's charter school legislation described charter schools as a way to "establish new forms of accountability" (Minnesota Statutes 2006, Ch. 124D §10). The same goal was incorporated into Texas' charter school law four years later. However Texas' statement of legislative intent further specified that while charter schools are expected to be fiscally and academically accountable, the charter school law "may not be applied in a manner that unduly regulates the instructional methods or pedagogical innovations of charter schools" (Texas Statutes Education Code 2006, §12.001). California's statement of legislative intent was more specific in its statement that charter schools are intended to facilitate a shift from "rule-based accountability to performance-based accountability" (California Education Code of 2006, §47601). Finally, Florida's discussion of charter school accountability was the most elaborate because it linked accountability with academic and fiscal outcomes. Charter schools are intended to "promote enhanced academic success and financial efficiency by aligning responsibility with accountability" (Florida Statutes of 2006, Title XLVII §1002.33). This discussion suggests that while "accountability" is consistently invoked as an important goal of charter school reform, there is little consensus around what charter schools will be accountable for and how they will be held accountable. I will return to this issue in chapter 6.

The statements of legislative intent provide insight into state lawmakers' goals for charter schools. They also illustrate how the policy talk around charter school reform coheres around a set of common goals (school choice, teaching and learning, accountability, and professional opportunities), yet how each of these goals is conceptualized varies considerably across state contexts.

Variation in Charter School Legislation

Once a charter school law has been enacted, charter school reform moves from policy talk to policy action in that state. Much like the statements of legislative intent that frame them, charter school laws also vary widely from state to state. To analyze charter school reform at the stage of policy action, I narrow the focus to three of the states with the largest shares of charter school students, California, Arizona, and Michigan, and compare features of the charter school legislation in effect as of September 2006. The information presented below was drawn directly from each state's charter school legislation, which was supplemented by documents that provided nonregulatory guidance from their respective state departments of education.

Who Can Authorize Charter Schools and How Many Charters Can Be Granted?

There is some variation across the three states in the types of agencies that are authorized to grant charters. In California, the majority of the charters are granted by local school districts, although county boards of education and the State Board of Education can also approve charter schools if a charter is denied by a local school district, or if the school provides countywide or statewide services that are not provided by local school districts. In Arizona, charters can be granted by school districts, the State Board of Education, and the Arizona State Board for Charter Schools, the state agency charged with overseeing charter schools. In Michigan, charter schools are called Public School Academies (PSAs) and can be authorized by local school boards and the governing boards of community colleges and state public universities. Michigan also has two additional types of charter schools: urban high school academies (UHSAs) and strict discipline academies (SDAs). UHSAs are PSA high schools located in Detroit; UHSAs can only be authorized by state public universities. SDAs serve students who have been suspended or expelled from other public schools and/or students who have been placed in the school by a court.

In all three states, school districts can only grant charters to schools that will operate within their boundaries. In Michigan this requirement also applies to community colleges, which are also prohibited from operating PSAs in first class school districts, or districts with over 100,000 students. There is only one first class school district in Michigan, the Detroit City School District.[5] There are no geographic restrictions on PSAs authorized by state public universities in Michigan. However, Michigan public universities are only empowered to authorize up to 150 PSAs. There are no limits on the number of PSAs that can be approved by the other PSA sponsors. There are no caps on the overall number of charter schools that can be authorized in Arizona. California's charter school law limited the total number of charter schools in the state to a total of 250 for the 1998–1999 academic year; in each subsequent year the cap is raised by an additional 1000 schools. In 2005–2006, the cap was 950 schools, which was far higher than the 542 charter schools in operation that year.

Private School Conversions and the Role of Religious Organizations

While California's charter school law specifically prohibits private school conversions, there are no similar restrictions in Arizona and Michigan. In the case of the latter, the nonregulatory guidelines issued by each state's respective departments of education noted that private schools wishing to convert to charter school status must follow their respective charter school law. In other words, they must be "reconstituted as public entities and accept the duties and responsibilities of becoming a public school academy" (Michigan Department of Education, 2005, 3; see also Arizona Department of Education, 2003). Moreover, both states expressly prohibit charter schools from charging tuition. In the 1999–2000 SASS, approximately 10 percent of all charter schools were private school conversions. Both California and Arizona's charter school laws specify that charter schools should be nonsectarian. Charter schools can partner with faith-based organizations in various ways, as was the case of Inspiration School, which was located on the grounds of a faith-based institution. In contrast, Michigan's charter school legislation makes the strong statement that "a public school academy shall not be organized by a church or other religious organization and shall not have any organizational or contractual affiliation with or constitute a church or other religious organization" (Michigan Rev. School Code, Act 451, §380–502).

Duration and Renewal of Charter

The three states vary in the length of the charter school contracts they grant to charter school operators. Once a charter school in California is approved, school operators have to renew its charter every five years. After January 1, 2005, unless it qualifies for the state's alternative accountability system, all California charter schools seeking renewal of their charters are required to meet one of three conditions related to the state's accountability system.[6] In California, all public schools, including charter schools, are required to administer state-mandated assessments to students in grades two through eleven. The results are used to calculate a school's Academic Performance Index (API), which is a score ranging from 200 to 1000. In addition, schools are ranked based on their API in two additional ways. First, all schools are ranked statewide by their API, divided into decile groupings and then assigned a number between 1 and 10 on that basis. Second, schools are ranked within cohorts of 100 schools that share similar characteristics. This process forms the basis for an additional decile ranking, the Similar Schools Index (SSI).[7] Each year, APIs are used to calculate growth targets for the school for the following year. Charter schools must either: (1) meet its growth target in two of the three years prior to renewal; (2) achieve 4 or greater on the API ranking; or (3) achieve a 4 or greater on the SSI ranking. Arizona grants charters for an initial period of fifteen years; a charter school can renew its charter for an additional fifteen-year term if the school and its sponsor determine that it is in compliance with its own charter and the state's charter school law. Arizona's charter school sponsors are required to review their charter schools every five years. Michigan does not specify the duration of contracts for PSAs or SDAs. Urban high school academies (UHSAs) are granted an initial ten-year contract.

Revocation of Charters

In California and Michigan, a charter school authorizers can revoke a school's charter if the school: (1) fails to meet the educational goals outlined in its charter; (2) does not comply with relevant laws; (3) has engaged in fiscal improprieties; and/or (4) violates a provision in its contract. In Arizona, a charter school sponsor can revoke a charter at any time if it determines that a school has violated its charter. In both California and Arizona, the charter school authorizer cannot revoke a charter unless it: (1) notifies the charter school operator of its intent to revoke the charter; (2) allows the school a period of thirty (California) or ninety (Arizona) days to address the authorizer's concerns; (3) and conducts a public hearing before the charter can be revoked. Michigan's law does not outline the procedures an authorizer must follow before it revokes a charter. In California, a county board of education can reverse a school district's decision to revoke a charter on appeal by the school, and the State Board of Education can reverse both a school district's or a county board of education's decision to revoke a charter. Arizona's charter school law does not stipulate whether or not a charter revocation can be appealed. In Michigan, once a charter school authorizer decides to revoke a charter, its decision is final and cannot be reversed by other state agencies.

Teacher Certification

Both California and Michigan require charter school teachers to hold state certification. Michigan's charter school law also contains provisions that allow the full-time faculty of universities and community colleges that are charter school authorizers to teach in the schools sponsored by their employers. Arizona's charter school law does not require that charter school teachers be certified.

Accountability

Although the statement of legislative intent that precedes California's charter school law notes that the charter school law was intended to facilitate a shift "from rule-based to performance-based accountability systems"

(California Education Code of 2006, §47601), California's charter school law has few provisions related to accountability. The Academic Performance Index (API) described above is the main means of holding all public schools accountable in California. The Public Schools Accountability Act (PSAA) of 1999 mandated the creation of the API, but all public schools are subject to the provisions of the PSAA. Indeed, the PSAA specifically states that "all references to schools [in this chapter] shall include charter schools" (California Education Code of 2006, §52051.5). As a result, the PSAA and later NCLB were much more significant than California's charter school legislation in fostering a shift from "rule-based to performance-based accountability" for all public schools (and not just charter schools).

Arizona's charter school law requires charter schools to design a way to measure their students' progress toward meeting state standards, administer state assessments, and participate in the state's report card system. According to the Arizona Department of Education, there are three types of charter school accountability: academic accountability, financial accountability, and general accountability (Arizona Department of Education, 2002). To be academically accountable, Arizona charter schools must outline performance standards and benchmarks and demonstrate how their curricula is aligned with state standards. To be financially accountable, charter schools must include business plans in their charter applications, have a certified public accountant conduct annual audits, submit annual budgets and financial reports to the Arizona Department of Education, and use a standard system of financial reporting. Finally, general accountability entails compliance with health, safety, and civil rights laws and regulations, and the Individuals with Disabilities Act (IDEA). Michigan requires that all three types of PSAs outline their educational goals, curricula, and methods of assessing student progress in their charters. In addition, "to the extent applicable," all PSAs must administer state assessments, including high school exit examinations, if relevant (Michigan Rev. School Code Act 451, §380–502, see also §380–522, §380–1311d). Once the charter is approved, the contract between a PSA and the authorizing agency must outline "the educational goals the public school academy is to achieve and the methods by which it will be held accountable" (Michigan Rev. School Code Act 451, §380–503, see also §380–523, §380–1311e).

What Do Charter Schools Look Like?

In this section I provide some basic information about who attends charter schools and where charter schools are located using the 2005–2006 Common Core of Data (CCD), which contains demographic information on schools and districts. For more detailed information about the characteristics of charter schools, and their principals, teachers and teachers' assessments of school climate, I use the 1999–2000 Schools and Staffing Survey (CCD). In these analyses I provide comparable figures for conventional public schools.[8]

Who Attends Charter Schools?

In table 1.2, I present a breakdown of charter school enrollment in 2005–2006 by race compared to public school enrollment in the forty states and the District of Columbia with operational charter schools. While charter schools and the conventional public schools located in the same states tended to enroll roughly comparable percentages of American Indian, Asian, and Latino students, overall charter schools enrolled more black students and fewer white students than conventional public schools. These nationwide figures, while useful, mask a considerable amount of variation across state contexts (see also Frankenberg and Lee, 2003). To illustrate, in table 1.3 I present the same figures for California, Arizona, and Michigan. In California, Asian students were underrepresented in charter schools compared to their population in the state as a whole. In both California and Arizona, the percentage of African American students attending charter schools was higher than the percentage of African American students attending conventional public schools, but the differences between the two sectors within each is less extreme than the difference between the two sectors nationally. However, in Michigan, African American students comprise 56 percent of all students attending charter schools and only 18 percent of conventional public student population, which suggests that black students were vastly overrepresented in charter schools. Likewise, in Michigan, white students were underrepresented in

Table 1.2 Enrollment by Race in Conventional Public Schools in Charter States and Charter Schools (2005–2006)

	Conventional Public Schools in the 40 States with Charter Schools and D.C. (%)	Charter Schools N (%)
American Indian	502,132 (1.1)	13,896 (1.4)
Asian	2,095,252 (4.7)	35,871 (3.5)
Black	7,606,149 (17.2)	321,873 (31.8)
Latino	9,196,788 (20.8)	223,996 (21.1)
White	24,557,198 (55.5)	406,000 (40.1)
Not reported	301,250 (0.7)	11,270 (1.1)
Total	44,258,769 (100.0)	1,012,096 (100.0)

Table 1.3 Charter School Enrollment in California, Arizona, and Michigan (2005–2006)

	California		Arizona		Michigan	
	Conventional Public Schools N = 9011 (%)	Charter Schools N = 542 (%)	Conventional Public Schools N = 1530 (%)	Charter Schools N = 494 (%)	Conventional Public Schools N = 3609 (%)	Charter Schools N = 263 (%)
American Indian	48,307 (0.8)	2,451 (1.3)	62,524 (6.2)	4,974 (5.5)	15,546 (1.0)	820 (0.9)
Asian	710,654 (11.6)	12,443 (6.4)	24,980 (2.5)	2,131 (2.4)	39,165 (2.4)	2,368 (2.6)
Black	471,191 (7.7)	23,766 (12.1)	50,832 (5.1)	6,031 (6.7)	293,947 (18.1)	50,802 (55.6)
Latino	2,928,332 (47.9)	75,189 (38.4)	397,337 (39.6)	29,359 (32.4)	68,813 (4.2)	4,907 (5.4)
White	1,839,746 (30.1)	75,703 (38.6)	468,184 (46.6)	48,102 (53.1)	1,194,783 (73.7)	32,248 (35.3)
Not reported	117,997 (1.9)	6,324 (3.2)	0 (0.0)	0 (0.0)	7,906 (0.5)	239 (0.3)
Total	6,116,227 (100.0)	195,876 (100.0)	1,003,857 (100.0)	90,597 (100.0)	1,620,160 (100.0)	91,384 (100.0)

charter schools. Seventy four percent of the students attending conventional public schools in Michigan were white compared to 35 percent of charter school students.

Urbanicity

As table 1.4 indicates, most charter schools were located in urban areas. Over half (54 percent) of all charter schools were located in cities.[9] Another 25 percent of charter schools were located in areas designated as "urban" by the U.S. Census. The same figures for conventional public schools are 26 percent and 35 percent, respectively. Likewise, compared to conventional public schools, a much lower percentage of charter schools were located in rural areas (15 percent of charter schools compared to 29 percent of conventional public schools). These differences in location do not fully account for the demographic differences in the student populations across the two sectors described above. To illustrate, in table 1.5 I provide a demographic breakdown of the populations of conventional public schools and charter schools located in cities. While African American students remained overrepresented in charter schools and white students

Table 1.4 Locale of Conventional Public Schools and Charter Schools (2005–2006)

	Conventional Public Schools N (%)	Charter Schools N (%)
Central city	21,007 (26.2)	1,998 (54.1)
Urban	28,335 (35.3)	928 (25.1)
Town	7,576 (9.4)	218 (5.9)
Rural	23,325 (29.1)	546 (14.8)
Total	80,243 (100.0)	3,690 (100.0)

Table 1.5 Demographics of Schools Located in Central Cities

	Conventional Public Schools N (%)	Charter Schools N (%)
American Indian	104,032 (0.8)	5,163 (0.9)
Asian	906,441 (6.8)	19,013 (3.3)
Black	3,619,223 (27.2)	243,508 (42.5)
Latino	4,288,054 (32.2)	144,119 (25.1)
White	4,312,391 (32.4)	156,267 (27.2)
Not reported	86,228 (0.6)	5,436 (0.9)
Total	13,316,369 (100.0)	573,506 (100.0)

were similarly underrepresented, the percentage differences across the two sectors were much less extreme than in all schools regardless of locale (see table 1.2).

Grades Offered and School Size

Table 1.6 provides a breakdown of the percentages of schools of each type that serves each grade from kindergarten to grade twelve. Rather than analyzing all possible grade configurations, for the purposes of brevity, I present an overview of how many schools of each type offered each grade from kindergarten to grade twelve. The figures in table 1.6 suggest that charter schools often serve wider grade ranges than the common grade configurations of conventional public schools (i.e., elementary, middle/ junior high, and high schools). For example, two of the case study schools described in the Introduction, Hearts and Hands Community School and Inspiration School, began as elementary schools and expanded over time to include the middle school grades. Notably, similar percentages of schools of each type (55 percent or higher) served kindergarten through grade five. In the middle school grades, the patterns diverged. While approximately half of charter schools reported offering grades six through eight, only 39 percent of conventional public schools offered grade six, and 27 percent offered grades seven and eight. Finally, while approximately 23 percent of

Table 1.6 Grades Offered by Conventional and Public Schools (1999–2000)

	Conventional Public Schools Weighted N = 54266 (%)	Charter Schools Weighted N = 1010 (%)
Pre-K	21.3	12.6
Kindergarten	54.8	55.7
1	57.0	57.6
2	57.4	57.7
3	57.8	57.3
4	56.4	56.7
5	55.1	56.3
6	39.1	58.7
7	26.9	53.1
8	27.3	48.9
9	23.2	37.9
10	23.5	36.7
11	23.7	34.9
12	23.6	32.8
Average Enrollment	573	264

conventional public schools served grades nine through twelve, between 33 percent and 38 percent of all charter schools served these grades.[10] The last line of the table provides the average enrollment of charter schools and conventional public schools as an indicator of school size. Charter schools tend to be considerably smaller than conventional public schools; on average, charter schools are about half the size of conventional public schools.

School Type

Table 1.7 compares conventional public schools and charter schools by school type. The vast majority of conventional public schools were regular public schools. In this particular question in the SASS survey, the term "regular" was implicitly defined by way of comparison with the other responses in this question (NCES, 2000). Regular schools were not: (1) schools with a special program emphasis offered school-wide; (2) a special education school; (3) a vocational/technical school; (4) or an alternative school which is "designed to provide alternative or non-traditional education" (NCES, 2000, Form 3A, p. 8). Charter schools were more likely to offer a special education program or an alternative education program. Similar percentages of charter schools and conventional public schools were vocational or special education schools.

What Instructional Programs Do Charter Schools Offer?

Table 1.8 provides an overview of the types of instructional programs offered in conventional public schools and charter schools. Over half of all charter schools (55 percent) offered programs with special instructional approaches, which included "Montessori, self-paced instruction, open education, ungraded classrooms, etc." (NCES, 2000, Form 3A, p. 10). While

Table 1.7 Conventional Public Schools and Charter Schools by School Type (1999–2000)

	Conventional Public Schools Weighted N = 54266 (%)	Charter Schools Weighted N = 1010 (%)
Regular Elementary or Secondary School	88.8	53.2
Elementary or Secondary with Special Program Emphasis	3.8	20.6
Alternative	5.4	23.3
Vocational/Technical	0.8	1.3
Special Education	1.2	1.5

Table 1.8   Instructional Programs Offered by Conventional Public Schools and Charter Schools (1999–2000)

	Conventional Public Schools Weighted N = 54266 (%)	Charter Schools Weighted N = 1010 (%)
Offers a special instructional approach	19.4	54.9
Talented/Gifted Program	70.8	32.2
Immersion in a foreign language	13.2	13.6
Advanced Placement (AP) Courses	14.2	18.5
International Baccalaureate	0.6	1.2
Specialized Career Academy	6.4	13.2
Specialized Tech-Prep	12.7	9.1

70 percent of all conventional public schools provided a gifted and talented program, just over 30 percent of charter schools did so. Roughly similar percentages of charter schools and conventional public schools offered foreign language immersion, advanced placement courses, the International Baccalaureate (IB), and specialized tech-prep programs (vocational-technical instruction during the last two years of high school). Twice as many charter schools as conventional public schools reported offering a specialized career academy program that "integrates academic and vocational courses, organized around broad career areas" (NCES, 2000, Form 3A, p. 10). However, the overall number of schools of this type is relatively low. Only 13 percent of charter schools and 6 percent of conventional public schools offered career academy programs.

Who Works in Charter Schools?

In tables 1.9 and 1.10 I present selected characteristics of conventional public school and charter school principals and teachers, respectively. Compared to conventional public school principals, on average, charter school principals tend to have less experience as principals and shorter tenures in their current positions. Likewise, charter school principals reported earning significantly less than their counterparts working in conventional public schools. The mean salary for charter school principals was $54,000 compared to $69,000 for conventional public school principals. Demographically, charter school principals are very similar to conventional public school principals, with the exception that a greater percentage of charter school principals were African American. Thus, charter schools might be serving as an alternative pipeline to the principalship for African American school administrators.

Table 1.9 Characteristics of Conventional Public School and Charter School Principals (1999–2000)

Variable	Conventional Public School Principals Weighted N = 53712 Mean (S.D.)	Charter School Principals Weighted N = 988 Mean (S.D.)
Years of experience as principal	8.9	6.9
Years principal at current school	5.0	2.3
Annual Salary	$69,000	$54,000
Age	50	48
Gender (%)		
Male	55.4	54.0
Female	44.6	46.0
Race (%)		
American Indian	0.4	1.5
Asian	1.0	1.8
Black	11.6	18.3
White	79.7	70.6
Hispanic	7.3	7.8

Table 1.10 Characteristics of Conventional Public School and Charter School Teachers (1999–2000)

Variable	Conventional Public School Teachers Weighted N = 2,014,596	Charter School Teachers Weighted N = 17,477
Years Teaching Experience	14.6	7.3
Years at Current School	9.1	3.6
Certified in Main Teaching Field (%)	93.9	73.1
Certification (%)		
Standard State Certificate	86.3	57.4
Probationary Certificate	2.6	4.9
Provisional/Participating in Alternative Cert. Program	3.0	5.7
Temporary (Requires Add'l Coursework)	1.1	2.9
Emergency/Waiver	0.9	2.1
Not Certified in Main Teaching Field	6.1	26.9
Age	42	37
Race (%)		
American Indian	0.7	1.1
Asian	1.9	2.5
Black	8.1	11.8
White	82.3	76.4
Hispanic	7	8.2

Like charter school principals, on average, charter school teachers tended to have less experience and shorter tenures in their current positions than conventional public school teachers. Fewer charter school teachers were certified in their main teaching fields, and of those that were certified, a much higher percentage of charter school teachers held provisional, temporary, or emergency certification. This finding is not surprising given that not all states require charter school teachers to be certified. For example, Arizona (a state with a large number of charter schools) does not require charter school teachers to be certified. On average, charter school teachers tended to be younger than conventional public school teachers (thirty-seven years compared to forty-two years). Finally, while the majority of the teachers in both charter schools and conventional public schools were white, a slightly higher percentage of charter school teachers were African American. The slightly higher concentration of African American principals and teachers in charters schools makes sense when we consider that, overall, charter schools tend to serve more African American students than conventional public schools.

School Climate

Finally, a set of questions from the SASS provides indicators of teachers' perceptions of school climate. Teachers were asked to rate the extent to which a series of issues, shown in table 1.11, were problems at their schools on a 4-point Likert scale (NCES, 2000). An answer of 1 indicated that the issue was a serious problem while a response of 4 indicated that the issue was not a problem (the full scale is provided at the bottom of the table 1.11). The responses were averaged for conventional public school teachers and charter school teachers. The closer the average to 1, the more teachers perceived this factor to be a problem in their daily work environments. I ranked the items based on the charter school teachers' average ratings from the issue that was rated as least problematic to the issue that was the most problematic. The last column in each table shows the difference in means across the two groups of teachers. A plus (+) indicates that the charter school teachers' mean was higher than the conventional public school teachers' mean. Conversely, a minus indicated that the mean responses for charter school teachers' were lower than those of conventional public school teachers. For example, in table 1.11, the difference of +.18 in the last row indicates that, as a group, charter school teachers felt that student possession of weapons was less of a problem than conventional public school teachers and the asterisks indicate the difference in means across the two groups was statistically significant at p ≤ 0.001.

The results presented in table 1.11 suggest that there is a good deal of consistency in teachers' responses across the two groups, particularly

Table 1.11 Teachers' Perceptions of School Climate (1999–2000)

	Conventional Public School Teachers, Charter States Only Weighted N = 2014596 Mean (S.D.)	Charter School Teachers Weighted N = 17477 Mean (S.D.)	Difference
Student possession of weapons	3.61 (0.61)	3.79 (0.49)	+0.18***
Student pregnancy	3.50 (0.81)	3.68 (0.71)	+0.18***
Student use of alcohol	3.29 (0.96)	3.57 (0.82)	+0.28***
Students dropping out	3.44 (0.85)	3.53 (0.81)	+0.09***
Students cutting class	3.36 (0.86)	3.52 (0.79)	+0.16***
Student drug abuse	3.28 (0.93)	3.52 (0.85)	+0.24***
Teacher absenteeism	3.28 (0.79)	3.40 (0.77)	+0.12***
Robbery or theft	3.24 (0.75)	3.35 (0.78)	+0.11***
Vandalism	3.18 (0.80)	3.35 (0.78)	+0.17***
Physical conflicts among students	3.04 (0.81)	3.19 (0.84)	+0.15***
Poor student health	3.04 (0.82)	3.13 (0.85)	+0.09***
Student apathy	2.50 (1.02)	2.73 (1.01)	+0.23***
Student disrespect for teachers	2.52 (0.94)	2.66 (0.98)	+0.14***
Student absenteeism	2.53 (0.91)	2.62 (0.92)	+0.09***
Lack of parental involvement	2.33 (1.00)	2.61 (1.05)	+0.28***
Student tardiness	2.65 (0.88)	2.60 (0.91)	−0.05**
Poverty	2.51(1.00)	2.60 (1.07)	+0.09***
Students come to school unprepared to learn	2.14 (0.94)	2.38 (1.01)	+0.24***

Note: *Scale*: 1 = Serious Problem; 2 = Moderate Problem; 3 = Minor Problem; 4 = Not a Problem.

in the items that teachers saw as a minor problem and those having no impact at their schools (the top eleven items in table 1.11 with means ranging between 3.04 and 3.79). On average, both conventional public school teachers' and charter school teachers' ratings indicated that they tended to see students' possession of weapons as the least problematic issue at their schools. Likewise, both conventional public school and charter school teachers ranked students coming to school unprepared to learn as the most serious problem at their respective schools. However, overall, charter school teachers tended to have a much more positive view of their school climates than conventional public school teachers, as indicated by the more positive scores on all measures except for student tardiness.

In table 1.12 I repeat the analysis, but here I focus only on teachers working in urban schools. There is less consistency between the average ratings of conventional public school teachers and charter school teachers working in urban schools, although the top-rated and lowest-rated issues are the same for both groups. More specifically, conventional public school

Table 1.12   Teachers' Perceptions of School Climate—Urban Teachers Only (1999–2000)

	Conventional Public School Teachers in Urban Schools, Charter States Only Weighted N = 551643	Charter School Teachers in Urban Schools Weighted N = 8271	Difference
Student possession of weapons	3.51 (0.69)	3.77 (0.51)	+0.26***
Student pregnancy	3.42 (0.90)	3.66 (0.73)	+0.24***
Student use of alcohol	3.37 (0.90)	3.61 (0.77)	+0.24***
Student drug abuse	3.30 (0.92)	3.54 (0.82)	+0.24***
Students dropping out	3.33 (0.96)	3.49 (0.85)	+0.16***
Students cutting class	3.20 (0.99)	3.48 (0.80)	+0.28***
Vandalism	2.98 (0.87)	3.32 (0.80)	+0.34***
Teacher absenteeism	3.13 (0.85)	3.31 (0.81)	+0.18***
Robbery or theft	3.10 (0.80)	3.29 (0.79)	+0.19***
Physical conflicts among students	2.83 (0.88)	3.13 (0.89)	+0.30***
Poor student health	2.78 (0.87)	3.02 (0.89)	+0.24***
Student apathy	2.39 (1.05)	2.69 (1.04)	+0.30***
Student absenteeism	2.31 (0.92)	2.57 (0.94)	+0.26***
Student disrespect for teachers	2.35 (0.97)	2.55 (1.02)	+0.20***
Lack of parental involvement	2.07 (0.98)	2.50 (1.05)	+0.43***
Student tardiness	2.41 (0.91)	2.47 (0.92)	+0.06*
Poverty	2.16 (0.99)	2.42 (1.06)	+0.26***
Students come to school unprepared to learn	1.90 (0.92)	2.26 (1.00)	+0.36***

teachers and charter school teachers both tended to rate student possession of weapons as a minor problem and students coming unprepared to learn as a moderate problem. As in the analysis of teachers across locales, teachers working in urban charter schools tended to have more positive perceptions of their school climates than their conventional public school counterparts. The latter finding could be attributable to selection bias in both teachers and students. In general, schools of choice tend to attract the most involved parents and students in a community regardless of socioeconomic status (Powers and Cookson, 1999), which could influence teachers' perceptions of their students and families. Likewise, charter schools could also be attracting teachers who are more committed to their schools' missions, educational approaches, and/or student populations, which may in turn influence their perceptions of their school climates. Finally, as table 1.6 indicated, charter schools tend to be smaller than conventional public schools, which may also explain why charter school teachers' tend to have more positive perceptions of their school climates.

Discussion

This chapter has provided an overview of some of the characteristics of charter school legislation and the schools created under its auspices. Not only do the goals for charter schools reform vary considerably from state to state, but there is also a considerable amount of variation in the specific provisions of the charter school laws that enable the creation of charter schools. In general, compared to conventional public schools, charter schools tend to serve more African American students and fewer white students. Charter schools also have wider grade spans and are more likely to offer specialized instructional programs than conventional public schools. Both charter school principals and teachers tended to have less experience and shorter tenures in their positions. In addition, charter school principals' salaries were substantially lower than that of their conventional public school counterparts. Charter school teachers tended to be younger and were more likely to not be uncertified in their main teaching field than conventional public school teachers. However, as a group, charter school teachers tended to have more positive assessments of their school climates than conventional public school teachers. In the next chapter, I turn to the issue of policy action to analyze some of the factors that shaped charter school legislation as it was being passed in three states, California, Arizona, and Missouri.

CHAPTER TWO
STATE LEVEL POLICY ACTION

In this chapter I continue to explore state level variation in policy action through brief case studies of the policy dynamics that culminated in charter school legislation in three states: California, Arizona, and Missouri. Because the case studies in the chapters that follow analyze charter schools located in California, I primarily focus on California's charter school law and use the other two states to draw contrasts.

The three states provide interesting comparisons because of the similarities and differences in their state policy contexts. California was the second state to pass charter school legislation in 1992; Arizona's charter school law was passed two years later in 1994. California and Arizona are also the two states with the most charter schools. Arizona has a greater number of charter schools and a higher percentage of its public school students attending charter schools, California has the largest number of public school students enrolled in charter schools. In contrast, Missouri's charter school legislation was passed in 1998 and is comparatively restrictive. Charter schools can only be opened in two cities: Kansas City and St. Louis. As I detail below, California's charter school legislation was tied to a state level school restructuring initiative and was also viewed by some proponents as a firewall against school vouchers. In contrast, Arizona's charter school legislation represented an effort to deregulate public schools and increase competition in public education when a voucher plan promoted by the governor and state legislators was not politically viable. Finally, Missouri's charter school law was incorporated into legislation that was part of an effort to settle two high profile desegregation lawsuits in Kansas City and St. Louis.

California's Charter School Law: Rooted in Restructuring

California's charter school legislation was rooted in the school restructuring movement. If *A Nation at Risk* marks the beginning of the first major "wave" of education reform in the late twentieth century, the school restructuring movement was widely considered the second "wave"[1] (Cookson, 1994; Elmore, 1990; Murphy, 1992; Timar, 1990; Tyack, 1990). In general, first wave reforms tended to be "top-down" reforms, such as increased graduation requirements, revamped curriculum standards, expanded teacher certification, and testing requirements. In contrast, restructuring was an effort to provide schools with more control over teaching and learning, a process described by Timar (1990) as "bureaucratic decentralization" (55).

Initial efforts at restructuring beginning in the mid- to late 1980s centered around efforts to empower teachers, parents, and students. However, by the late 1980s and early 1990s, a more radical form of restructuring gained increasing prominence, which Cookson (1994) argued is a third wave of reform.[2] This latter version of restructuring centered around policies aimed at giving parents and children increased control over schooling through market-driven choice policies (for a discussion of market-driven choice, see Powers and Cookson, 1999). More recently, in NCLB (2002), the term restructuring has been used to describe the last stage in a series of consequences for schools that do not make adequate yearly progress (AYP).[3] Elmore (1990) remarked that school restructuring was an attractive reform proposal because it accommodated multiple meanings and a wide range of changes at the school site. As a result, restructuring had broad political support as a reform movement (see also Olsen et al., 1994).

During the second wave of reform in the mid- to late 1980s, many states and school districts undertook high profile efforts at restructuring. For example, Massachusetts, Arkansas, and Washington adopted restructuring reforms (Timar, 1990). In their study of twenty-one districts in six states, Firestone, Bader, Massel, and Rosenblum (1992) reported that thirteen districts in their sample were involved in restructuring. Of these, eleven initiated reforms that involved teachers in site-based management. Dade County, Florida and Rochester, New York were among the most widely cited examples of districts that implemented restructuring reform (e.g., Cookson, 1994; Grant and Murray, 1999; Timar, 1990). Chicago and Boston were also engaged in restructuring reform.

In California, school restructuring became policy action through SB 1274, which provided funds for a limited number of schools to implement restructuring plans (Connor and Melendez, 1994; Kingsley, 1993). Sponsored by state Senator Gary Hart, SB 1274 was the outcome of a long process of collaboration between state legislators, the Superintendent of Public Instruction, and business leaders represented by the California Business Roundtable. The California Business Roundtable is comprised of the chief executive officers (CEOs) of the largest corporations in California; the organization's mission is to "provide essential leadership on high priority public policy issues" (California Business Roundtable web site). Alarmed by what it saw as a decline in the quality of California workers, the Roundtable first became involved in education reform in the early 1980s when it commissioned a report that was highly critical of public education and proposed a series of reforms that became the basis for its legislative agenda.[4] The report galvanized the public and legislative support for education reform that helped pass SB 813 in 1983 (Berman and Clugston, 1988; MacGuire, 1990; Timar and Kirp, 1988; Toch, 1991). An example of "first wave" reform (Elmore, 1990, 1), SB 813 was a large-scale legislative package that provided new funding for schools and created a foundation for subsequent reforms, which included raising graduation requirements, revising state curriculum frameworks and the state's testing program, and creating a mentor teacher program, among others (Mitchell, 1986).

The Roundtable's advocacy on behalf of SB 813 established the Roundtable as a major player in state efforts at school reform.[5] The Roundtable's involvement in SB 1274 followed the same pattern as its involvement in SB 813. The organization commissioned a second report entitled *Restructuring California Education* that proposed over seventy reforms organized into six broad policy proposals (Olsen, Chang, Salazar, Leong, Perez, McClain, and Raffel, 1994; see also Berman, Weiler Associates, 1988). The scope of the reforms advocated in *Restructuring California Education* was wide-ranging and encompassed reforms aimed at schools to changes in state policy (Berman, Weiler Associates, 1988).

Two of the six policy proposals are particularly pertinent to the present discussion. The first was to "establish accountability based on performance and choice" (Berman, Weiler Associates, 1988, 3). *Restructuring California Education* argued that California's public education system had become increasingly centralized and overly regulated. In response, the Roundtable argued that the state should: (1) set performance goals for schools and students; (2) create accountability systems that will assess how well schools and students meet these goals; (3) create provisions for intervening in schools that do not meet performance goals; and (4) increase parental choice. *Restructuring California Education* proposed that once standards and accountability systems were in place, schools could be deregulated. For example, students would take exit tests rather than fulfill graduation requirements. Likewise, teachers and administrators would have more flexibility to create policies to help students meet performance goals. In addition, expanding school choice would have two related benefits: "introducing competition and putting pressure on weak schools to do better" (Berman, Weiler Associates, 1988, 15). This latter claim anticipated some of the themes of charter school policy talk I described in chapter 1.

A second overarching goal for reform was to "establish school autonomy, and empower parents, teachers, principals" (Berman, Weiler Associates, 1988, 3). There were three proposed areas of reform: (1) provide schools with more control over their budgets; (2) create opportunities and structures for parents, community members, and teachers to participate in school governance; and (3) expand the career ladder for teachers by creating positions for teacher leaders and reorganize schools to allow teachers to collaborate in teacher teams. This latter set of recommendations became the focus of SB 1274 traveled through the legislative process (Olsen et al., 1994). After *Restructuring California Education* was released, the Superintendent of Instruction, California Department of Education staff, the Business Roundtable Education Committee, and the research team met and created the legislative strategy that culminated in SB 1274 (Olson et al., 1994). As noted above, the central component of the bill was to create school restructuring demonstration projects. The Roundtable initially proposed implementing restructuring on a large scale in the hopes that it would foster systemic reform beyond the participating schools (Olsen et al., 1994). Another bill proposing a more comprehensive reform package ultimately did not pass.

While SB 1274 in its final form was much more modest than the Roundtable had hoped—the scope of the program was reduced and a school choice proposal was dropped—the organization's influence was crucial in passing the legislation. Not only did the Roundtable lobby for the bill, the individual companies that comprised the organization were active advocates. The Business Roundtable also supported charter school reform in the years after California's charter school legislation was passed. For example, the Roundtable underwrote a discussion paper on the first year of charter school implementation in California and provided financial assistance and consultants to schools, including Hilltop Charter School (Premack and Diamond, 1994).

Funding for SB 1274 was limited. As a result, a relatively small number of schools received funding—ninety-two planning grants and 140 demonstration grants were awarded, totaling approximately 20 million dollars.[6] Kirst (1992) described SB 1274 as a "small demonstration project that provide[d] planning and seed money for local restructuring," which paralleled reforms underway in Massachusetts and Washington (31). The Department of Education also established two restructuring centers and regional restructuring networks (Olson et al., 1994). A 1994 study of restructuring schools concluded that the legislation had a broad impact on school restructuring in California beyond the participating schools (Olsen et al., 1994).

Like SB 1274, the bill that became California's charter school law, SB 1448 was sponsored by state Senator Gary Hart. SB 1448 was one of two charter school bills that were simultaneously being considered in the Senate and the Assembly (both of which were controlled by Democrats). The second bill, AB 2585, was sponsored by Assembly Member Delaine Eastin. There was a considerable amount of overlap between the two bills. Both bills prohibited private schools from converting to charter schools. In addition, both Eastin and Hart's bills contained: (1) provisions for accountability based on student achievement; (2) a requirement that charter schools reflect the racial and ethnic composition of their sponsoring districts; (3) an appeal process for parties denied a charter; and (4) a five year chartering period (Amsler, 1992).

Yet there were also some important differences between the two bills. Eastin's bill (AB 2582) limited the total number of charter schools to fifty; no more than five charter schools could be approved in a single district. Hart's bill (SB 1448) limited the number of charter schools that could be created to 100 schools. Eastin's bill had a more elaborate approval process. All charters had to be approved by the State Superintendent of Instruction who would then submit the charter to the sponsor district for approval. Conversion charter schools also had to be approved by their schools' teachers union representative and a majority of the school's teachers and parents. In contrast, Hart's bill required that charters be approved directly by the sponsor district; proposed charters had to be signed by 10 percent of the teachers within the district or 50 percent of the teachers within a single school. Eastin's bill stipulated that charter schools could only be attended by students who lived within the boundaries of its sponsor district; Hart's bill did not contain geographic restrictions on charter school attendance other than that conversion charter schools had to grant enrollment preference to students living within their attendance boundaries. Finally, the two bills differed in their provisions for collective bargaining. Eastin's bill stipulated that charter school teachers had to be certified and also that teachers would remain employees of the district for collective bargaining purposes, whereas Hart's bill contained no such provisions.

While both bills were approved by the California Assembly, Governor Pete Wilson, a Republican, vetoed Eastin's bill citing its "excessive controls" noting "[t]he essential elements of the charter school concept are freedom from state regulation and employee organizational control, and choice on the part of parents, pupils, teachers and administrators…on all accounts, this bill fails to embrace the basic ingredients of the charter school concept" (Wilson, 1992). Interestingly, while the limit on the number of charter schools in Hart's bill has since been expanded, most of the other provisions of Eastin's bill that Wilson described as "excessive controls" have since been incorporated into California's charter school law by state lawmakers.

Many commentators viewed charter school reform as the next logical step for school reform in California after restructuring in its early 1990s form. For example, in a briefing book for legislators and their staffers reviewing a decade of education reform in California, both SB 1274 and SB 1448 (Hart's charter school bill) were described as "a shift from a system of accountability based upon rules to a system of accountability based upon student performance" (Connor and Melendez, 1994). The connection between restructuring and charter school reform was also highlighted by an early document on charter schools by the California State Department of Education:

> The starting point for many charter proposals will be to ask: What is our vision for our school and its students.... The SB 1274 restructuring proposals which many schools wrote in the course of last spring asked schools to begin with an analysis of the most pressing problems, gaps, or issues the school faces in providing quality learning for all students. (Kingsley, 1993)

Likewise, Hilltop Charter School's 1993 charter drew similar connections between the two pieces of legislation, and also invoked themes characteristic of first wave restructuring:

> Passage of the California School Restructuring Act [SB 1274] and subsequent approval of the Charter Schools Act [SB 1448] represent landmark achievements in the history of education reform because they finally authorize a grassroots revolution, conferring local autonomy over school programs and policies, and therefore assuring that schools can respond to the special needs of their communities. This legislation assures that the actual "stakeholders" and real change agents—teachers, staff, parents, community, students—are finally in charter of the systemic and local reforms which will restore California's schools' productivity and competitiveness. We can now stop talking and start translating the noble rhetoric into significant action. (Hilltop Charter School, 1993, 1)

Finally, in the request for proposals for the Public Charter Schools Grant Program administered by the California Department of Education, *Restructuring California Education* was cited as a key influence on the charter school movement because it was one of the earliest state level policy reports to advocate for a "performance-based" education system (California Department of Education, 2000, 19).

California's charter school law requires all charter school petitions to include sixteen elements. First, charter school petitioners are required to describe the school's education program, the specific population the school is targeting, and the school's educational goals or "what it means to be an 'educated person' in the 21st century, and how learning best occurs"

(California Education Code of 2006, §47605). The law further specifies that "[t]he goals identified in that program shall include the objective of enabling pupils to become self-motivated, competent, and lifelong learners" (California Education Code of 2006, §47605). Elements two and three focus on standards and accountability. Charter schools must define "measurable pupil outcomes," or the ways their students will demonstrate that they have achieved the educational goals outlined in Element One and how student progress will be measured. As I noted in chapter 1, in California, charter schools were intended to be different from other public schools because they were (at least in theory) accountable for student performance rather than how well the school complies with the regulations governing public schools. The remaining elements focus on the nuts–and–bolts issues of school management. Among other things, charter school organizers must outline: the procedures for school governance, the qualifications for employment, employees' rights, student admission procedures, how financial audits will be conducted, and the steps that will be followed should the charter school close.

Thus, while California's charter school legislation requires that charter schools articulate their educational goals, it does not prescribe how these goals should be accomplished. Decisions about charter schools' missions, curricula,[7] and governance structures are largely the responsibility of the individual schools and their sponsor districts. As the case studies in chapter 3 suggest, since 1992, California's charter school legislation has provided a broad legal framework for the establishment of schools with a wide range of missions and structures.

Vouchers as a Policy Threat

While restructuring was an example of a policy action that directly influenced charter school reform in California, a school voucher proposal that never made it to the stage of policy action also shaped California's charter school legislation. Proposition 174 was a statewide ballot initiative that was defeated at the polls by voters in November of 1993. If passed, Proposition 174 would have added an amendment to the California Constitution providing all school-age children with a scholarship worth half of the average amount of state and local government spending on K-12 education (estimated to be $2,600 at the time). Families would use these scholarships at private and public "scholarship-redeeming schools." Private schools would have been immediately eligible to be designated as scholarship-redeeming schools; the initiative also contained provisions directing the state legislature to establish a procedure for public schools to be designated as scholarship-redeeming institutions.

Proponents of charter school reform were mindful that Proposition 174 could have been approved by voters. For example, in an article detailing the history of California's charter school legislation, State Senator Gary Hart described how he wrote his charter school legislation as a response to the voucher referendum.

It was almost like playing Russian roulette with public education, except instead of having a one-in-six chance of being hit by a deadly blow, the odds were closer to 50–50. Something had to be done to respond to the public's frustration with public schools, and it seemed possible to us to craft a legislative proposal that did not sacrifice the attractive features of the voucher movement—namely, choice of schools, local control, and responsiveness to clients—while still preserving the basic principles of public education: that it be free, nonsectarian, and nondiscriminatory. (Hart and Burr, 1996, 38)

In a *Los Angeles Times* editorial that appeared the day following the election, Hart wrote that Proposition 174's defeat was "not a victory but a wake-up call" for the "educational and political establishments" and advocated three reforms in response: choice, school restructuring, and accountability. Hart specifically highlighted the role of charter schools in providing "meaningful choice" and a means by which parents and teachers can build "local educational models and approaches" within public education (Hart, 1993, B7). Similarly, the Geary Unified School District's school board voted to approve Hearts and Hands Community School's charter on the same day that California voters were voting on Proposition 174—before the election returns were announced. According to a newspaper article reporting on the unanimous decision, a school board member explained her vote by noting that a Waldorf school would increase school choice options within the district and commented that even if voters did not approve Proposition 174, "it would be back in another form."

Interestingly, there were some connections between California's restructuring reform and Proposition 174. The leader of the campaign for Proposition 174 was Joseph Alibrandi, a defense industry executive. Three years earlier, Alibrandi was the chair of the California Business Roundtable's education task force that produced the 1988 report *Restructuring California Education* discussed above (Woo, 1988). Alibrandi's advocacy for school vouchers is perhaps not surprising given that vouchers were among the issues considered by the Business Roundtable as it initially became involved in education reform. However, as an organization, the Roundtable remained neutral on Proposition 174 (Kerchner and Menefee-Libey, 2003). According to a contemporaneous interview in the *Wall Street Journal*, Alibrandi decided that the public schools could not be fixed "from within," and he began to organize the campaign for what became Proposition 174 (Ferguson, 1991). Alibrandi's campaign brought together prominent libertarians who authored the proposition—including economist Milton Freedman who worked on a draft of the initiative—and veteran Republican political campaign consultants (Morain, 1993).

Subsequent efforts at creating a statewide voucher plan via a voter referendum were unsuccessful. In December 1993, just over a month after Proposition 174 was defeated, another voucher referendum was submitted to the California Attorney General for the 1994 ballot. Unlike Proposition 174, which would have provided a scholarship to all school-age children in California, the new initiative specifically targeted low-income and disabled students in its first year of operation. The referendum was ultimately withdrawn by its proponents who decided to postpone their campaign until 1996. Two additional referendum campaigns for statewide voucher programs were initiated after Proposition 174 was defeated. An organization called the Council for School Change conducted some exploratory research to assess the viability of a voucher referendum for the 1996 ballot, and ultimately determined there was insufficient public support for such an effort. Finally, Proposition 38, a ballot initiative that would have made a voucher of $4,000 that could be used to pay tuition and fees at a private school available to every school-age child, was defeated by voters in November 2000.

The Evolution of California's Charter School Legislation

As noted above, charter school legislation continues to evolve across the country, and California is no exception. Most of the changes to California's charter school legislation were relatively minor from 1993 to 1998 (Premack, 1997; California Department of Education, 1999). However, more substantive changes to the Charter School Law were made in 1998 and 1999 starting with AB 544, which took effect on January 1, 1999.

This legislative revision to charter school law was initially spearheaded by Technology Network, a bipartisan political organization of Silicon Valley technology firms led by Reed Hastings, an entrepreneur who became president of the State Board of Education in 2001. With the help of Don Shalvey, an early California charter school activist, the group employed a tactic described by Gerber (1998) as indirect modifying influence. Technology Network authored and gathered signatures for a ballot initiative intended to facilitate the growth of the charter school movement (Morain, 1998). When a bill containing almost the same provisions was passed by the state legislature in the spring of 1998, the group dropped their ballot initiative (Johnson, 1998).[8] Technology Network members also spent a considerable amount of time meeting with legislators to get the legislation passed. As the bill's sponsor noted "[t]hey were willing to get their hands dirty in the legislative process" (Simon, 1998, A15). AB 544 made a number of significant changes to the 1992 legislation. It lifted the 100-school cap, reduced the requirements for granting charter petitions for both start-up and conversion charter schools, and required that all charter school teachers hold a teaching credential or qualifications commensurate to those of a public school teacher. While the provision in the original law prohibiting a private school from converting to charter schools status remained in force, the new legislation allowed charter schools to be constituted as nonprofit corporations. AB 544 also empowered the State Board of Education to: (1) grant charters; and (2) intervene in instances of financial mismanagement, inappropriate use of funds, or if a charter school "jeopardizes the educational development" of its students (California Education Code, §47604.5).

AB 544 and a subsequent bill (AB 1115) also phased in changes to charter school funding intended to ensure that charter schools would receive the same funds that a school district would receive for their students. Prior to AB 544 and AB 1115, charter schools in the Geary Unified School District were funded like other public schools in the district under the revenue limit model; schools were allocated a certain number of positions for the year (teachers, administrators, aides, and so on) based on the number of students enrolled at the school on October 1. Schools also received a portion of categorical funds based on the number of students at the site eligible for these programs. Under this system, charter schools were granted more flexibility in their spending than conventional public schools because they could opt to take the money for a particular position and re-designate it toward other expenses.

The new legislation required all charter schools that had been approved by the state and assigned a charter number before June of 1999 to switch to a direct funding model by the 2001–2002 school year. Under direct funding, California's charter schools receive funds directly from the state in the form of a block grant based on their average daily attendance (ADA). Block grants include both monies from local property taxes and state apportionments; the funds are deposited in an account for the school in the county treasury. The legislation also established an intermediate local funding model where the same formulas used in the direct funding model determined the amount of funding the school received, but the monies were allocated to the sponsor district.

Finally, AB 544 also included a particularly notable addition to the statement of legislative intent—a clause stating that California's charter school law is intended to "provide vigorous competition within the public school system to stimulate continual improvements in all public schools"

(California Education Code of 2006, §47601). While symbolic, this change highlights how charter school reform is flexible enough to accommodate both restructuring and market-driven choice.

Arizona's Charter School Law: Market-Driven Choice as Policy Action

As noted above, many commentators have argued that market-driven choice is another strand of the restructuring movement that emerged in the late 1980s and early 1990s. A hallmark of market-driven education reforms is the argument that market principles such as competition can be used to foster education reform. The publication of John E. Chubb and Terry M. Moe's *Politics, Markets and America's Schools* (1990) under the auspices of the Brookings Institution provided important theoretical and empirical support for market-driven choice.

Chubb and Moe viewed democracy and markets as two competing models of school organization. Public schools are democratically organized, whereas private schools are organized around a market model. Yet Chubb and Moe (1990) argue that in reality, public schools are less democratic and equitable than private schools. Like other democratic systems of school governance, public schools are "coercive" because in a system of majority rule, the "loser" not only has to go along with the majority, but is forced through public financing to pay into a system that to some degree or another does not match her/his needs or interests (28). The fundamental problem with public schools, then, is that the direct beneficiaries of school services—parents and students—are one of the least powerful constituencies among many that are jockeying for control over school policies. In contrast, market forms of governance are "radically decentralized" (Chubb and Moe, 1990, 29). While governments create the legal parameters within which markets operate, once markets are formed, they enable voluntary transactions between providers (school operators) and consumers (parents and students).

Chubb and Moe argued that while it appears as if parents and students would have less influence in a private school than a public school because the owners of a school have formal authority over school policy, three characteristics of markets ensure that parents and students have more influence in a private school. First, a private school needs to not only attract parents and students but also keep them satisfied in order to retain them. Second, one of the fundamental characteristics of markets is that consumers have the "exit option"—if a school is not meeting their needs, parents and students have the freedom to change schools. Finally, if a school does not retain enough parents and students, it will be forced to close. As a result, a private schools has a strong incentive to become competitive, or they will go out of business.

Chubb and Moe (1990) further claimed that these issues of power and authority in school governance have implications for school organization. As creatures of majoritarian politics, public schools have an inherent tendency toward bureaucratization. Each winning faction in successive political contests around education policy creates rules to enforce its own interests. Because political power in a democratically organized system is often temporary (or dependent on the outcome of the next election), there is a strong incentive for officials to protect their policies from being overturned or undermined by creating a complex regulatory structure that specifies how policies should be implemented. As a result, public schools are governed by an elaborate and layered system of regulations that hamper learning because they interfere with teachers' abilities to use their best professional judgment to address the needs of their students. In contrast, because private schools need to be attuned to their market (parents and students), there is a strong tendency toward decentralization. Because they have to deal with fewer administrative rules, teachers in private schools have the latitude to more effectively meet their students' needs.

Drawing on these theoretical arguments, Chubb and Moe conducted an empirical analysis using a nationally representative sample of public and private high schools that examined the relationship between school organization and student achievement. Based on their findings, they argued that school organization as measured by an index comprised of variables related to goals, leadership, personnel, and practice had a strong and statistically significant effect on student achievement. More specifically, student achievement was higher in effective schools—schools that had shared goals, high academic standards, strong leadership, highly professional teachers who cooperate and are collegial, and orderly classrooms focused on academic work. Because private schools were more likely to be effective schools, market forms of school organization were more likely to support student achievement. Chubb and Moe (1990) concluded:

> The structure of school control is critical, then, not only for the autonomy of schools but for the development within schools of the requisites for school success. Clear academic goals, strong educational leadership, professionalized teaching, ambitious academic programs, teamlike organizations— these effective schools characteristics are promoted much more successfully by market control than by direct democratic control. The kinds of qualities that contemporary school reformers would like to develop, private schools have developed without any type of external reform at all. Bureaucratic autonomy and effective school organization are natural products of the basic institutional forces at work on schools in a marketplace. They are

products of school competition and school choice. Success is built into the institutional structure of private education. As public education is now structured, institutions make success almost unnatural. (181–183)

While Chubb and Moe's (1990) empirical and critical arguments have been amply criticized elsewhere, their arguments outlined the main assumptions behind some of the policy talk that linked school choice with competition and provided school choice advocates with the "research legitimation the school choice movement [was] waiting for" (Glass and Matthews, 1991, 26; for additional critiques, see for example, Cookson, 1994; Elmore, 1991; Henig, 1994; Meier and Smith, 1995; Rasell and Rothstein, 1993). Chubb and Moe's arguments resonated in Arizona in the early 1990s when state lawmakers tried to create a school voucher program. When that was unsuccessful, they turned to charter school reform as a compromise. Thus, as in California, in Arizona the threat of school vouchers was a significant factor in facilitating the passage of Arizona's charter school law. However, a key difference between Arizona and California was that Arizona's voucher plan was promoted by the governor and other state legislators rather than by actors largely outside of the political system (i.e., through a ballot referendum). At the time Arizona's charter school law was passed, Republican lawmakers controlled both houses of the state legislature (Timmons-Brown and Hess, 1999), and the governor, Fife Symington, was also a Republican.

State lawmakers had been exploring the possibility of creating a voucher program in Arizona as early as 1991 (Timmons-Brown and Hess, 1999). In 1991, the Governor's Task Force on Education Reform recommended an open-enrollment plan for Arizona schools that included private and parochial schools, which would have been able to enroll low-income students using state vouchers ("Public schools get first priority," 1991). After public opposition to the voucher proposal, the task force scaled back the plan to include only public schools for the first two years after open enrollment was implemented, and then gradually expand the program to include private schools. In a report analyzing the Task Force's report, which drew from the arguments he and Chubb presented in *Politics, Markets and America's Schools*, Moe (1991) argued that choice should be the centerpiece of the group's proposal because it would best promote systemic reform, and that private schools should be included in any choice plan:

> Many private schools, especially those that are religiously affiliated, are eager to participate in a system that would provide them with funding in return for minimal regulation. Their participation, all by itself, would increase the numbers and types of desirable schools available for choice by students. At the same time, it would put heavy competitive pressure on

the public schools to become more effective and responsive. In addition, the availability of new funding will almost surely stimulate the emergence of a great many new private schools of all shapes and sizes—enhancing choice, heightening the incentives for effective organization, and injecting tremendous dynamism and innovative potential into a system that has so long been mired in inertia. (7)

A year later, a second school reform proposal promoted by the Arizona Business Leadership for Education (ABLE) proposed a plan to decentralize public education by allowing open-enrollment, creating school site councils that would have more control over school budgets and policies, and the creation of charter schools ("Businesses offer school-funding plan," 1992). As with the compromise plan proposed by the Governor's Task Force, private school vouchers were not part of the plan, although Symington continued to support the open enrollment plan that included a private school voucher component (Meissner, 1992).

Symington opened Arizona's 41st legislative session in 1993 by proposing a school voucher plan that included private schools (Cook, 1993). At the same time, a group called Citizens Taking Action was beginning a campaign to put a number of issues on the 1994 ballot, including a school voucher proposal (Fischer, 1993). By March 1993, state lawmakers had introduced two competing bills in the state legislature, SB 1200, a charter school bill, and HB 2125, a bill that proposed a series of reforms including open-enrollment, school accountability, programs targeted at at-risk students, charter schools, and school decentralization through the creation of school site councils (O'Connell, 1993). SB 1200 passed the Senate but was not taken up by the House (Timmons-Brown and Hess, 1999). The main opposition to HB 2125 focused on the decentralization proposals. The Arizona School Boards Association opposed the bill on the grounds that the school site councils took too much power from local school boards. A compromise bill scaling back the decentralization provisions was crafted with the support of ABLE, but was never passed because of the prohibitive cost of the other new programs HB 2125 proposed.

In 1994, Symington and Republican lawmakers tried unsuccessfully to build support for a small pilot voucher program that would have allowed 8,000 low-income students to attend a private or parochial school for up to three years. Once again, two competing bills, HB 2505 and SB 1375, were proposed in the House and Senate, respectively. Both bills included charter school and open-enrollment provisions. However, the Senate bill did not contain the pilot voucher program and proposed considerably less spending than the House bill. In general, the debate split along party lines. Republicans wanted a voucher plan included in any education reform package, whereas Democrats and their allies (the teachers unions, the

Arizona School Boards Association, the Arizona School Administrators) were opposed to vouchers (Timmons-Brown and Hess, 1999). On the last day of the legislative session, HB 2505 (the broader reform package) passed the House by a two-vote majority but was rejected in the Senate by three votes. During the legislative debates, state legislators who were unwilling to support a voucher program indicated they were willing to support charter schools (Graham Keegan, 1999).

In a special legislative session, Lisa Graham Keegan, the chair of the house Education Committee, proposed HB 2002, which was a scaled-down version of HB 2505, in April 1994. The new bill did not contain the voucher program, but it did include the charter school provisions, decentralization, and open-enrollment. Endorsed by the teachers unions, the Arizona School Boards Association, and the Arizona School Administrators, HB 2002 was passed by the legislature and signed by the governor in June 2004. Arizona's first cohort of charter schools opened their doors in September 2004. Graham Keegan commented later that she had included the charter schools provision and the voucher program in the same bill because she had anticipated that the voucher plan would make the charter school proposal more palatable to potential opponents such as the teachers unions (Timmons-Brown and Hess, 1999).

A few features of Arizona's charter school law are worth noting. First, Arizona created a separate entity, the Arizona State Board for Charter Schools, which was empowered to grant charters. Graham Keegan, the bill's sponsor, explained that this provision was intended to facilitate the expansion of charter school reform. According to Graham Keegan (1999), in other states, charter school reform had been hampered by district sponsorship because "[c]harter school entrepreneurs had to go before their school board and basically say 'I divorce you. Now please approve my new school'" (190). Local school districts and the State Board of Education were also given the authority to grant charters. Second, Arizona's charter school law requires that charter schools: (1) comply with federal, state, and local health, safety, and civil rights laws; (2) are nonsectarian; (3) provide a "comprehensive program of instruction" for the grades they serve; (4) administer state assessments; (5) follow the fiscal reporting and accounting rules required of school districts; (6) comply with federal and state laws for serving children with disabilities; and (7) create a governing board that is responsible for school policy (Arizona Revised Statutes, §15–183E, 2007). Aside from these requirements, Arizona's charter schools are "exempt from all statutes and rules relating to schools, governing boards and school districts" (Arizona Revised Statutes, §15–183E, 2007).

The political dynamics that created California's and Arizona's charter school laws share some important similarities. Both were efforts at decentralization, and both bills passed as voucher proposals were gaining momentum. However, there are also some important differences in how these processes played out in each state. While decentralization in California was an effort to reduce bureaucracy to empower teachers (Hart and Burr, 1996), decentralization in Arizona was an effort to reduce bureaucracy to empower consumers. As Tom Patterson, one of the bill's proponents in the Arizona Senate, noted:

> [C]harter schools are in a way a test of an entirely different accountability method which is decentralized, which depends, rather than on bureaucratic rules and regulations, on first of all these being schools of choice. It's accountability that comes from the parents and the consumers. (Patterson, 1998, quoted in Garn, 1999, 21)

Likewise, in the case of California, Senator Gary Hart, the bill's sponsor, saw charter school reform as a "firewall" to protect public education from what he saw as a more harmful voucher proposition, the proponents of Arizona's charter school law saw it as a first step toward the creation of school choice policies that included private schools. Indeed, while California's charter school law expressly prohibits private schools from converting to charter schools, Arizona's charter school law did not have similar restrictions. Thirteen of the fifty-one schools in Arizona's first cohort of charter schools were private school conversions (Arizona Department of Education, 1995).

Missouri: School Choice as a Tool for Racial Integration

Missouri's charter school law presents an interesting contrast to both California's and Arizona's charter school laws. In Arizona and California, charter schools can be established in any school district across the state. In contrast, Missouri's 1998 charter school law limits the establishment of charter schools to the Kansas City and St. Louis school districts. The charter school act was part of a larger legislative package (SB 781) crafted by the Missouri General Assembly designed to end court-ordered segregation in these two urban districts. While there were legislative efforts to pass charter school reform and voucher programs before 1998, none of these gained political traction. Instead, as I will explain below, desegregation tended to dominate education policymaking in Missouri in the 1980s and 1990s and was also a significant issue in statewide political contests (West, 1992). In Missouri, charter schools (and before them magnet schools) were aimed at fostering racial integration rather than restructuring or creating an education market.

Before 1954, the Missouri Constitution required the state to maintain separate public schools for "white and colored children" ("40% of Public School Pupils," 1954, 21). After the Supreme Court's decision in *Brown v. Board of Education*, the Missouri attorney general did not actively attempt to desegregate, but instead let local city and school district officials retain control over the degree and scope of integration (Morantz, 1996). In Kansas City, the school district had created two sets of attendance zones, one for white students and one for African American students (Moran, 2005). After the Supreme Court declared segregation unconstitutional, the Kansas City Missouri School District's (KCMSD) research department created a desegregation plan that was accepted by the school board in March 1955. The two sets of segregated attendance zones were replaced with a single attendance zone system where students were required to attend the school closest to their homes. The new plan also maintained the school district's permissive transfer policy, which allowed students to transfer out of their neighborhood schools and into a different school.

Because of residential segregation, there were large sections of the city that were not affected by the new desegregation plan. However, in areas where the new attendance boundaries traversed racially segregated residential neighborhoods and white students were assigned to formerly black schools, whites used the transfer policies to avoid attending their newly assigned school. Moran (2005) notes that while the plan was technically in compliance with the Supreme Court's decision in *Brown II*, Kansas City schools continued to be segregated. In the two decades after Brown, the district's demographics shifted; white students were moving to the surrounding suburbs and the black population was increasing. Although the transfer policy allowed white families to avoid integration, district officials resisted changing it because they were afraid that without the transfer policy, white flight to the surrounding suburbs would accelerate (Moran, 2005).

In the 1970s, the federal government began to require that KCMSD comply with Title VI of the Civil Rights Act in order to receive federal funds. At the request of the Office of Civil Rights (OCR), KCMSD discontinued the transfer program, reformed its teacher assignment policy, created a comprehensive, district-wide school assignment plan, and bused white and black students to achieve racial balance (Moran, 2005). It also converted predominantly black schools to magnet schools to attract white students. However, these desegregation reforms were the result of a long period of negotiation and compromise with OCR, and, as Moran (2005) points out, were implemented after a considerable amount of white flight had already occurred. In 1960, almost three-quarters of the students attending Kansas City public schools were white; by 1975, white students comprised less than one-third of the districts' students. In May 1977, after a board-sponsored task force determined it would be difficult to achieve meaningful integration without expanding desegregation programs to include schools in the predominantly white suburban districts surrounding Kansas City, the KCMSD school board filed a lawsuit in federal court against eighteen neighboring districts in Kansas and Missouri, the states of Kansas and Missouri, and the federal government, requesting the authority to create an interdistrict desegregation plan (Morantz, 1996).[9]

Citing the Supreme Court's decision in *Milliken v. Bradley* (1974),[10] Judge Russell Clark rejected the plaintiffs' argument that federal agencies and the suburban districts had engaged in actions that facilitated racial segregation in KCMSD (*Jenkins v. State of Missouri*, 593 F. Supp. 1485). Instead of creating an interdistrict desegregation plan, the court mandated the creation of a large-scale magnet school plan in KCMSD that was funded by the state and an increase in local property taxes (Morantz, 1996). The goal of the magnet school program was to increase the enrollment of white students in Kansas City schools. Developed in the 1970s as a voluntary integration strategy, magnet schools offer distinctive education programs and open-enrollment to students outside of their attendance zones. In this case, the goal was to enhance the capital facilities and education programming in KCMSD schools in the hope that these would attract white students. Over time, Clark approved plans for facilities renovations, remedial programs, instructional improvements, and teacher salary increases (Morantz, 1996; Green and Baker, 2006). When the local property tax levies Clark imposed in Kansas City did not raise sufficient funds to pay for the costs of the court-ordered reforms, the state was required to fund the balance. Between his 1985 decision outlining his initial remedy order and his last decision in 1997, Clark had approved reforms that incurred a total of approximately $2 billion dollars in new spending, the majority of which was funded by the state (Ciotti, 1998).

Like Kansas City, in the pre-Brown era, the St. Louis School District assigned students to schools by race (Wells and Crain, 1997). After the Supreme Court's decision in *Brown*, students were assigned to neighborhood schools. However, most of the district's schools remained segregated because of residential segregation and gerrymandering. The majority of the new attendance zones either excluded black neighborhoods from the attendance boundaries of all-white elementary schools or maintained the segregation-era attendance zones of all-white elementary schools. The school board also changed high school feeder patterns to ensure that students attending black elementary schools would attend one of the two black high schools (Wells and Crain, 1997). In addition, like Kansas City, St. Louis had a liberal transfer program that many whites used to avoid attending black majority schools.

The transition from de jure to de facto segregation in St. Louis was exacerbated by a demographic shift in the city's population; the *Brown* decision occurred in the middle of a period of black migration to the cities and white flight to the suburbs. As Wells and Crain (1997) point out, residential segregation in St. Louis County (which encompasses the central city and the outlying suburbs) was facilitated by the policies of federal, state, and local housing agencies (see also Lipsitz, 1998). Between 1942 and 1967, the percentage of white students attending St. Louis city schools declined from 78 percent to 37 percent of the total student population (Wells and Crain, 1997). As the city's schools transitioned from predominantly white to predominantly black, and black schools became increasingly overcrowded, the school board altered school attendance zones to preserve predominantly white schools or purposely built new schools in segregated neighborhoods. In addition, in the 1950s and early 1960s, the district relieved overcrowding in black schools through "intact busing" (Wells and Crain, 1997). Black students were bused and placed in predominantly white schools in separate classrooms, and they followed a different schedule so the two groups of students never mixed.

During the 1960s, black parents started to organize and protest the school board's policies (Wells and Crain, 1997). The parents' grassroots organizing culminated in *Liddell v. Board of Education of the City of St. Louis,* a class-action lawsuit filed in 1972 in an effort to force the school board and the state of Missouri to desegregate the district's schools. *Liddell* has a long and complex history, which is recounted in detail in Wells and Crain (1997). In one key decision, the Eighth Circuit Court ruled in 1980 that the state and the school district were responsible for maintaining and exacerbating segregation in St. Louis schools and ordered the school district to create an interracial committee that consulted with experts to create a desegregation plan. The district court was charged with overseeing the implementation of the plan (*Adams v. United States,* 620 F.2d 1277). However, in the process of developing the plan, the school district realized that integration would be difficult without the involvement of the surrounding suburban districts. On the advice of Gary Orfield, one of the court-appointed experts, the district court approved the implementation of St. Louis' plan to promote segregation within the district, but also directed the parties to develop a voluntary county-wide desegregation plan (Wells and Crain, 1997).

Because of residential segregation, the St. Louis plan left about two-thirds of the city's black students in segregated schools. Armed with the lower court's directive, the NAACP filed a motion to expand the original *Liddell* lawsuit to include the suburban school districts in St. Louis County and two neighboring counties (Wells and Crain, 1997). Ultimately, all of the parties involved (including the suburban districts) reached a settlement that was first implemented in 1983–1984 and later upheld by the Eighth Circuit Court in 1984, which included: (1) an interdistrict transfer program that allowed St. Louis students to attend schools in the sixteen school districts that had the lowest percentages of African American students; (2) the creation of a magnet school program in St. Louis that included transfer provisions allowing suburban students to attend city schools; and (3) educational and capital improvements for St. Louis schools (Wells and Crain, 1997). As in Kansas City, the state funded the majority of the costs of the desegregation programs.

While a detailed review of both cases is outside the scope of the discussion here (for detailed reviews of the litigation in Kansas City and St. Louis, see Baker and Green, 2006 and Wells and Crain, 1997, respectively), a few brief points are worth noting. The court-ordered desegregation plans absorbed a large share of state education funding and as a result were politically unpopular outside of Kansas City and St. Louis (e.g., West, 1992). In the early 1990s, state lawmakers began what became a long effort to settle the lawsuits (see, for example, Dvorak, 1992; Horsley 1995). Charter school reform was rolled into SB 781, the massive education reform bill passed by the Missouri Assembly in 1998 to settle the desegregation lawsuits in both districts. The charter school portion of the bill originally began as a stand-alone bill and was subsequently incorporated into the desegregation bill. In the original version of the bill, any district in the state could sponsor a charter school. In the final version of the bill, charter schools could only be established in "a metropolitan school district or in an urban school district containing most or all of a city with a population greater than three hundred fifty thousand inhabitants" (Missouri Revised Statutes of 2007, §160.400). Only two cities in Missouri have more than 350,000 residents, Kansas City and St. Louis.

Discussion

In chapter 1 I highlighted how the goals of charter school reform and the specific provisions of charter school legislation share some common themes, but also how they vary considerably across state contexts. The analysis presented in this chapter suggests that some of these differences may be attributable to differences in state political contexts. In each of the three states, charter school legislation was shaped by issues that were dominating the broader education reform agendas in each state. For example, unlike in Missouri, desegregation was a far less salient political issue in state policymaking in California and Arizona. As a result, the charter school legislation in these two states was very different than in Missouri. Likewise, in

California, a key goal of charter school reform was to empower teachers. The state legislature passed two charter school bills; the governor used his veto power to enact the bill with comparatively fewer restrictions on charter schools. In contrast, Arizona's charter school law was more squarely an effort to deregulate public schools and create an education market. In the next chapter and the two chapters that follow, I turn to the issue of charter school implementation. What happens after charter school legislation becomes law, when the work of lawmakers is largely finished?

Chapter Three

School Level Implementation: Charter School Reform "On the Ground"

In this chapter I focus on implementation in charter schools by examining how the principles outlined in the three case study schools' charters were enacted in daily practices at each school. I use the concepts organizational structure and school culture as anchors for the analysis and to facilitate comparison across the three schools. In the two chapters that follow, I move beyond features of school organization to further develop an issue I touch upon throughout the analyses presented in this chapter—how organizational structures and school cultures are shaped, and in some cases reshaped, by features of the schools' policy context, that is, state and district policies. Organizations are commonly defined as a collection of social relationships consciously formed and maintained for the purpose of accomplishing one or more goals (Selznick, 1948; Stinchcombe, 1965).[1] The term organizational structure draws attention to the regular features of school life—how instruction (the type of curriculum being taught and the technology of teaching), governance (the distribution of power), and resources are organized within a school. School culture highlights the importance of the collective nature of organizational life—the complex chemistry of social interactions and social structures that creates a community ethos that is more than the sum of its parts.

In conceptualizing school culture, I draw from Swidler's (1986) definition of culture as a "tool kit" comprised of "symbolic vehicles of meaning, including beliefs, ritual practices, art forms, and ceremonies, as well as informal cultural practices such as language, gossip, stories, and rituals of daily life" (273). Actors select from this array of cultural tools to devise "strategies of action" (Swidler, 1986, 276). Yet, as Swidler notes, the range of cultural tools that actors can draw from in this process is large, diverse, and often contradictory. While Swidler's framework is useful because it highlights the role of human agency, we are still left with the question of *how* individuals or groups chose from an array of equally viable cultural tools to determine how to act. I argue that organizations help to mediate the relationships between individuals and the larger society. That is to say, in modern societies, as individuals go about their day-to-day routines within an organization, the many possible elements of their "tool kits" are filtered—some cultural tools become more viable than others as "taken-for-granted" choices as they construct strategies of action (March and Olson, 1986). In this case, the school—and within the school the features of school organization—influences how teachers select and utilize cultural tools to enact and frame charter school reform. Thus, focusing on the organization helps us connect the day-to-day interactions between individuals within the social spaces of school life to broader cultural discourses about education reform.

As the discussion above suggests, while I draw a conceptual distinction between organizational structure and school culture, in practice the two concepts are interrelated. If culture is forged in the crucible of social interaction, it is the structure of an organization that sets the parameters for social interaction by participants. Or, to put it another way, a school's organizational structure enables some activities and hinders others. Organizational structure, then, provides a broad framework within which actors construct more detailed sets of norms and beliefs that guide the action that takes place within it (see Sarason, 1972; Meyer, 1977; Swidler, 1986; Simpson and Rosenholtz, 1986; Rosenholtz, 1989). In the case of organizations such as schools, these can comprise such elements as ideas about how participants in the organization should act and interact, teach and be taught, assumptions about what constitutes "learning" and "good teaching," who should be making decisions for the school, and the processes by which decisions should be made. Finally, there can also be multiple cultures within an organization that may or may not coexist harmoniously, a dynamic we will see in chapter 4 in the analysis of Hearts and Hands Community School. For example, several subcultures may compete for dominance within an organization. Similarly, the dominant culture within an organization at one point in time can be displaced by another as the organization develops and evolves over time (Rao, 1998).

California's charter school legislation requires a charter school to describe its pedagogical and operational philosophies and procedures in a charter that is endorsed by a governmental agency empowered to approve charter schools. However, drawing from the insights of organizational theorists that have questioned the tight link between a formal organizational chart and the activity that takes place within organizations, and constructivist accounts of culture, we might understand a school's charter as the blueprint of the abstract ideas and principles behind school culture that must continually be brought to life by participants. As McDermott and Varenne (1995) point out: "Culture is not so much a product of sharing as a product of people hammering each other into shape with the well-structured tools already available" (326).

Hilltop Charter School

If you were to walk around Hilltop Charter School during a formal instructional day, it would not seem very different from any other school in Geary Unified School District. Children lined up for recess and lunch and ate cafeteria food that looked almost exactly the same as the food I ate in elementary school over twenty years earlier on the other side of the country. Yet appearances can be deceiving, because if you scratched below the surface sameness of the bulletin boards that displayed student work, the alphabet strips hung at the top of blackboards, and the jackets and colorful cartoon-emblazoned backpacks that dangled from racks outside classroom doors, there was much that was different about Hilltop Charter School.

The first indication was the designation "California Charter School" on the marquis. I began to learn about the more distinctive aspects of Hilltop School during my first few weeks at the school. On my first day, a teacher graciously spent part of her weekly two-and-a-half-hour preparation period telling me about the school and invited me to sit in on her classroom cluster meeting. During this meeting, she and the two other teachers in her classroom cluster who taught combined K-1 classes shared teaching strategies, discussed their students, and planned a joint activity for their three classes commemorating the hundredth day of school:

> Ms. Landry suggested that they use *Wolf's Chicken Stew*, because the number 100 was featured prominently throughout the book. The book told the story of a wolf who was trying to eat a chicken and couldn't because he was won over by the hen's 100 chicks who covered him with 100 kisses. The story ends with the wolf making 100 cookies for the chicks. The three teachers brainstormed ways to use the story as a "Read Aloud" by identifying prompts in the illustrations that would help students guess the plot. For example, in one illustration, the wolf was wearing a chef's hat and holding a spoon or a spatula, a clue that the wolf wanted to eat the chicken. The teachers also discussed how the students could also compare the plot of this story to others they read earlier in the school year, such as the *Three Little Pigs*, which also featured a wolf.

In addition, the teachers planned tactile and physical activities around the number 100 that involved counting (each student would receive 10 pieces of 10 kinds of snack food such as peanuts and pretzels) and running 100 short laps. Because the teachers mixed their classes during regularly scheduled times throughout the week, they were familiar with all of the students in the three classrooms. During the meeting one of the teachers discussed her frustration with Guided Reading; she felt that while the technique was effective with her first-grade students, her kindergarten students were still struggling. This teacher also described how she felt pressured by the district to move ahead with the strategy even though she thought this might not serve her students well. As I noted in the Introduction, Read Alouds and Guided Reading were techniques heavily promoted by the Geary Unified School District as part of the district-wide literacy reform.

During another early visit to the school, I was advised to attend the next regular meeting of the Finance Committee, which met weekly before school. At that meeting, staff members on the committee decided to spend about $10,000 on computer equipment and maintenance needs. In addition, some new funds from the school district were made available and the committee discussed how to assess the staff's needs and spend the funds accordingly in a relatively short period of time. A few days later, the principal suggested that I attend the Principal's Evaluation Committee meeting, which was a representative committee at the school charged with outlining a site-specific process to evaluate the principal.[2] Mrs. Carmichael, the principal at the time, described this committee to me as very "charter." Thus I was introduced to the complexities of Hilltop Charter School as an organization. I now turn to a more detailed analysis of the school's organizational structure and school culture.

Organizational Structure

Unlike schools where teachers teach a single grade and are isolated in their classrooms during the instructional day (see Johnson, 1990, for example; Eisner, 1991 makes a similar point), Hilltop Charter School was organized into multiage classrooms. Ideally, students were to be grouped into two-grade classrooms ranging from K-1 to 4–5. Each multiage classroom was part of a three classroom cluster comprised of an English, a sheltered,[3] and a bilingual classroom. In practice, the organization of grades and classroom clusters depended in part on the mix of students at the school in a given academic year. In some instances, single-grade classrooms were created, as well as classroom clusters of two and four classrooms in various combinations. Each classroom cluster was organized into grade clusters: Early Primary (K-1), Primary (2–3), and Elementary (4–5). The school's weekly schedule was structured so that teachers had blocks of common time to meet in these groupings to plan. Teachers also team-taught within their classroom clusters. In addition, each teacher led a "family" comprised of students across the schools' K-5 grade span, which met once a week. All students were assigned to a family when they joined the school community that they would remain in for their tenure at Hilltop Charter School.

Data from the SASS can help us place the organization of teaching at Hilltop Charter Schools within a wider context. A series of questions on the school questionnaire provides information about students and classroom organization. To be consistent with the analyses presented in chapter 1, I limited the analysis to charter schools and conventional public schools in charter states. In addition, because my goal was to understand how Hilltop Charter School's organizational structure compared to that of other similar schools, I further restricted the sample to include only conventional public schools and charter schools that served all of the grades between kindergarten and fifth grade that were identified as either a regular elementary school or an elementary school with a special emphasis (e.g., science, math, or language immersion).[4] While the survey did not have a specific question related to the use of multigrade classrooms, 88 percent of conventional public schools reported using traditional grades to organize their classes compared to 74 percent of charter schools. This suggests that Hilltop Charter School was unusual because the entire school was organized around multigrade classrooms. Likewise, team-teaching was not very prevalent in either conventional public schools or charter schools. Paired or team-teaching was used at 48 percent of conventional public schools and 56 percent of charter schools. Finally, only 15 percent of conventional public schools and 32 percent of charter schools reported that they had students organized by grades or groups into "houses" or "families."

At Hilltop Charter School, all teachers and full-time employees were organized into committees that carried out aspects of the school's work. There were eight standing committees: Assessment, Budget, Director Evaluation, Parent Involvement, Human Resources, Education Program, Second Language, and Technology/Library. Most of the committees were staffed on the basis of participants' interests, although each committee was required to have one representative from each grade cluster, with the exception of the Human Resources and Director Evaluation Committees, which were elected by the School Site Council (SSC). Committee work was a condition of employment at the school. While anyone could join or attend any committee meeting, every full-time employee was required to participate on at least one committee.[5] Ad hoc committees were also created on an as-needed basis. All committees reported to the School Site Council (SSC), the governing body of the school, which was chaired by two staff members elected to staggered two year terms. In addition to these committees, which were predominantly run by teachers, there were also two parent-run groups, the Hilltop Charter School Supporters and the

Parent Advisory Council. The latter was comprised of bilingual parents. The SSC, the Human Resources Committee, and the Director Evaluation Committee all had parent representatives and, while it often went unfilled, the SSC also had a seat available for a community representative.

Organizational Structure and the Forging of a Distinctive School Culture

Hilltop Charter School's organizational structure as described above served instructional and administrative purposes explicitly defined in the school's charter: developmental learning, bilingual education, team-teaching, and shared decision-making. While analytically these purposes can be separated, they often blurred in practice. For example, decisions about the school's instructional program had to be brought to the SSC for approval. Likewise, the classroom clusters supported the school's bilingual instructional model and team-teaching.

Developmental Learning

A key assumption of the "developmental model" that was the core component of the school's educational philosophy was that "children grow and develop as whole beings, not one dimension at a time or at the same rate in each dimension" (Hilltop Charter School, 1998, 4). Staff members commonly referred to this understanding of human development in shorthand as the "whole child." Instruction should be aimed at developing students' academic skills and also meeting students "social, emotional, physical, and aesthetic needs" (Hilltop Charter School, 1998, 4). The charter identified seven "critical" components of an effective developmental education program: (1) developmentally appropriate educational practices; (2) multiage grouping; (3) continuous progress; (4) authentic assessment; (5) qualitative reporting methods for documenting student progress; (6) professional teamwork and collaboration; and (7) positive parent and community involvement. Note that the predominant emphasis here is on *how* to teach, rather than on *what* should be taught or, in other words, the technology of teaching rather than content. While other components of the charter were changed over two revisions, this section of the charter remained fairly stable.[6]

Hilltop Charter School's charter explicitly linked the school's developmental focus to reform-initiatives that were underway in the Geary Unified School District when the school was founded, and in particular the work of a task force focused on reforming primary education that released its findings in the spring of 1992, right before the school reopened. Distributed to teaching staff during the school's planning phase and quoted in the charter, the Developmental Primary Task Force's report described the declining academic achievement among the district's youngest students and the high levels of retention among "at-risk" students and concluded that the "present curriculum and testing practices are inappropriate for the developmental needs of the primary age child and current interventions are not working" (Task Force Report, 1992, 4). Drawing from a range of extant policy talk on reforming primary education, the task force recommended reconfiguring early primary and primary education to provide a "developmentally appropriate," experiential education program for students. While a detailed discussion of the task force's findings and recommendations is beyond the scope of this analysis, a few points are worth noting here because the education program outlined in Hilltop Charter School's charter can be read as an effort to enact the recommendations of the task force.

Developmental learning was defined as providing to children active learning experiences that, while planned and facilitated by teachers, were focused around allowing even very young students to make choices about their educational experiences. Such an approach will enable "children to start 'wherever they are' on the developmental continuum, to grow and learn at their own pace" (Task Force Report, 1992, 8). The report recommended de-emphasizing teacher-centered instruction and seatwork and instead advocated the following teaching practices: reconfiguring classrooms to allow students to work in different ways, creating activity centers for students that allow students to work independently, using small and large group strategies flexibly to introduce concepts, rotating students between work at centers and more focused instruction in small groups throughout the day, and integrating academic subjects through thematic instruction. In this setting, students' progress should be evaluated continuously using both formal and informal assessments. Moreover, students should be assessed in relationship to their own growth and not in comparison to other students or an "arbitrary standard" (Task Force Report, 1992, 17). Finally, teachers should have opportunities to team teach and plan. As I discuss in greater detail in chapter 5, these recommendations were echoed by a state task force on elementary education in a report released the same month entitled *It's Elementary*. This report, described as a "Bold Blueprint" for elementary education in the headline of the front page story in *The Los Angeles Times* announcing its release, was distributed to all elementary teachers in California (Asimov, 1992, A1).

Hilltop Charter School worked hard to implement and maintain many of these practices school-wide. By the time of the fieldwork—in the school's seventh and eighth years—many of the practices described in the task force document and the original charter were still regularly in evidence at the school, particularly in the early grades, which was the specific target of the district task force report. The most significant departure from the developmental education program described in the original charter was a relative de-emphasis on thematic instruction, which was implemented schoolwide for about five years.[7] During the school's early years, the science and social studies curricula were integrated through a site-created "thematic matrix"—school-wide themes that spanned grade levels. Each trimester was structured around a topic (environment, expressions, enchantment). During each trimester, each grade cluster studied age-appropriate subjects related to that topic in a two-year cycle. For example, in the first year, early primary students would study their home and community, primary students would study the environment, and elementary students would study world geography as part of the unit on the environment. Over time, the school-wide themes became increasingly difficult for the school to maintain because of factors internal and external to the school site: high teacher turnover, and pressure within and outside the school to move to a standards-based curriculum.

Many analysts have documented the high rates of teacher turnover at high poverty urban schools, much of which can be explained by conditions within schools (Shen, 1997; Ingersoll, 2001; Loeb, Darling-Hammond and Luczak, 2005). Hilltop Charter School fits this broad pattern. Two separate periods of crisis at the school, which I describe in more detail in chapter 4, each of which culminated in the reassignment of the school's principal, resulted in staff turnover. The teachers who left tended to be the more experienced teachers on staff, many of whom were founding members of the school community. The staff turnover had a large impact on this component of the academic program. Both new and experienced teachers reported that, as the more experienced teachers left the school, the teachers who were hired in their places did not have the training, curricular materials, and/or experience to implement the school-wide themes. In this context, district and state standards and textbooks provided important teaching resources. Ultimately the thematic matrix as it was originally configured was discontinued schoolwide. However, Hilltop Charter School remained committed to thematic instruction. Over approximately a two-year period, the Education Program Committee worked from state standards to create a new thematic matrix. During this process, after reviewing the state standards for grades four and five, the Education Program Committee decided that the social studies standards for each grade were too specific to fit into a two-year cycle (e.g., California missions are to be studied in the fourth grade), so they reverted to grade-level standards for the elementary cluster.

At the same time, the preceding discussion suggests that state standards were stable. However, in the years after Hilltop Charter School was founded, the state content and teaching standards were revised for all major subjects. As I detail in chapter 5, the state's subject matter standards or "curriculum frameworks" had been revised in the late 1980s and early 1990s as part of the broader array of reforms initiated in the wake of *A Nation at Risk* by State Superintendent of Instruction Bill Honig (Ravich, 1993). By 1995, controversy around the California Learning Assessment (CLAS), the performance-based assessment aligned with the curriculum frameworks, and the state's poor performance on the National Assessment of Educational Progress (NAEP) initiated another round of revisions to the curriculum frameworks (Gardner, 1997). During this period, the State Board of Education adopted the SAT-9 for assessment purposes.

The shift at Hilltop Charter School—from a site-created thematic matrix to a standards-based program taught developmentally—suggests that there is a complicated relationship between aspects of the school's policy context and internal organizational dynamics. Staff turnover in tandem with changes in state policy were all factors that propelled the school to move from a more "locally" created curriculum to one that was more tightly aligned with state standards. I expand on this point in chapter 5 when I compare the effect of these shifts in state testing policies on Hilltop Charter School and Inspiration School.

A widely shared understanding of Hilltop Charter School as a "developmental" school was a key component of the school culture at Hilltop Charter School. Staff members readily used the term in the daily life of the school— in interviews, at staff and SSC meetings, in informal discussions, and in situations where the staff described the school to outsiders—to describe the school's broader educational approach and specific policies and practices. However, at one of our first meetings, Mrs. Carmichael, the principal at the time, commented that, instructionally, Hilltop Charter School was not that different than other schools and that the use of developmental teaching strategies at the school varied across classrooms. This assessment was consistent with the comments made by teachers during formal interviews and informal discussions. While teachers were too professional to "name names," they were aware of and actively assessed the degree to which their past and present colleagues taught "developmentally." In some cases, they also assessed their own teaching in these terms. On one hand, this could be viewed as participants' knowledge of the gap between "theory and practice." On the other hand, the fact that these conversations took place was significant in and of itself because they reflected how deeply embedded this concept was in the normative life of the school. Thus, even if teachers were not formally sanctioned for not being "developmental" enough (although one teacher reported experiencing some peer pressure in her first years at the school), teaching "developmentally" was one of the parameters of appropriate action within the school.

Bilingual Education: Teaching English Language Learners

As I noted in the Introduction, from its inception, Hilltop Charter School served a large population of English language learners (ELLs). In 1999–2000, 61 percent of Hilltop Charter School's students were identified as ELLs and 77 percent of these were Spanish speakers. This feature makes Hilltop Charter School distinctive among both charter and conventional public schools. In contrast, in the 1999–2000 SASS, 7 percent of students attending conventional public schools were ELLs, compared to 5 percent of students attending charter schools. Among the same sample of schools roughly similar to Hilltop Charter School, very few schools—only 5 percent of conventional public schools and 6 percent of charter schools—had student populations in which greater than 50 percent of their students were identified as ELLs.[8]

To address the needs of these students, Hilltop Charter School implemented a developmental model for bilingual instruction. The aspect of school organization that best reflected the emphasis on bilingual education was the classroom cluster structure, which grouped a bilingual, sheltered, and English classroom. Bilingual classrooms were comprised of Spanish-speaking students who were taught in Spanish for part of the instructional day. Non-Spanish speaking ELL students taught in sheltered classrooms in English were provided with support in their native language by the second language "sweep team" that pulled children out of the classroom for one-on-one lessons throughout the day. Finally, classrooms with fluent English speakers comprised the third component of the classroom cluster.

The classroom cluster structure served two purposes: to integrate the English-dominant and ELL students throughout the school day and to provide teachers an opportunity to work together as a team. I will discuss the latter in more detail below. During most days there was a specified time when students would rotate among the classrooms in their classroom cluster for subject area lessons (e.g., social studies, science) taught by the three teachers in their classroom clusters. Rather than move as a classroom, students in each classroom would be divided into thirds and mixed to create three groups comprised of students from a fluent English, sheltered, and bilingual classroom. This technique was also used to mix students within their classroom clusters for once-a-week "rotations"—a two and a half-hour block when the students attended music, physical education, or library classes that were taught by resource teachers. Some of the lower grade classroom clusters also combined their students in this way for at least one hour a week during "PDR," or Perform, Do, Review, or less structured play-oriented activities in centers. In addition to these more structured opportunities for interaction, some teachers in classroom clusters also mixed their classrooms on a more informal basis.

As a result, students of different levels of English language proficiency had multiple opportunities to interact with their peers in academic activities, which teachers described as more meaningful than if students of different language backgrounds only interacted during lunch and recess. Some teachers would direct students to choose students from other rooms as their partners during these lessons to facilitate this process. Teachers often pointed out that during these lessons English was the only common language among the students. In addition, another benefit of this aspect of school organization was that students had the opportunity to work with a wide range of teachers as they progressed through the school. The frequent mixing of students was a feature that many staff members described as distinctive about the school. Bilingual teachers often pointed out that in more traditional schools, their students would be isolated from the rest of the school in separate classrooms for most, if not all, of the day. These themes come together in a Bilingual teacher's description of the school's language program, which began as a discussion about what is different about Hilltop Charter School and why she came to work there:

> [I]t would provide [students] real opportunities to work in academic areas in English and also support their primary language. But not be the sort of isolation model that I had taught in for so long. It was the model at [conventional district schools] where they would have the majority of their day in Spanish and a pull-out program for ESL or a half hour a day where they did formal English instruction. The plan here was to have more of their time spent with sheltered, SDAIE [Specially Designed Academic Instruction in English] strategies where the kids would be involved in real activities with English models mixed in with other kids, not so isolated. And having vocabulary and the concept instruction in their native language and also in English. And I am not so sure that is happening today in all classroom clusters. But that was the original way it was done. That is why it was so important that we had to work closely in classroom clusters. Because we had to be on the same concept. [I]f we were doing patterning, colors and classification in the afternoon with the mixed grouping, then I had to be doing that in the morning [in Spanish] so that the kids had the concepts. So in afternoons [when] they mixed up in their workshop groups to work on activities in English-speaking classrooms with English-speaking teachers with other English-speaking kids, or with kids [where English] was their only common language—because we also had the sheltered kids—they would know what was going on. Even if they couldn't understand everything that was said, the workshops were done with manipulatives, visuals. Things that the kids could tie into. They could get then the vocabulary for the concept that they already had in Spanish that they already understood.

Teachers across the three types of classes viewed this practice as beneficial to *all* students because it exposed them to other peers and teachers and helped to create a positive community-oriented environment on the campus (although one teacher was critical about the extent to which students interacted in less teacher-directed activities).

> When we mix the kids up and they go into other classrooms for different activities. You can't do that in a lot of other schools because the kids just don't know how to react when they step outside of the boundaries of their own classroom door. Our kids, you can send them anywhere and put them anywhere and they are very flexible and very respectful generally. And I think that is a success. I think that we have created that kind of a community for these kids where they can walk into any school and find their own way.

Indeed, staff members frequently cited the comments made by people who worked with many different schools, such as art instructors, substitute teachers, and performers, about the positive affective environment they encountered at Hilltop Charter School, which staff members largely attributed to the classroom cluster arrangement.

The emphasis on the school's language program also represented the teachers' efforts to enact a program that valued students' home languages and experiences, a goal that was made increasingly difficult in California in the late 1990s after ballot referendums such as Proposition 187 (which barred illegal immigrants from using public services) and Proposition 227 (which mandated the virtual elimination of bilingual education) were passed by voters. Indeed, staff members—particularly those who taught bilingual or sheltered classes—explicitly described the charter as the vehicle that allowed them to maintain their bilingual program in the face of these shifts in state policy.

The classroom cluster arrangement as envisioned in the charter was difficult for the school to maintain consistently, in large part because of changes in district and state policy. When the school first reopened, at the request of the original principal, Geary Unified allowed the school to cap its enrollment by classroom type so that new students would be admitted in the middle of the year only if there was space available in an appropriate classroom. For example, if the only openings were in bilingual classrooms, English-speaking students would be sent to another school. This policy was eventually discontinued because of demographic changes, overcrowding in central city schools (for example, a school that was opened in the mid-1990s was overenrolled from the first day), and, according to some staff members, Mrs. Carmichael was less willing to negotiate with the district to maintain the enrollment caps. As a result, in some years it was difficult for the school to maintain a balance between the three types of classrooms. For example, one year two bilingual classrooms were paired and while these teachers often mixed their students, the students did not have the benefit of consistent exposure to English-speaking peers.

Maintaining this configuration was even more difficult after 1996 when the California state legislature passed a law requiring class size reduction in kindergarten through third grade, and classrooms at these grades were limited to no more than twenty students. As new students came in to the school, existing students often had to be shuffled between classrooms so that all students were appropriately placed within the arrangement of classrooms at the school. At the end of the 1998–1999 academic year, the teachers spent hours in "configuration" meetings examining the projected enrollment of new students, the placement needs of their continuing students, and the credentials and training of the teaching staff in an effort to recreate the multigrade classroom cluster structure for the following school year. In some cases, teachers physically switched classrooms to accommodate the changes they made—no small task considering that years' worth of teaching materials had to be packed, moved, and reorganized in their new classrooms during their summer vacations.

Team Teaching

As noted above, the classroom cluster structure reflected the strong emphasis and importance placed on bilingual education. Another aim of the classroom cluster structure was to facilitate team-teaching. Once a week, while the students attended "rotation" activities (music, physical education, or computer lab), classroom cluster teachers had a common two-and-a-half hour preparation period to plan lessons together and share information about students and teaching strategies. Mixing students for the afternoon activities within the classroom clusters had additional advantages for teachers. First, it allowed teachers to specialize on different subjects within their classroom cluster. Second, it reduced the number of lessons teachers had to plan since they would teach the same lesson to the three groups. In addition, for some teachers this structure also seemed to facilitate collaboration over and above the regularly scheduled opportunities for mixing their classrooms.[9] In addition to classroom cluster meetings, teachers also met regularly in grade clusters, which were designated as time for curriculum planning "instructional conversations," and deciding how monies budgeted for curriculum materials should be spent. Each grade cluster had a "chair" that met with the director and assistant director on a biweekly basis and ran these meetings based on a common agenda.

Both classroom and grade cluster meetings were spaces for teachers to trade ideas, plan lessons together, and receive other types of support. Over the course of my time at Hilltop Charter School, I observed teachers negotiate the division of labor around planning activities and fieldtrips, share teaching strategies and lessons, discuss articles they read as a group, assess the strengths and weaknesses of professional development workshops, discuss problems with students, train each other on new systems the school was implementing, develop and refine rubrics for assessing student writing, and assess student work based on the rubrics.

Like teaching "developmentally," team-teaching was a strong norm at the school, although there were no formal sanctions for not participating on a team—although some teachers advocated policies that required their peers to work in teams. Similarly, teachers were aware of resistance to the group norm, which they discussed in interviews and informal conversations:

> There are people that work together well and there are people that don't. If you are going to be at this school you are going to be expected to work on a team and you are not a team player... maybe you just need to move on and it is probably the best thing for you, and for everybody involved if you go back to a self-contained classroom and work by yourself. You know, close your door and you can do what you want. But when you are in a classroom cluster and you are on a team and you have a program that impacts each other, you have to be able to work together.

This teacher referenced the conventional norm of teaching where a teacher is isolated in his or her classroom to point out how Hilltop Charter School departed from that norm. Likewise, while teachers with a longer tenure at the school often described the school's early years nostalgically by commenting that teachers were not working together as closely as in prior years, they were nonetheless positive about the benefits of teaming, even in this (apparently) more limited form. Like the school's developmental model of teaching and learning, maintaining teacher teams was challenging due to high staff turnover. As a result, teaching teams did not remain stable. In some instances, the school was not always able to hire teachers with the same strong commitment to team-teaching as some of the core teachers at the school. Moreover, the school was small enough so that even though the absolute number of staff members who were resistant to these strongly held tenets of school life was not large, their influence was strongly felt.

Even more substantively, over time, many of the more experienced teachers at the site left the school. Most of the teachers that were hired to replace them over time were newer teachers. This change in the composition of the teaching staff made it difficult to staff the classroom clusters with the mix of experienced and inexperienced teachers that one veteran teacher described as an ideal arrangement for team-teaching:

> When we opened the school we made a very conscious effort. It was very well thought out, that we had a balance between what we called expertise and energy. That we have the old teachers with a lot of experience who were maybe a little burned out and not very energetic [laughs]. And then we have the young people with the fresh ideas and the energy to go, but they don't have the experience of what can work and what can't work....So the working together was wonderful. And we lost our balance. We don't have enough expertise working here, enough experienced teachers. We have wonderful teachers. I am not saying that they are not. But I think you need to have that balance. And I think you need to have, teachers that are experienced that aren't just struggling with just the management of their classrooms....just running a classroom. Managing. Ordering. Figuring out curriculum, growth records, cum. Just getting down the nuts and bolts of it takes 90 percent of your time. And once you get past those first five, ten years you have more time to devote to things like developmental [teaching]. And when you are a new teacher, you don't have time. What you want is, OK, like show me the guide, give me my worksheets. And you can't blame them because they are struggling with, OK, how do I take roll, and just day-to-day management issues. They can't develop a developmental program, walk into a classroom where there are no textbooks and there are no worksheets and expect them to be able to write a curriculum. But when we had the balance, we would have the more experienced teachers to be able to help out with the management issues, and help to develop that program, the developmental, the hands-on. A very developmental program takes a lot of work, a lot of work. And new teachers just don't have the time. Even if they have the expertise they just don't have the time.

Thus, as the school lost many of the core teachers at the school that were well versed in developmentally appropriate teaching practices, it became more challenging for the school to maintain its instructional philosophy school-wide. While this attrition of faculty was occurring, the policy support for developmentally appropriate instructional practices was declining. I discuss these policy shifts in greater detail in chapter 5. In addition, after the Geary Unified School District's reform initiative was underway, there was less institutional support in the form of professional development and training within the district for this instructional model.

The Distribution of Power and Resources: Shared Decision-Making

In the section detailing school governance, Hilltop Charter School's charter states that the school will "concentrate decision-making and resource authority in the hands of the 'service providers,' the people who work with and care for children all day every day" (Hilltop Charter School, 1998, 10). The Finance Committee and the Principal's Evaluation Committee meetings I described in the opening vignette are examples of how "shared decision-making," as it was called at Hilltop Charter School, worked in practice. The governance structure based on shared decision-making or site-based management at Hilltop Charter School can be traced to national, state, and local efforts at restructuring contemporaneous to the school's founding. I discussed school restructuring legislation as an important precursor to charter school legislation in California in chapter 2 and will expand on how these trends played out at Hilltop Charter School in chapter 4.

As the statement in the charter suggests, a core value at Hilltop Charter School was staff-governance via shared decision-making through the SSC and its committees. Every week had a "minimum day." Students were dismissed early, which allowed the teachers a two-hour time block each week for school governance. The SSC, grade cluster, and committee meetings were allotted the equivalent of a two-hour time-block a month to meet during this time. Every staff and parent member of the SSC was issued a "grey binder" that they were expected to bring to SSC and committee meetings and refer to as needed. The grey binders contained a copy of the charter, the SSC bylaws, the staff handbook, a statement from each committee outlining its membership, mission, and yearly goals, and sections for the agendas and minutes of the various meetings.[10]

The SSC was a hybrid governing body that combined both large-scale participatory and representative forms of membership with the balance in favor of the teaching staff (both classroom and support teachers). The Director, the Assistant Director, all teachers, and other full-time staff members (support staff, the counseling office staff, and the building services supervisor) were members of the SSC. In the bylaws, parents and community members were represented on the SSC by elected terms, although the school consistently struggled to find enough parents to fill the eight seats on the council allotted to parents. As a result, teachers predominated in both the composition of the SSC and in voting power. The Director, and all of the committee and grade cluster chairs were expected to report on their activities to the SSC during the regular monthly meetings. Most instructional decisions were delegated to these groups and reviewed at the monthly SSC meetings. The regular reports to the SSC by committees and grade clusters meant that staff members were reasonably informed about school activities beyond their classroom, and also that inactivity was publicly admitted and recorded in the governance minutes.

School-wide decisions were brought to the SSC by any "stakeholder"— any staff, parent, or community member—through a proposal. Once a proposal was brought to the SSC, the group was required to come to a consensus on whether or not the proposal should be approved through a series of highly formalized steps for talking through the proposal, called the proposal process. The norm for decision-making was that consensus on a proposal should be reached among those present without a formal vote. As staff members explained, everyone gets a say. This process might be best described as a kinder, gentler form of majority decision-making. If a staff member "cannot live" with a particular decision, then the staff member was expected and often encouraged to state her or his opinion, even if it was a minority opinion. In this case, the issue went to a formal vote, and a 75 percent majority was required for the proposal to pass. The goal of this process was to build strong support for decisions. If a decision was thoroughly talked through and everyone got to "say their piece," then regardless of their positions during the debate, all staff members were expected to support the final outcome. If a SSC member was not present during the meeting where a decision is made, they lost their right to participate in the decision-making process in the event the issue was resolved.

The importance of the consensus-based decision-making process at Hilltop Charter School was reflected in an exchange at a SSC meeting when the community representative (a relative newcomer to the group) suggested that the group use Parliamentary procedures to reach decisions—thus questioning the group's accepted practice. In response, two teachers with a long tenure at the school responded that consensus was part of the charter, and if staff members did not agree with a decision it was their responsibility to say so. This belief that staff members were expected to raise concerns about decisions was reflected in a phrase often repeated at the school—"silence means consent." Likewise, it was not unusual for a SSC member to remind the group that they have departed from their accepted decision-making procedures by saying that they were not "following process," or to explicitly reference the steps of the proposal process in her/his comments. Similarly, if a decision was made outside of the proposal process, it was often criticized even if it was eventually ratified by the SSC.

Hilltop Charter School's complex governance structure provided channels for staff members and parents (and to some extent community members) to become deeply involved in the school's day-to-day management. For example, staff members ranging from new teachers to the building maintenance supervisor sat on the Finance Committee, which was chaired for three years by the full-time music teacher. The latter joined the committee out of interest, and in the process gained a considerable amount of expertise as he learned to navigate the complexities of charter school financing. The list of proposals from a representative SSC meeting suggests a similar conclusion. Four proposals were approved: (1) the

Technology Committee's request to begin planning a computer lab; (2) the Budget Committee proposal to hire a financial manager; (3) a second Budget Committee proposal to buy an office copier (expenses of about $43,000 and $3,500, respectively); and (4) a proposal by a group of teachers to form an after-school homework club for students. An additional proposal to purchase a test preparation program for the upper grade classrooms was tabled because consensus was not reached.

The range of decisions here and in other meetings I attended throughout my time at Hilltop Charter School suggests that teachers at Hilltop Charter School were broadly empowered across the four domains identified by Marks and Louis (1997): school operations, students' school experiences, teachers' work life, and classroom instruction. Studies of teacher authority suggest that Hilltop Charter School was unusual in this regard. For example, Shen (2001) found that elementary school teachers had a great deal of control over instructional decisions within their classroom, but much less influence on school-wide issues such as hiring, budget, and teacher evaluation (see also the review in Mueller, 1998). As one teacher commented:

> It does take a long time, it is time consuming. . . . [Although] sometimes individuals don't agree with what the group has decided, it is still, in my opinion a more democratic way of governing. I was always very bored when I taught at other schools and we had staff meetings and we sat in rows. And the principal stood in front of us and just talked all the time. And we either said yes, we said yes most of the time because we were told what to do. Here, each individual has the opportunity to present new ideas by following the process that exists, and that is getting proposals, presenting them to the SSC, and allowing the rest to participate in making a decision.

I will expand on this issue in greater detail in chapter 6 when I use data from the SASS to compare charter schools and conventional public schools on decision-making and accountability.

Finally, one ritual that took place during the SSC meetings at Hilltop Charter School provides a good illustration of how organizational structure and school culture, the two concepts I introduced at the beginning of this chapter, are tightly linked. That is, how the school is organized provides a framework within which the beliefs and values of participants are shaped and in turn the school culture, while certainly not static, is reconstituted. The first ten minutes of every SSC meeting were spent reading a section of the charter aloud and briefly discussing it, although the time-constraint prohibited in-depth discussion. The stated goal of this practice was to make sure that everyone was minimally familiar with the charter. The following excerpt from field notes provides a glimpse of how this worked in practice:

> Mr. Arden, the Director began reading from the charter document starting from where the group concluded at the prior SSC meeting. Someone asked what "the province of the Developmental Learning Program" meant and the Assistant Director responded that it meant that the school's priority is its developmental program. Because this sentence was unclear, someone suggested rewording and the Assistant Director, who was also co-chairing the meeting, responded that the SSC meeting was not the time to reword. Ms. Landry, who has been critical of this practice [reading the charter during the SSC meetings] asked "why do we do this" [if we are not rewording]. Mr. Arden read further, and changed the word "Principal" to "Director" as he read, reflecting the recent change in the job title for the position. Mr. Jones asked what "transformation leadership" meant. Ms. Landry replied that "when we wrote that," we meant that the Principal/Director would take us into the "charter future" and have vision. Mr. Arden read a section enumerating the "areas of shared decision-making." Ms. Landry commented that personnel was not an area of shared decision-making, but Ms. Larson responded that the members of the Human Resources Committee are approved by the SSC. Ms. Baxter added that the SSC also approves the creation of staff positions.

This exchange reveals how this regularized practice of reviewing the charter served the function of reproducing and, I would also argue, recreating school culture. Far from being an empty ritual—although some staff members complained that the practice was tedious—reviewing the charter helped to reproduce the school culture by ensuring that new staff members understood the importance of the charter as a document that outlined the school's vision and operational plan and also had some basic knowledge of the content of the charter. This practice recreated school culture by giving continuing staff members the opportunity to revisit the most up-to-date version of the charter, which had been revised considerably since the school opened. Most importantly, this ritual was also a forum for all of the "stakeholders" at the school to discuss their interpretations of the charter as a group. For example, in the exchange above, Ms. Landry both interpreted a section of the charter for someone and had her own understanding of the charter clarified. Notably, Ms. Landry was a critic of this practice because she felt that it was too superficial and instead advocated for more substantive and philosophical discussions about the charter. At other SSC meetings, this ritual highlighted areas where a common understanding of key concepts in the charter, such as developmental learning, needed to be reached.

Hearts and Hands Community School

Hilltop Charter School was a school that had developed a fairly coherent school culture built around the principles outlined in the school's charter. In contrast, at Hearts and Hands Community School, there was a more divided school culture. The main fracture line was around the balance the school was maintaining between the two main elements of its "Waldorf-inspired" curriculum, which was a blend between the secular components of the Waldorf curriculum (and the philosophy that underpins it) and district and state standards. While reaching an optimal balance between these two elements appeared to be a long-term issue the school had been struggling with, this existing tension in the school's culture was exacerbated when the Geary Unified School District initiated a large-scale systemic reform effort, the centerpiece of which was the Balanced Literacy approach, a literacy reform based on specific teaching techniques. Where some staff members were perceived was pushing the staff toward adopting the district reform and following district policies, others viewed this as an erosion of the school's autonomy and, more importantly, the school's Waldorf-inspired curriculum.

On my first day at Hearts and Hands Community School, I observed one of the two kindergarten classrooms. Two pans of bread the class made earlier that morning were rising in a small, improvised kitchen area; these would be served as the next day's snack. As I arrived, students were in the process of writing a sentence they composed together after looking at a hand-drawn picture of a bird. When they finished, the students rearranged their chairs and the tables and created a long banquet-style table. Singing out commands, the teacher called the students to a carpeted area for a song and dance activity. In the meantime, a parent volunteer, a few students, and I dished out macaroni in bowls for the students' snack and filled twenty small jars that served as glasses with water, which we placed on napkins that served as placements.

After the song and dance, the students found their chairs—each chair was marked with a symbol drawn by each child that also marked their hook on the coat rack area—and sat down to eat. As they ate, the teacher told the students to look at the shape of the macaroni (farm animals) and reminded the class that they had talked about farm animals in an earlier lesson. After their snack, students had recess. After recess, the students cleaned up the classroom while their teacher emphasized how important it was that they return everything they used during their play back in its proper place. As we watched and assisted, Mrs. Jewel, the parent volunteer, and I chatted informally. Mrs. Jewel discussed her belief that children can learn through playing and commented that Hearts and Hands

Community School offered an important choice in the public sector. While this vignette is largely illustrative of how Waldorf-inspired education is practiced at Hearts and Hands Community School, a vigorous debate was also occurring at the school about how to blend this educational model with the relatively faster paced academic model promoted by Geary Unified School District described in the Introduction. I discuss the conflict between the two instructional models in more detail in chapter 4. In this chapter, I focus on the aspects of school culture related to Waldorf education.

Organizational Structure

The most salient feature of Hearts and Hands Community School's organizational structure was the curricular model, which was described in school materials and in many instances of school life as "Waldorf-inspired"—a blend of a secularized version of the Waldorf educational philosophy and state and district curriculum frameworks. What this meant in practice was perhaps best reflected in the combination of artifacts visible around the school. One of the first things a visitor walking through the main entrance would see was a poster outlining the Waldorf curriculum hung on a bulletin board outside the main office. Many classrooms displayed watercolor paintings using a wet-on-wet technique characteristic of Waldorf education. In two classrooms, the alphabet strips at the top of the blackboard were made from paper painted in this manner. Many lower grade classrooms had nature tables on display—a small table with carefully arranged natural artifacts such as tree branches, dried flowers, and stones.

However, also readily apparent were the sets of textbooks from a recent district textbook adoption. In one classroom, children busily worked on the portfolios required as a component of the district's assessment system. At various points during the year, teachers in the lower grades tested their students one-on-one using the Developmental Reading Assessment (DRA), another district assessment. Inside at least some of the classrooms there were also elements associated with the district's literacy reform: posters outlining "Conditions for Learning," word walls, and, in one classroom, a block in the daily class schedule posted on the wall designated for Genre Studies, a component of the literacy reform for upper-grade classes.

Aside from the curricular model, however, other aspects of the social organization of teaching at Hearts and Hands Community School resembled that of many other small elementary schools. Because of class size reduction, there were two classrooms at each grade in grades K-3. In addition to one classroom that combined the fourth and fifth grades, there was one classroom for each successive grade through grade eight. The seventh and eighth grade classrooms were commonly referred to as the middle school or the "junior high." At the end of sixth grade, students received certificates to mark their transition from the elementary school to the middle school. All of the classrooms were largely self-contained; the school's organizational structure did not foster much collaboration outside of the initiative of individual teachers. Only two of the pairs of classrooms in the lower grades worked together as a team consistently throughout the year. For example, the kindergarten teachers worked together to create a coherent kindergarten program across their two classrooms that was consistent with the Waldorf model. Two other teachers in the upper grades switched their classes for at least one main lesson block during the school year.

However, a local adaptation of a practice in private Waldorf elementary schools set the school apart from conventional public schools. In private Waldorf elementary schools, teachers remain with their classrooms from the first through eighth grade, an educational practice commonly described as "looping." The first five years the school was open, continuing teachers would loop with their students. For example, one teacher worked with the same class from first grade to sixth grade. Starting in 1998–1999, the school was divided into three loops after kindergarten: first through third grade, fourth through sixth, and seventh through eighth grade. In this system, teachers still moved with their classes, but only within their loop. Once their class reached the end of this smaller loop, teachers would return to the grade at the beginning of their loop and bring another class through. While in conventional public schools teachers sometimes teach a class for two consecutive years, what was notable here is that, like the emphasis on multiage classrooms at Hilltop Charter School, looping was a school-wide practice at Hearts and Hands Community School.

School governance was carried out through a complex committee structure. One teacher served as the head of the faculty, which was comprised of the teaching staff. The faculty chair conducted bimonthly faculty meetings and the "whole-school" meetings that were attended by teachers, administrative staff and administration, and teachers' aides. In addition, there were two other standing committees that were largely comprised of the teaching staff and, in some cases, administrative staff: the Budget Committee, and the Curriculum Committee. There was a Parent Involvement Committee that was comprised of parents and served the function of a Parent Teacher's Organization. In addition, the chairs of the latter two committees, the faculty chair, and a parent member of the Site Management Team described below served as the Executive Committee. This latter committee was created at the beginning of the 1999–2000 school year to address what many participants saw as gaps in the school's organizational structure. The

Executive Committee had two main functions: (1) serving as a centralized system for forwarding information and requests to the relevant parties; (2) and acting as a liaison between the school and the district. Finally, two committees that had been in operation at the school in the past, the Evaluation Committee and the Personnel Committee, were also reconstituted in 1999–2000. In addition to these formal committees, three ad hoc committees were created that year to manage the following tasks: (1) organizing a school-wide retreat and two follow-up meetings; (2) researching the implications of the school's decision to accept the local teacher's union as its collective bargaining unit (a response to changes in charter school legislation that had recently taken effect); and (3) creating an employee handbook.

All of these committees fell under the purview of the school's Site Management Team (commonly referred to as Management), which consisted of four parent members, three faculty/staff members, a classified staff member and the two administrators, a Director of Finances, and a Chief Educational Officer (CEO). While there was some flux in the composition of this group, with the exception of the two seats for the administrators, staff (either teaching or support staff) and parents were required to have equal representation on this body, which, according to the parent handbook, was charged with overseeing "the affairs and overall business management of the school." Most committees ran on staff and parents' commitment and energy. With the exception of faculty and whole-school meetings held on the school's minimum day, most committees met after school hours and often in the evenings.

Organizational Structure and School Culture

In contrast to Hilltop Charter School, where the technology of teaching was a key influence on the school's organizational structure and school culture, at Hearts and Hands Community School, the curriculum based on the Waldorf educational model fundamentally drove the school's organizational structure and the school culture(s) it engendered. Historically, the Waldorf educational model was propagated by independent private schools based on the ideas and philosophy of Rudolf Steiner. As it has evolved, Waldorf education has come to comprise a specific curriculum sequence and technology of teaching, and also site-based management. While the latter is rooted in Steiner's critique of the role of the state in education, it is also compatible with the assumptions of the restructuring movement and the charter school movement. In the section that follows, I provide a brief overview of Waldorf education to help contextualize Hearts and Hands Community School.

Instruction in the Waldorf Educational Model

The first Waldorf school was founded in 1919 in Germany by Rudolf Steiner, an Austrian philosopher, scientist, and educator. Since then, Waldorf education has developed into an international movement. In general, Waldorf education can be characterized by the following features: an integrated, arts-infused curriculum where students learn subject matter through the arts, a developmental view of children's development, and site-based management coupled to a belief in the importance of fostering a sense of community within the school (Uhrmacher, 1995). Despite its long history, there has been little scholarly work evaluating Waldorf education. Most of what has been written about Waldorf education consists of Steiner's voluminous writings and lectures, and analyses of Steiner's ideas by adherents, which range from discussions of practical applications in a range of settings to philosophical interpretations. Many of the latter are books produced by presses and training institutions affiliated with the Waldorf School movement.

Underpinning Waldorf education is a specific vision of human growth and development that emphasizes childhood as a formative stage in a person's life. Childhood is understood as having three distinct physical stages (Edmunds, 1975). The first stage spans from birth through about age six or seven, when the child's adult teeth develop. The second stage begins from age six or seven to age fourteen, or the beginning of puberty. The final stage of childhood is puberty. Each of these physical stages has corresponding cognitive and emotional stages. Because Hearts and Hands Community School is an elementary/middle school (K-8), I focus specifically on the first two stages and the educational practices viewed as appropriate for each stage.

According to Waldorf adherents, in the first stage of development the child's entire being is focused on physical development, although cognitive and moral development is also occurring in the background (Edmunds, 1975; Uhrmacher, 1995). As a result, Waldorf educators believe that a young child in this stage should not be introduced to more "intellectual" forms of education such as reading, memorization of facts, and abstract concepts because this will divert energy from her/his physical development and thus have a negative impact on the child's overall development:

> If we introduce intellectual forms of education before the change of teeth, we can certainly effect results, but only at great cost, because we are working against nature; we are drawing into consciousness, into the nervous system, forces that should still be working unconsciously, and thus we vitiate the development forces needed for the future. Human beings then tend to grow up prematurely intelligent but so much weaker in physical constitution, in character, and in will. (Edmunds, 1975, 31)

As a result, in Waldorf education, kindergarten is viewed as a transitional grade that bridges the home and school; this view is reflected in the practice of having the children wear slippers in the classroom. Texts on Waldorf education (Edmunds, 1975; Clouder and Rawson, 1998) describe the ideal Waldorf kindergartens as places where children are engaged in a variety of activities—free play, art or craft activities, listening to stories told orally by the instructor, recitation of songs and rhymes—that occur at regularly scheduled times throughout the day and/or week. For example, while play and oral activities might be scheduled each day, children in a Waldorf kindergarten might also participate in particular handcraft activities on a weekly or biweekly basis at a designated day and time.

Instead of formal academic lessons, children in kindergarten classrooms engage in what Clouder and Rawson (1998) describe as "constructive play." Children play with natural or unfinished objects that are meant to spark their imaginations (Edmunds, 1975). Imitation of adult activities is another important aspect of play; here the teacher is an important role model. Cleaning up after play is also an important task—as important as the play itself—which the children are expected to participate in. The students also set the table with placemats and place settings for the daily snack, which the children eat together after reciting a brief verse of thanks. All of these activities—which primarily focus on motor skills—are viewed as providing a foundation for children's subsequent intellectual development:

> By learning how to grasp and manipulate in a meaningful way with the hands, a functional basis is formed in the child's mind for the later development of 'grasping' the world through concepts. By modeling their behavior on those around them, children acquire skills in the same way that they acquire their mother tongue, not by being taught but through imitation combined with the unfolding of innate interest-driven formative forces. The learning environment is wholly integrated rather than compartmentalized and subject based. This is achieved by the 'natural' homey atmosphere of the kindergarten. The development of mathematical, conceptual or coordination skills arises experientially out of the practical activities, such as those described above. (Clouder and Rawson, 1998, 43)

In subsequent grades, lessons based on the Waldorf educational model are delivered utilizing a specific technology of teaching, the main lesson, a two-hour period that opens the day. During main lesson, students concentrate on a subject or age-appropriate theme for a four-week block. Activities during the main lesson are varied. Students listen to and discuss lectures delivered orally by their teachers, participate in rhythm and recitation exercises related to the main lesson, and work individually on their main lesson notebooks or workbooks where they record what they learn and essentially create their own textbooks (Edmunds, 1975). In the early grades, students are expected to learn by imitating their teachers and copying pictures and texts. Over time, students are given more freedom to create their own individualized main lesson books.

Generally whole-class activities, main lessons focus on a subject or age-appropriate theme. However, a main lesson should also be integrated, that is, it should incorporate activities that develop skills in other subjects as well. Teachers are also discouraged from using textbooks because they promote passive learning, and instead are expected to deliver lessons orally and use rhythm and tempo to convey meaning (Uhrmacher, 1995). Rhythm is also used to teach mathematics through activities that involve clapping and stomping. In the early grades, many lessons are built around stories and narratives that provide both moral lessons and an entry point into other subjects (Clouder and Rawson, 1998). For example, in the third grade, students learn creation stories, which are meant to teach children lessons about the relationship between humankind and nature and the responsible use of resources (Edmunds, 1975).[11] These lessons are expanded and elaborated in lessons on farming and shelters, and can also be extended to include grammar lessons about constructing sentences using active verbs. Finally, throughout the Waldorf educational process, lessons are expected to start from the child's concrete experiences, and use the child's concrete experience to introduce more abstract concepts.

While the Waldorf school movement has been primarily a creature of the private sector in the form of independently run private schools, Hearts and Hands Community School was the product of more recent efforts to integrate the practices of Waldorf education into public school settings. This trend began in 1991 when a Waldorf magnet school was opened in inner-city Milwaukee (Byers et al., 1996). Two years later when a parent began the chartering process, the Milwaukee school was the organizational model for Hearts and Hands Community School. Teachers at Hearts and Hands Community School reported visiting this school annually and described the Milwaukee public Waldorf school as the model for the school they were striving to create. Subsequently, other public schools patterned after the Waldorf educational model have been opened as either magnet schools or charter schools. At the time of the fieldwork there were twelve Waldorf-inspired charter schools in California. To capitalize on this trend, at least one Waldorf training institute was offering classes for teachers in public Waldorf-inspired schools.

Waldorf-Inspired Education in Practice at Hearts and
Hands Community School

As I noted above, signs of Waldorf-inspired education were readily apparent in classrooms throughout the school. For example, the kindergarten classrooms shared most, if not all, of the features described above, including: a very structured schedule, daily snacks where children would participate in setting the table and cleaning up, and periods of unstructured play. Many classrooms had large chalk pictures related to the current "Main Lesson" block prominently on display. At various points in the day (usually morning) students could be seen working on Main Lesson books, which students and teachers would readily and proudly show off. In most classrooms, students' desks held square beeswax crayons, recorders, and handmade pencil cases.

In the mornings, students participated in "circle activities," which included songs and poetry related to past and present main lessons. For example, one class recited a poem by Langston Hughes and a poem about a local Indian tribe—the latter was part of their main lesson block on California history—and participated in math-related movement activity. It was also common to see kindergarten and first-grade students walking through the corridors en route to lunch or recess, led by their teachers or instructional aides singing songs. Students attended weekly gardening classes in areas around the school designated as "class gardens" (for example, the second-grade garden) and also had regular handwork classes. Both of these classes were taught by specialty teachers. Classroom teachers provided music lessons on recorders and art lessons, such as wet-on-wet watercolor painting and beeswax modeling.

More fundamental, however, was the influence of the Waldorf curriculum on the technology of teaching through the organization of instructional time and subject matter in "Main Lesson" blocks taught in every grade with the exception of kindergarten.[12] In Hearts and Hands Community School's charter, the main lesson was described in the following way:

> The key to the program is the main lesson block format: intensive study on a core subject for an extended period of time, usually three to four weeks. These blocks are rotated throughout the year according to grade level, with eight to ten blocks per school year. (Hearts and Hands School Charter, 1998, 12)

While main lesson books focus on a particular subject or even a particular topic, teachers emphasized that one of the key features of main lessons is that they are integrated, that is, the main lessons also incorporate other subjects into the lesson. For example, one teacher commented:

> What is Waldorf-inspired education? In my classroom it is clearly that I am integrating language arts, math, science and social studies in a thematic block. So with Aesop's Fables we were also doing math. We were bringing in math aspects of Greece and the first numbers and where they came from and how people counted in those days. That is history. . . . [W]e were learning to borrow and carry along with that. Earlier in the year we had multiplication along with a Native American unit where I [taught] American Indian stories about animals. For me that is the way that works.

Another teacher with more extensive Waldorf training highlighted similar themes and also talked about the importance of engaging multiple intelligences.

> Number one, it is a given, that we are teaching to all of the multiple intelligences, and that every lesson, whether it is main lesson or a special subject has to incorporate, we call it a three-fold when we talk about head, heart and hands. So you are working with the will, in some way doing something. And you are working with the imagination, the feelings. And you are also working with the thinking. So even when you are painting, you have to bring in the thinking element. We work with what you might call thematic units. We focus on a topic for month. We give a two-hour lesson every day that includes this multiple intelligence aspect, lots of kinesthetic work, visual intelligence, musical intelligence. You know, the whole nine yards. And it is an integrated thematic unit where there is history, literature, science or geography. So it is going to involve literacy, it is going to involve usually some mathematics, it is going to involve research hopefully. All these different aspects. And definitely the whole curriculum is taught through the arts. So you might call it a creative arts curriculum.

Similarly, in classroom observations and as teachers discussed their main lessons in formal interviews and informal conversations, it was evident that many of them were following the basic frameworks for main lessons outlined in the current version of the school's charter (at the time the original charter had been revised and renewed), which were adapted from both Waldorf curriculum frameworks and the California state curriculum frameworks. This third grade teacher's description of his schedule for the main lesson blocks for the year is also strikingly similar to the description of the third-year curriculum in texts on Waldorf education, which describes lessons on creation stories, farming, and shelters (Clouder and Rawson, 1998).

> This year I have [pulls out schedule]. We teach in blocks. In September my math block, I integrated math [and] form drawing with fables. And we did

a lot of review in the first month. The second month I taught, October—the blocks last three to four weeks, depending if I get stuck on it or do extra things—language arts, we did a lot of creation stories. [Lists main lesson blocks by month.] Science, we did the grains. I should have switched these back and forth. It was a science main block, but I focused on grains. And I am always integrating math. We use a lot of math. Math, there is a math block. We worked on measurement, the metric system. Language Arts in March. And the focus is local native people's stories. And we read a lot of stories, we did a lot of projects and things on language arts. And it is integrated everything at the same time. Geography, science, math, but the main focus is language arts. Geography, we just finished that one, [the main focus] was shelters. Shelters from around the world. So we did projects where kids actually picked a country, and they built a shelter from that country. And they had to bring it in and write a report on it. And describe it and talk about the whole area.

Teachers that taught third grade in other years also described doing main lesson blocks on grains with their students. While one fourth-grade teacher described teaching a main lesson block on California history—a key component of the fourth-grade history standards—another main lesson block was on animals, which is a main lesson in the fourth-grade Waldorf curriculum. Likewise, in the latter's class, the end of the year class play was "Thor's Hammer," which the class performed for the entire school. The play was based on a story of the Norse gods, another component of the fourth grade Waldorf curriculum (Clouder and Rawson, 1998).[13] As this discussion suggests, the curriculum at Hearts and Hands Community School outlined in the charter and in practice in many classrooms followed the broad outlines for Waldorf education outlined in texts aimed at a practitioner audience.

While the tangible product of the main lesson is the main lesson book made by each student, and is more concretely the "stuff" of school, that is, reading, writing and artwork, the "circle" exercises discussed briefly above were also an important part of each day's main lesson activities. Students gathered in a circle inside their classroom or outside in the playground and recited poetry, math exercises (e.g., multiplication tables), and participated in movement activities. Sometimes these were combined. For example, fourth-grade students learning multiplication had to take turns around the circle reciting the multiples of seven while clapping and moving to a rhythm—"stomp-stomp-clap-7, stomp-stomp-clap-14"—which required students to say the correct number during their turn at the appropriate beat. In a more complex rhythmic activity, students had to take seven steps backwards and clap, then move six steps forward and clap twice and continue with this pattern until they reached one step backward, clapping seven times. According to their teacher, these activities served social and academic purposes:

> It is really to have them move, to integrate the right and left side of their body, which is how, their brain is doing the same thing. To speak in chorus, to speak clearly, because I think people would say that spelling is atrocious in our country as a whole. And in our district even that is one of the lower points in the testing. But children's speech is lazy. They don't say the final sounds. So you are working on clear speech. Speaking together.... [W]hen I started with this class, there were several children who would speak faster than everyone else, things I would never imagine people would do. Or not speak clearly. So it is really good too for social interaction. Also standing in a circle, they look at each other. They have to hold hands. It is not about cooties. Some days it is, but usually it is not. They just have to learn not to tolerate each other but to accept each other, and respect that we all have an important place in this classroom and no one is more important that the rest of us. I even tell them that I am not more important or less important, but I just have a different job to do. And then the verses are to enhance the main lesson. Whatever subject we are learning. And I do math every morning, rhythmically, because I think it just helps the children settle into their bodies as we get ready for the day.

While these are the more readily visible aspects of the Waldorf educational model, other teachers emphasized the importance of oral storytelling, particularly for younger students. One teacher drew on the Waldorf educational philosophy to explain this practice: Stories told orally are an effective way to engage children's imaginations because they are not "bombarded" with the images the illustrator creates, and thus the children are freer to imagine the story in their own terms. Notably, oral storytelling was one of the criteria for assessing teachers on a site-created teacher evaluation form. Likewise, in discussing their classroom practices, some teachers—particularly those with the most training in Waldorf education—described the school's practices in terms of the philosophical underpinnings of Waldorf education. For example, as part of a longer discussion of the "Waldorf-inspired" components of the curriculum, one teacher described the importance of the specialty subjects in the following way:

> The fact that we have gardening, that we really want the children to have the connection to the earth, that handwork again is to learn the skill, to work those fine motor skills, but it is also that we can produce things that are practical and useful to us. So the self-sufficiency. I think as teachers we don't always see the results. I think we are teaching to the thirty-year-old more. What we are doing today will come into fruition much later down the road. I remember one little boy, he had set everything out. He had made

a pencil case, a recorder case, and there was one more object that we were using in the classroom for things we had, and he said, teacher, I made all of these. So to me, that said, oh, this is such an important part of the program, to feel, OK I can take care of myself, I can do this.

As a final point, the Waldorf-inspired curriculum was highly teacher-driven. Unlike a curricular program or "package" with a manual, teachers had to compile the information students used to create main lesson books, and plan the accompanying activities (i.e., the circle, oral storytelling). Moreover, because the teachers "looped" with their students, until they completed their loop with their class and returned to the initial grade in their loop with a new class, teachers had to repeat this process for each grade—they could not revisit the lesson plans they developed the previous year.

Teaching With Beauty as an Aspect of School Culture

One aspect of school culture that emerged from the interviews and fieldwork was the importance for things to be "beautiful" and to be done beautifully—even down to the most mundane and routine classroom activities, such as in this instance, where students were making a chart about pronunciation:

Ms. Hardy told the class that they would be making a chart to keep that would tell them how to pronounce the letter "c" with different vowel combinations which would be "really, really beautiful with colored pencils." She directed the students to get out their pads of paper. Because the room was noisy, she commented "I'm sorry second graders, this isn't working" and then told the students to pull their chairs all the way in and sit up straight. She stood up at the board and modeled each step for them. "In the center make a beautiful 'C.'" Ms. Hardy told the students to go over their "C" several times and then "very carefully" make a little box around it to show their readers that the page is all about the letter "C." She proceeded to draw two each of "k" and "s" around the C, enclosing them in boxes and making arrows to join them with the C. As she wrote the letters students made the sounds to pronounce them (k-k-k). Working at the board, she told the students that they should make a "nice circle" around "k" and draw a "beautiful s." Around the side she wrote vowels to indicate how the C would be pronounced, and students were told to find words that matched each pronunciation and write them in the correct place. One student asked, "Can we put a border?" [main lesson books characteristically have a colored border around each page]. Ms. Hardy responded yes and told the students to make their charts "beautiful so we can laminate it...make the color stand out and the spelling correct." She informed the students she wanted the students to use their nicest handwriting and that they should "please be willing to do it again," and to be sure that they have "checked every word."

One teacher, Mr. Healy, described the emphasis on beauty and the use of the arts in the curriculum as the hook that will get students engaged in the learning process. In this context, the arts were not a luxury in an age of high standards, but a fundamental part of the best teaching and learning, and for this particular teacher, the best way to engage inner-city children:

> You have to integrate all that [arts in the curriculum, communicating with parents and getting them engaged and involved], and make the school a beautiful place for kids to come. Where they want to come, where they want to open their minds up, and they want to just absorb as much as they can. That is where I see Waldorf is, you make education beautiful to them, and not just words on the board and looking up this. You've got to make it relevant to their lives, and beautiful for them. They get enough out there on the streets, on TV and all that mess.

Yet in Mr. Healy's classroom, this orientation was coupled to high academic standards. In this example from field notes, he directed his third grade students to incorporate complex vocabulary into their Main Lesson books:

> With the students gathered around his chair on the floor, Mr. Healy read the class a story entitled *Come on Rain!* written from the perspective of a young Black girl living in a city during a hot summer. After finishing, he picked up another book, telling the students that "this is heavy science, so you better listen." Before reading he asked the class "what is water." Students gave a variety of answers, including "a combination of things" "H_2O" and "liquid." After a few more student responses—"drink, liquid, good for you" "two hydrogen cells and an oxygen" (this latter response started as one hydrogen and two oxygen), Mr. Healy asked the class "what is a cell?" At this point, the students were getting silly. He commented to the students that it was a "crazy Monday" and added that while the students were pleased they were getting out of school early [the students had early dismissal because of parent conferences], during the parent conferences later that afternoon he would be able to remember these incidents to report them to their parents. Telling them they needed to put their names on the front covers, he handed out their main lesson books. Because he had to look inside each book to find out who it belonged to, he also commented on the quality of the student work (i.e., if it was sloppy or neat). He directed them to turn to the next clean page and copy the drawing of the water cycle on black paper with chalk that was taped to the board. On the next page they had to define the three words in the water cycle written on the drawing (precipitation, evaporation, and condensation) and retell the story *Come on Rain!* in their own words. He reminded them that he wanted neat work from them, which included a border and cursive writing. After consulting the book he had planned to read, he added transpiration to the list, and told the class: "there is another [word] we are going to do because we are

all going to college. Are we going to college?" The students responded in unison "Yes."

For these teachers, then, teaching "with beauty" or teaching with the arts did not mean little substantive content. Instead, the arts were an integral part of the academic curriculum because they made lessons more meaningful for students. As another teacher commented:

> The key component is that you have to be able to know how to integrate the disciplines—math, science, and literacy—in every aspect of the work that you do every day. We don't teach math for twenty minutes, grammar for twenty minutes. But lessons have to be really alive with all of those elements. And they have to be done enthusiastically, actually orally, and tied to a story element that engages the children.

Notably, the teachers that came to Waldorf education through their association with the school—and learning about Waldorf education on the job—described being challenged as teachers and as individuals because everyday teaching required a level of artistic competence they did not have when hired:

> *Teacher*: [I]n three years I have developed a lot more skills in block crayons and pencils and main lesson books and drawings. You noticed that map of Africa that I did on black construction paper?
> *Jeanne*: I don't think I got to see that.
> *Teacher*: It is by the door...
> *Jeanne*: By the Kwaanza [display]?
> *Teacher*: It is my handiwork. I did that. I can't believe I did that. I am amazed at myself. ...And it never would have happened if I hadn't been challenged by this. And so I have learned and experimented and grown from that.

However, effectively incorporating art into the curriculum and using Waldorf techniques was generally much easier for the teachers with specialized training in Waldorf education. Yet teachers were not required to have Waldorf training as a condition of being hired. And aside from a small stipend to attend summer workshops once teachers were employed, the school did not offer teachers much professional development and training in the Waldorf curriculum. By the end of the academic year, there had been considerable discussion among the teaching staff about the need for mentoring within the staff around the more specialized aspects of the Waldorf curriculum (e.g., beeswax modeling). Ultimately, the expectation that teachers' lessons should incorporate the Waldorf-inspired curriculum and technology of teaching coupled to minimal institutional support for training in the Waldorf model created a rift among the faculty, which I discuss in more detail in chapter 4.

While the Waldorf model was clearly an important feature of school life, it was not rigidly implemented at Hearts and Hands Community School. For example, the Association of Waldorf Schools of North America (AWSNA) recommends limiting young children's exposure to electronic media because the barrage of images it provides constrains the development of children's imaginations. Similarly, AWSNA also recommends that students wait until high school to use computers because they hinder the social interactions that support learning. However, in the course of an interview and discussing student work, Mr. Healy described a web site he had created for his third-grade students so that they could do academic work over the summer:

> I don't know how many [students] have computers. And this is not the Waldorf way, computers, but there is so much on the Internet. I have several pages already. And I am going to give them a password. During the summer, if they really want to study, I am going to have some problems on the board. [...] I am going to try to do it in a beautiful way too. So have some nice things on there to go to. Talk to their parents, make sure their parents know. And I am going to have some sites where they can go to and just study. Some art. A lot of things they can do.

Similarly, another teacher described integrating the techniques of Writer's Workshop (an activity used by teachers at other schools, including teachers at Hilltop Community School) into the process of creating Waldorf main lesson books with her students:

> Why was I using Writer's Workshop? I was experimenting. I sort of feel like a mini-laboratory, because I have kind of exported myself out of the mainstream of Waldorf education, after having been in it most of my adult life. And I am trying to apply the principles, because the idea of Waldorf is really not to apply a dogmatic method but to apply the principles of the method to whatever situation you find yourself in, whether it is in Brazil, or Israel, or South Africa. So here I am in [Geary City] with inner-city kids with all of these constraints. So I decided I wanted to focus on writing, and I wanted to empower them. So I decided to experiment with this tool, this instrument of Writer's Workshop. ...So I have completely adapted the material that I would be bringing anyway. And all I have done is introduce the concept of brainstorming and prewriting, which I think that probably a lot of Waldorf teachers could well use. And do use at older grades but perhaps haven't considered using them [in lower grades].

Finally, one key similarity between Hilltop Charter School and Hearts and Hands Community School was that both schools' systems of school governance shared an emphasis on site-based management, there were also some important differences between the two schools. Where Hilltop Charter School's educational model fits squarely into what were, at the time of its founding, cutting-edge policy trends in elementary education, Hearts and Hands Community School represents an effort to bring alternative educational models into public education. I expand on this last point when I discuss the schools' early histories in chapter 4. In contrast to both schools, Inspiration School, founded four years after Hilltop Charter School, reflected some of the shifts in education policy that occurred statewide in the mid-1990s, and also provides an example of a charter school structured around a more "traditional" educational model.

Inspiration School

During one of my first visits to Inspiration School, I attended a staff meeting held in an impressive looking conference room. We gathered around the large conference table, which dominated the room. Nine boardroom-style chairs were lined up on each side of the table, with two additional chairs at the end. We began by reviewing the agenda, which started with a team-building exercise. At the time, this very businesslike setting seemed very much in keeping with the mission of the school's parent company, which emphasized applying the market model to school administration. It also presented a stark contrast to meetings I have attended at other schools, where we often sat in the school library or a classroom. In elementary schools this often meant sitting on undersized chairs. As I was to find out, this first impression not withstanding, Inspiration School was in some ways more complicated, and in other ways very much like a traditional school.

Organizational Structure: Reproducing the Traditional School

Unlike the education program at Hilltop Charter School, which was structured around a specific technology of teaching, Inspiration School's education program was structured around a nationally known "back to basics" curriculum model, Grand Heritage, that was being implemented to some degree or another in public and private schools in forty-six states.[14] Grand Heritage consists of a set of content standards that is expected to provide half of the curriculum. The standards for each grade level are detailed in a series of mass-market press books, which are intended as guides for both teachers and parents. There are no other formal texts for the program, although the standards, guides, and other materials available from the organization include lists of recommended books for each topic. In addition, Grand Heritage's developer has authored two books outlining the theoretical rationale for the approach. The program is fundamentally content-driven. Promotional materials for the program explicitly stated that the content standards lend themselves to a variety of teaching methods.

As Tyack and Cuban (1995) note, policy talk about education reform tends to move in cycles, and some policy prescriptions recur more frequently than others. In particular, two themes in policy talk have tended to recur in tandem: "traditional" and "progressive" educational models.[15] Inspiration School's effort to implement a standards-based curriculum fits squarely into one of these cycles in policy talk. While I explore these policy dynamics in more detail in chapter 5, a few points are worth noting here as a backdrop. The dominant education reforms of the early 1980s, standards-based reform and an emphasis on standardized testing, can be generally characterized as traditional reforms (Cuban, 2000). In the late 1980s, there was a resurgence of interest in more progressive reforms, such as structuring curricula around concepts rather than facts, collaborative learning, and the use of performance-based assessments. Many of these trends were reflected in the organization of teaching and learning at Hilltop Charter School.

By the middle of the 1990s, a new cycle in policy talk was underway and there were renewed calls for more traditional education reforms. The revisions in California's curriculum framework during this period reflected this reorientation of state education policy toward an increased emphasis on "basic skills" (Colvin 1995, 1996). Concurrently, a growing number of critics were questioning the efficacy of "progressive" education reforms for poor and minority students. For example, Lisa Delpit has written a series of articles that raised cogent questions about whether or not progressive educational methods that primarily focus on "process" help poor and minority students develop the skills they need to effectively participate in what she describes as the "culture of power" (Delpit, 1995).[16] Similar—although less nuanced—arguments have been made by the main author and advocate of the Grand Heritage curriculum.

At the time of the fieldwork, the school was at the beginning stages of implementing the Grand Heritage curriculum; a few teachers and the principal had attended a national conference on the curriculum model. Some teachers were also using the mass-market press books as guides for structuring lessons. By the beginning of the next year, the entire staff had attended an in-service on the curriculum, although some teachers reported informally in the context of a staff meeting that the training did not further their knowledge and capacity to implement the Grand Heritage curriculum. In addition, the school planned to send most of the teaching staff to a regional conference on the curriculum in a nearby city. Teachers described the Grand Heritage curriculum in highly positive terms. At the same time, many teachers felt that this gradual implementation was proceeding too slowly. In particular, teachers reported that they had too few materials and too little planning time to implement what they saw as a complicated education program.

While in the process of implementing the curriculum described above (which was also explicitly referenced in the charter), the school was also utilizing another language arts program that was also well known and marketed as a "back to basics" model. At the time, this program was not among the Geary Unified School District's 1998–1999 textbook adoptions, although the district and the state of California subsequently adopted the company's phonics program for the early elementary grades. Finally, the school was at least nominally implementing the three-hour literacy block associated with the Geary Unified School Districts systemic reform effort. Teachers tended to describe the literacy block as constraining and as an example of how the school was too much of a "district" school—that is, closely following district policy—rather than a charter school. However, within the basic structure of the literacy block—a morning period designated for language arts activities—teachers tended to utilize a range of teaching methods based on their own preferences rather than the techniques associated with the Balanced Literacy approach described in the Introduction.

Aside from the curricular model, the organizational structure at Inspiration School was very similar to a traditional school. Teachers were relatively isolated in their classrooms, although the school was transitioning toward a more departmentalized model for the upper grades to handle the school's projected expansion. Teachers reported more informal instances of teaming among themselves, which they also tended to describe as something they undertook on their own. In general, the school structure did not provide formal support for teaming and other types of collegial relationships between teachers, and even mitigated against them. The instructional day (8:00 to 4:00) was longer than that in most schools, and teachers had one hour per week of preparation time during their students' regularly scheduled physical education class. Because there was only one physical education teacher, teachers did not have common preparation time during the school day. Some teachers emphasized that this one hour of preparation time per week was far short of the time they needed to prepare, and also pointed out that the charter stated that teachers were supposed to have ninety minutes each day for "teacher planning and professional development."

A minimum day once a week provided time for staff meetings, but teachers reported that these meetings generally followed a set agenda, which did not really allow much discussion outside of the agenda items. Similarly, a few teachers also described spending extensive time tutoring students outside of the formal instructional day, which made after-school meetings more difficult. Teachers also shared lunch and recess duty responsibilities on a rotating schedule, which made it challenging for teachers to eat lunch, never mind check in with one another (although some did manage). There was a small teacher's lounge that was generally kept locked and did not appear to be used very often. Instead, teachers would congregate in the classrooms with microwaves and refrigerators. Lunch periods were also staggered by grade level, which also made it difficult for teachers to check in with one another across grades. One teacher predicted that this lack of common time would hinder the long-term success of the school. This teacher's comments are also telling when read in the context of the school's charter, which stated that the education program will include structures that will encourage teaming among the teaching staff.

> *Teacher*: In a charter school, unless it is done properly, you end up burning your teachers out. There is no prep time, there are no breaks. You are on the playground during lunch time, you don't get to eat. It is not set up properly. And I think if it was set up properly, if they had people come in to do lunch, and whatever. The teachers should not have to be on the playground. So I think that is a big facet of it. I think if we had more prep time, I think that we could really sit down and plan things accordingly for the school here. And I think that is where a school starts to become effective.
>
> *Jeanne*: And time to plan things together as a group?
>
> *Teacher*: Right, as a group. Do some team-teaching or do whatever you are doing. Right now we don't have that. Everyone is just kind of on their own doing whatever. Until we get to that point where you can work as a team, then, I truly don't know how effective the school is going to continue to be.

Thus, unlike Hilltop Charter School where individual classrooms were formally organized into teaching teams, the organization of teaching at this charter school is perhaps best characterized by Bidwell's (1965) term "structural looseness," with teachers isolated in their classrooms. Also notable is how this teacher saw this feature of Inspiration School as a general quality of charter schools. One teacher described this structure in highly positive terms, reporting that he valued the freedom to teach what he wanted in his own classroom. In contrast, other teachers, such as the teacher above, reported wanting more opportunities to work with their colleagues. Both the isolation of teachers and an education program that was silent on what "good teaching" looked like seemed to contribute to an eclectic "technology of teaching" across classrooms that, on the whole, tended toward seatwork and whole-class, teacher-directed instruction.

School Culture: The Market Model in Theory and in Practice

The atomized structure of teaching at Inspiration School also provides a good example of the relationship between organizational structure and school culture, although seen here as a "negative" case. With the school day tightly organized so that staff members had relatively limited time to meet together as a group, it is not surprising that many teachers reported that the school did not have a shared mission or vision, aside from the very general mission of being committed to the education of their students.

> I think they would like to have a vision but I don't really think they know what it is at this point in time other than to be successful. But to me a vision is not just being successful. So I think they really need to make a true statement and come up with their own vision of what they would really like to see the school become.

Likewise, an administrator noted that the school's mission was "developing," which he attributed in part to the lack of planning time:

> I think because of the age of the school and the newness of the school and basically the lack of staff planning time and staff development. I think that it is still developing so that it is across the board, and I don't feel like it is where it needs to be. Even myself, I don't feel like it is where it needs to be.

The absence of a shared mission or a vision could also have been a consequence of the chartering process. A nonprofit parent company, Educational Enterprise Corporation, partnered with the faith-based organization to secure the charter for the school. The school charter approved by the school district was almost identical to charters submitted to other school districts by Educational Enterprise Corporation. As a result, the charter was something the staff had to implement rather than create. This may be why two teachers commented that the school had a mission statement they had not seen. I discuss the school's relationship with the parent company in more detail in the section that follows.

One caveat to this latter point bears discussion. Teachers and other staff members at the school tended to emphasize that there was a shared sense of the importance of having high standards for the students and pushing the students to achieve academically. Some staff members described this as the school mission, while others (like the teacher above) felt that the school mission should be more elaborate. The importance of high standards was reflected in daily practices at the school. For example, teachers would routinely comment to their students during lessons that they were engaged in work that was above their respective grade levels. In this excerpt from field notes, a first grade class was in the middle of a whole-class lesson in math. Earlier in the lesson, the teacher, Ms. James, gave the students eight problems to solve, which required them to add three digit numbers. Here the class was reviewing their work as a group:

> Turning to the fourth problem, Ms. James said "I am waiting for someone to tell me what to do." A student responded, "start at the one's column." Ms. James reminded students to write the one when carrying the one. Another student noted that she had to "identify the sign," and again Ms. James asked "where do I start" and a student responded "at the one's column." Then Ms. James told the class "this is second grade work, not even your grade level. Go over there [second grade] and represent me well." The next problem was 100 + 500 and a student called out "too easy." With 519 + 181, Ms. James had them look at the sign and then said "9 + 1 equals" and the students called out in unison "10." Ms. James then said "write the..." and the class responded "0" "carry the..." and the class responded "1," etc. One student commented "Ms. James give us hard ones." Ms. James called four students up to the board to solve the problems. Once they were done, she asked the students whether or not their peers came up with the right answers.

Some of the teachers and other staff members linked the emphasis on high standards with the racial demographics of the student body, the overwhelming majority of which were members of an "underrepresented" minority group. Noting that these and students from other minority groups often "fall through the cracks" in conventional public schools, staff members saw the school as an effort to address the achievement gap between white and minority students, a long-standing concern within the Geary community.[17] For example, one support staff member who had many years of experience working in conventional public schools described why she started working at Inspiration School.

> I thought it was a great opportunity to get in this community to work in a charter school. Since they have quite a few things I like about charter schools. Helping our students to achieve our goals. It was important for me to see our students reach the highest goals possible. Be encouraged to go to college and get the encouragement that they need for their education. Sometimes that is missing in other schools. They are not encouraged to do these things. [When I asked her if she was referring to the minority students served by the school, she responded yes, but later broadened her comments beyond this particular group to include minority students more generally.]

Invoking the Market Model

One of the most interesting features of Inspiration School as an organization was something that was not immediately obvious to school visitors. Indeed, given the school's location, it would be easy to draw the conclusion that the faith-based organization that housed the school was its primary partner. However, another organization—the school's "parent company," Educational Enterprise Corporation—also had an important role at the school. Inspiration School was one of the first schools founded by Educational Enterprise Corporation, and the first of four within the Geary Unified School District. Educational Enterprise Corporation—which explicitly referred to itself as a company—sponsored additional schools in California, including three schools in another urban district in Northern California where a charter for a fourth school had been approved by the school board. Finally, Educational Enterprise Corporation also operated charter schools in a Midwestern state and was submitting charter petitions to school districts across the country in an effort to expand its operations.[18] In a promotional brochure, the Educational Enterprise Corporation projected that it would be operating forty schools across the country at the end of three years.

According to the company's mission statement, Educational Enterprise Corporation's goal was to apply market principles to public education:

> To improve student performance through the development and operation of charter schools by applying free-market solutions, communicating the effectiveness of the solutions, and serving as a catalyst for the systemic reform of public education.

Educational Enterprise Corporation's web site included a brief overview of the organization with the following subheadings: history and purpose, vision, philosophy, company description, strategy, marketing potential, marketing plan and organization, and financial summary. The discussion of the company's purpose began with a statement of the problem it aimed to address, the "crisis" in public education: student achievement has been declining for two decades despite changes in how schools are funded and high profile reform efforts. In response, Educational Enterprise Corporation argued that "systemic reform" through "choice and competition for all customers" was the "only solution" to this problem. More specifically, the company's goal was to develop charter schools to address the needs of "children trapped in historically low performing schools." Three key themes were invoked throughout the discussion: (1) students and their families are reframed as "customers"; (2) choice and competition will foster school reform; and (3) education is a market that is both underdeveloped and has enormous financial potential. The latter two themes were combined in the discussion of "Market Potential":

> The potential market base for quality education nationally is staggering ($384 billion). As mentioned, the continual decline of the public education system is escalating the need for alternative solutions. Charters, Vouchers, and Tax Incentives are methods of providing choice and competition that are becoming popular. Policy shifts that expand the above and create equity in financing create instant markets. As the public becomes more informed of the critical status of education and the success of free market solutions, this market should increase exponentially.

Educational Enterprise Corporation's market argument had deep roots in the policy talk that propelled the charter school movement. As I discussed in chapter 2, in California the charter school movement was an outgrowth of the restructuring movement, which many analysts characterized as the "second wave" of school reform after *A Nation at Risk*. Here, Tyack and Cuban's distinction between policy talk, policy action, and implementation is useful to help us sort out these complex policy dynamics. Many schools that were part of the first cohort of charter schools in California (i.e., the early implementers of charter school reform) had also participated in restructuring and framed their arguments for restructuring—and subsequently reorganizing as a charter school—around the need to empower teachers and/or parents to make decisions for their respective schools. However, the *policy talk* that generated the political momentum for restructuring as policy action (i.e., SB 1274, which created the grant program to fund restructuring projects) contained themes related to teacher empowerment but also included arguments for market-driven school choice. More specifically, the California Business Roundtable's report *Restructuring California Education* (1988), described in chapter 2 as one of the factors that generated the momentum for the restructuring legislation, anticipated the market language of charter school policy talk by arguing that increased choice in public education was a way to "introduce competition" into public education and ultimately increase student performance by pressuring "weak schools to do better" (Berman, Weiler Associates, 1988, 15).

As I discussed in chapter 2, another key instance of policy talk that presented an argument for reorganizing public education around the market model was Chubb and Moe's (1990) *Politics, Markets and America's Schools*. Chubb and Moe's arguments were widely circulated and debated in the national media at the time the book was published. In the six months after the book was published in 1990, thirty-one stories in thirteen major newspapers discussed the book's major arguments and findings, including five guest opinion pieces written by one or both of the authors. Chubb and Moe's argument was explicitly linked to the charter school movement in California in a 1996 report on charter schools by the Little Hoover Commission,[19] *The Charter School Movement: Education Reform, School By School*. While the Commission noted that it was too early to assess charter schools on the basis of academic achievement, overall, charter schools were successful in other areas, including parent satisfaction, academic innovation, and providing opportunities for teachers. More importantly for the discussion here, the specific findings of the report are framed by a brief overview of charter school reform, the first section of which is entitled "Charter School Theory."

The Hoover Commission's argument in "Charter School Theory" is an interesting example of charter policy talk because of the way it framed charter schools in relation to the "social problem" of failing public schools. The discussion began with the conventional account of the origins of the charter school movement I noted in the Introduction; that is, Al Shanker's role in taking Ray Budde's idea to a wider audience. The Commission noted that Shanker's proposal was appealing to reformers who were interested in using "private sector concepts like competition" to reform public schools and also remained committed to the democratic ideal of public education. Drawing on Chubb and Moe's argument to support its assertion, the Commission argued that charter school reform was important because of the bureaucratic nature of public education that stifles promising reform efforts. Charter schools are important, then, because they were a move toward decentralization and would therefore create the conditions where innovations can flourish. Notably, the Commission concluded with former state senator Gary Hart's description of charter schools as a "license to dream." Recall from chapter 2 that Hart was the author of California's charter school legislation. This final rhetorical flourish can be read as an instance of the "repackaging of choice" where less politically popular market-oriented forms of choice were harnessed to existing programs with wider public support (Henig, 1994, 79).

While Educational Enterprise Corporation's marketing materials and executives emphasized school reform through choice and competition, it could be argued that by partnering with a prominent community organization, Inspiration School was to some degree buffered from competition for students. More specifically, by virtue of its standing within this particular minority community beyond its members, the faith-based organization that hosted the school provided a steady pool of potential students. One teacher described it this way in an interview:

> *Teacher*: I first heard of Inspiration School. I didn't know about Inspiration School, but when they said [names faith-based organization], I knew about it. Do you know what I mean?...
> *Jeanne*: Yes. It gives you a sense of place and position in the community.

Teacher: Because [names faith-based organization] itself is a
Jeanne: Prominent institution?
Teacher: Right.

However, competition was an important theme in school life, primarily through Educational Enterprise Corporation's emphasis on standardized testing. I address this topic in more detail in chapter 5.

Bureaucracy Without Democracy or Autonomy?

While the discussion above focused primarily on the policy talk of Inspiration School's parent company, in its implementation, Inspiration School might be viewed as a partial example of the market model school described by Chubb and Moe because it was buffered from democratic participation. Yet unlike market model schools, Inspiration School was not fully autonomous. Decision-making power was largely concentrated at the level of the corporation. According to Inspiration School's charter, Educational Enterprise Corporation had "general responsibility" for the operation of the school (Inspiration School Charter, 1997, 16a). The charter outlined a system of school governance based on a Board of Directors and two advisory boards. The Board of Directors, which was designated as legally and financially responsible for the school, was to be chaired by the CEO of Educational Enterprise Corporation. The chair would in turn choose the other members: two community members (including one parent), a business leader from the surrounding community, and an educator. The two advisory boards were to be composed of educators and parents, respectively. According to the charter, the latter two provided input on issues related to school discipline, curriculum, and "governance ideas for increasing performance" (Inspiration School Charter, 1997, 16). A second parent group was intended to function as a parent-teacher association.

Thus, in the governance structure outlined in the charter, Educational Enterprise Corporation retained much of the control over decision-making at the school. However, by the end of the school's second year, other constituents were not participating in school governance—even in the highly constrained advisory role.[20] Only a parent group that functioned like a parent-teacher association was up and running. While there were more informal committees comprised of teachers, parents, and administrators at Inspiration School, which worked on school issues such as a discipline plan and the school calendar, for the most part teachers reported having little say in the more substantive issues of decision-making, such as budgetary decisions. For example, one teacher commented:

> We have no governance team. It is written into the charter, but there has been one governance team, in, one meeting in [the time] that I have been

here. There is supposed to be a teacher representative, a parent representative, but there is no real governance team here.

Moreover, in the school's charter, the relationship between the Inspiration School, its Board of Directors, and Educational Enterprise Corporation was ambiguous. For example, the Educational Enterprise Corporation was designated as responsible for the "day-to-day" management of school operations, while the Board of Directors was responsible for "fiscal and educational programs," which included: setting general policies, budgetary oversight, applying and managing grants, administering personnel policies, contracting for audits, and hiring the principal. The school would be responsible for hiring teachers and other consultants, although some teachers reported being hired by Educational Enterprise Corporation. Educational Enterprise Corporation was designated as responsible for making salary recommendations to the school's board of directors. The charter also stipulated that employees would be evaluated by the principal using Educational Enterprise Corporation's "performance appraisal framework and system" (Inspiration School Charter, 1997, 31). Another California school district, Easterly School District, denied a petition for a charter school sponsored by Educational Enterprise Corporation in 2001, citing the ambiguous relationship between the school, the corporation, and the school district as one of the reasons it withheld approval. The official minutes of the Easterly School District suggested that Educational Enterprise Corporation's relationship to the proposed school would be similar to its relationship with Inspiration School. Easterly School District was concerned that it would not have sufficient input into the proposed school's operations.

Thus Inspiration School illustrates how, in some cases, it is difficult to draw a clear boundary around organizations (Pfeffer and Salancik, 1978). In addition to the school district, a parent company had a great deal of authority over the operation and management of the school. Unlike Hilltop Charter School and Hearts and Hands Community School, where the respective staffs were empowered to make decisions regarding personnel, most of the major decisions about personnel at Inspiration School were made by Educational Enterprise Corporation. Moreover, teachers were unsure about the parameters of the relationship between the school and Educational Enterprise Corporation and, in particular, the extent to which decisions about the school's operations were being made on site. Some teachers also reported that they had anticipated participating in school decision-making, but their experiences at the school had not matched these expectations. Perhaps ironically, a contemporaneous newspaper article by two members of the corporation's executive staff advocated more on-site decision-making in an editorial on school reform:

> In order to meet new and higher standards, the [public education] system will have to change from what it is designed to do—to become what the future demands. One such demand requires schools to allow for greater levels of participation in the decision-making process. What this means is that parents, teachers, community members, and the principals must work together to make important decisions about how to improve student achievement.

While Educational Enterprise Corporation was a nonprofit organization, the schools it managed paid for its management services. According to 1999 tax documents, Educational Enterprise Corporation collected $280,875 from the four schools it was operating in California at the time.[21] Based on California Department of Education enrollment figures at these schools that year, I estimated this sum to be approximately $234 per child served, which was approximately 5.6 percent of Inspiration School's $4,177 per pupil allotment.[22] These figures were consistent with reports about Educational Enterprise Corporations operations in other districts. One staff member, understandably reluctant to be too critical, commented that the organization took more than it gave back to the school and questioned the organization's business practices. While the management fees were relatively nominal, Educational Enterprise Corporation's major source of income in the same fiscal year was a grant of just under $2,700,000 from a single donor.

The Limits of the Market Model "On the Ground"
Finally, Inspiration School provides an example of how the ideological principles expressed in a school's charter may not animate daily practices and belief systems within a school. Put differently, cultural ideas have to be enacted. While Inspiration School's charter and Educational Enterprise Corporation's literature and corporate executives promoted applying a "business model" to education, Inspiration School's teachers tended to be less sanguine about the efficacy of the business model as it was practiced at Inspiration School. For example, one teacher commented:

> I think that the school needs to be run as a school and not necessarily as a business. Because you don't have customers and clients here, you have children and you are dealing with their lives. I think that some charter schools are looked at strictly as a business and not actually as a school and I think they need to really step back and hire some educators that really understand what needs to be done in these charter schools, and not all of

these business people that have never stepped foot in a classroom and are making decisions.

Likewise, another teacher echoed these concerns by implying that as a teacher she felt that kids' needs should be the foremost concern rather than a strict bottom line:

> They [Educational Enterprise Corporation] have done great things for us, they have come up short for us. But you know, whenever we try to talk to them about it, it is all budget. Which I guess I understand, and I guess that is why I am a teacher and why I am not running something like Educational Enterprise Corporation because, don't tell me the budget. I am telling you what my kids need.

Both teachers suggested that the goal of creating a "child-centered" education program conflicted with running a school strictly on business principles. They also asserted a moral claim: children's educational needs are more important than the efficiency argument implied in the business model. Similarly, teachers also questioned why Educational Enterprise Corporation was opening additional schools, because in their view Inspiration School had not received sufficient resources and support from the company. Thus the market model, which suggests that expansion would be a positive virtue, provided a rationale for expansion at the "corporate" level of the organization. Yet classroom teachers, the constituents at the center of the organization's technical core, perceived the corporation's expansion as a constraint because they viewed it as a major factor behind the lack of resources at their own school. For example, one teacher reported having to buy crayons for her classroom. Other teachers reported waiting months—well into the school year—to receive books for their classrooms.

On one hand, the issues described above could be explained as part of the growing pains of a new school—and as I will discuss in the next chapter, not unusual among charter schools. Both Hilltop Charter School and Hearts and Hands Community School had their share of turmoil in their early years. Yet evidence from another school managed by Educational Enterprise Corporation suggests another picture. Located in a Midwestern state, Greenacres Elementary was plagued with problems from its first year, including rapid turnover of school leadership—by the end of its second year, three principals had worked at the school. These details about school management came to light in June of 2001 when the school's sponsoring agency voted to revoke its charter as a result of ongoing problems with fiscal management and school governance.

According to a press release by the sponsoring agency, Greenacres Elementary was put on probation after its first year for similar problems that were apparently never resolved. These issues, coupled to serious violations of school safety codes, culminated in the revocation of the charter. Local school officials attributed the issues the sponsoring agency identified to Educational Enterprise Corporation and severed its ties with the organization. After obtaining a stay on the revocation from a judge, and later reaching an agreement with its sponsor, Greenacres Elementary remained open and began to operate independently. Notably, when the sponsoring agency's governing board voted to revoke the school's charter, its report described the positive educational impact the school was having on its students and emphasized that lapses in management triggered the sponsor's action.

As I suggested above, on one hand we might see these issues as common to many charter schools as the "storming" part of an organization's developmental cycle (Tuckman, [1968] 2001).[23] On the other hand, we might also see the problems in Educational Enterprise Corporation's schools as surprising. Unlike charter schools run by educators and parents, such as Hilltop Charter School and Hearts and Hands Community School, Inspiration School was operated by a management company with the explicit goal of demonstrating the efficacy of market principles in school management. As a teacher from Inspiration School noted:

> And if this is their business—because that is really how they look at it—if this is their business, it is like if you own a restaurant, you never go to that restaurant. If you own a business you've got to be there. You've got to see what is going on. And I know they leave that up to the principal, but still. And also if we are in the red, and this school is in the red, then why are they opening up more? And I don't get that and I am not a business-minded person, so I am sure there is some reasonable explanation for it, but it does not make sense to me. If I didn't have money to do something, I wouldn't do it. And it does not seem like they are trying to make this school the best that they can. It is quality, not quantity. Take care of what you have, and then build from here.

The issues raised by these apparent problems in management might also make us think more deeply about the relevance or applicability of the business model to educational settings. In the business world, rapid expansion might be considered a legitimate strategy. But if unsuccessful, using this strategy in educational settings can have deleterious effects on children's educational careers. Take, for example, Greenacres Elementary, which was serving "at risk" students but was faced with the threat of closure because of poor management. What if those students, many of whom were apparently thriving, had to find and adjust to a new school? Likewise, if teachers do not have books for the first few months of school and still manage to help their students perform well academically, what might these same teachers accomplish if they started the school year with the books and other supplies they needed? Certainly many of these issues are not unlike those facing more "traditional" schools. For example, some teachers working in conventional public schools in the Geary Unified School District also reported that before the district-wide reform they had few books in their classrooms aside from those they had purchased themselves. However, Educational Enterprise Corporation was "marketing" the market model as a more effective way to run public schools. Corporate executives were presenting at state and national conferences and advocating expanding the use of market-based reforms—including school vouchers—in public education.

Discussion

As I discussed in the Introduction, in California, there are two main types of charter schools: "brick and mortar" charter schools and distance learning/independent study charter schools. Comparing Hilltop Charter School, Hearts and Hands Community School, and Inspiration School, the considerable diversity within the former category of schools, which primarily target traditional student populations. The three schools described here had different educational models and also contrasting forms of school governance. For example, Hilltop Charter School's educational model was based on a developmental understanding of learning and was primarily focused on the technology of teaching. In contrast, Hearts and Hands Community School's educational model was based on a specific curricula and technology of teaching patterned after the philosophy and pedagogy of Waldorf schools. At both Hilltop Charter School and Hearts and Hand Community School, staff members were involved in school governance, although the two schools had very different ways of implementing site-based management. At Hilltop Charter School, the SSC comprised the entire staff and also included representatives of other constituent groups (parents and community members), while Hearts and Hands Community School's Site Management Team was a representative group with a balance of staff and parent members. Finally, Inspiration School was implementing a back-to-basics curriculum and was also run by Educational Enterprise Corporation, a nonprofit educational management organization. While teachers had a great deal of autonomy within their classrooms—indeed, many felt too isolated and unconnected from the rest of the teaching staff—they had little influence over school decisions. They were also highly critical of one of the key tenets of Educational Enterprise Corporation's philosophy, the notion that schools should be organized around market principles. While this chapter focused on analyzing charter school implementation through the lenses of organization structure and school culture, throughout the analysis there were instances where the policy context influenced school-level implementation processes. In the next chapter, I expand on this theme in greater detail by focusing on school foundings and how the schools responded to the reform initiative undertaken by the Geary Unified School District.

Chapter Four
How Policy Contexts Shape Implementation

While the concepts of organizational structure and school culture provide a conceptual window into school life, they are insufficient for analyzing the complex set of influences on implementation. Individual schools are bound into complex relationships with other organizational entities, which include: district, state, and federal education agencies; business organizations; professional organizations; and judicial and legislative bodies. Thus it is important to be attentive to the structural and institutional settings within which schools operate (Cuban, 1995; Talbert, McLaughlin and Rowan, 1993). I use the term context to highlight the complex and organized environments that shape the work of schools.

In this chapter and the one that immediately follows, I focus on the relationships between the schools and a specific component of a school's context, the policy context. My analysis draws from neoinstitutional accounts of schools as embedded within broader, nonlocal contexts, and places a particular emphasis on state regulations and the agencies created to enforce them (Arum, 2000). In addition to broad and widely shared cultural norms and beliefs about schooling (Meyer, 1977; Tyack and Cuban, 1995; Weick, 1976), national, state, and district education policies—the products of organized processes within these bodies—are viewed as environmental factors that both enable and constrain processes occurring at the school site. Meyer, Scott, Strang, and Creighton (1988) described these multiple and intersecting policy contexts in the following way:

> Consider the programs resulting from the recent concerns about educational quality, for example. There is much national discussion, a bit of legislative activity, a few national commissions, and a little money. But this has fueled a huge industry at the state and district level as these more sovereign units employ the general concerns to expand their own domination over the local scene. (164)

More specifically, I argue that these policy contexts are a significant source of imprinting where charter schools acquire features at their founding that remain relatively stable over time (Stinchcombe, 1965; Hannan and Freeman, 1989). Yet as Hannaway (1993) reminds us, even within institutional structures there is a considerable amount of room for local variation. Charter school reform is premised on local variation, yet as chapter 2 illustrated, the state contexts in which charter school reform becomes policy action vary widely. At the implementation stage, this diversity is further multiplied. Within a single state, especially a large state such as California, school districts vary considerably. In this chapter I explore how aspects of the schools' policy contexts shaped each of these schools. For both Hilltop Charter School and Hearts and Hands Community School, I focus on the local policy context. In the case of Inspiration School I discuss the local and extralocal ties between the school and the voucher movement. I also examine the local dynamics of marketization, the schools' responses to the Geary Unified School District's systemic reform initiative described in the Introduction, and the similarities in teachers' perceptions of charter school reform across the three settings.

Because charter school reform is clearly an effort to change the organizational structure(s) of schools, charter schools are a particularly interesting site to study the relationship between internal features of the school (here conceptualized as organizational structure and school culture) and the overlapping and intersecting external contexts in which the schools are situated. One of the general features of charter school reform is that it is an effort to create new organizational forms. Indeed the chartering process requires that schools and the actors that animate them be self-reflexive about these features of their internal organization.

Yet, the policy talk promoting charter school reform tends to be silent about how this lofty goal should occur. As a result, it could be argued that charter school reform is conceptually empty. This feature of charter school policy talk is best reflected in the description of charter school reform in the *Request for Applications for California's Public Charter School Grant Program* (California Department of Education, 1999). Unlike other reform efforts such as Success for All or the Coalition of Essential Schools, charter schools are "not limited to any specific educational vision or approach. Instead, a charter is a powerful organizational tool that can be used to effectively implement virtually any educational vision" (California Department of Education, 1999, 20). Thus, it is not surprising that once implemented, charter schools often reflect broader ideological struggles over the form and meaning of schooling in a democratic society: What should the relative balance of power between stakeholders within a school be? Can a private school model with religious overtones be used in public schools without violating the principle of separation between church and state? Should parents and families be given vouchers to attend any public or private school of their choice? How will students most effectively learn literacy?

Hilltop Charter School

Looking more broadly at the relationship between organizations and their environments, Stinchcombe (1965) made the straightforward observation that "organizational forms and types have a history," and Hilltop Charter School was no exception (153). Hilltop Charter School was a site where national, state, and local restructuring reforms intersected. In general, restructuring refers to the process of decentralizing decision-making within an organization. This reform proposal gained a significant amount of traction as policy talk in business and educational settings in the late 1980s and early 1990s. As I described in chapter 2, restructuring became policy action in California through SB 1274, the legislation that established a grant competition for school restructuring. In the section below, I describe restructuring as policy action and implementation in the Geary Unified School District to highlight how one of the key features of Hilltop Charter School's organizational structure I described in chapter 3—shared decision-making—was shaped by the district policy context.

Restructuring and Charter School Reform in the Geary Unified School District

By the time SB 1274 was passed in 1991, restructuring had been underway in the Geary Unified School District for about five years. In May 1986, Carl Nelson, the superintendent of the Geary Unified School District convened a task force to create a vision for school reform in the district. The task force issued a report in 1987 entitled *Moving Forward: New Directions for the Geary Unified School District.* Drawing upon a range of national and state level policy statements on education reform, and citing contemporaneous efforts at restructuring in other cities, *Moving Forward* proposed restructuring Geary's public schools to more effectively respond to changing economic and demographic conditions (Geary Public Schools Task Force, 1987). With the support of the Board of Education, Nelson appointed a leadership team comprised of teachers, administrators, parents, and community members that was charged with implementing the Commission's plan. Restructuring became the overarching frame for all of the district's reform efforts. As Nelson (1991) described the reform effort in a letter to constituents:

> School restructuring does not lend itself to a single, simple definition. It is a process, not a product. Restructuring involves shifting the decision-making responsibility to the local school level. Schools are encouraged to involve teachers, other staff members, and parents in deciding how teaching and learning will be enhanced and how resources will be allocated, rather than having those decisions made centrally and handed down from the top. (3)

In a 1989 newsletter about school reform in California, the Geary Unified School District's restructuring reform was highlighted by the state Superintendent of Public Instruction. The article described how one of the key features of Geary's restructuring effort was a "focus on change in the central office" rather than on change within individual schools (Honig, 1989, 6). More specifically, district administrators were to serve as "supporters," "collaborators," and "facilitators" of reform. Contemporaneous district documents suggest that the process of shared decision-making was proceeding less than smoothly on the ground, largely because there were few policies and procedures in place to guide schools undergoing the restructuring process. A task force was convened in 1990 that created a set of guidelines for shared decision-making that was adopted by the school board in early 1992. Of note is the brief rationale for convening the task force:

> The main issue was that school staff did not have procedures or guidelines for systems of governance and were seeking assistance to establish shared decision-making procedures. Questions raised included: What roles should various site personnel (Teachers? SDTA site representative? Principal? PTA President? Classified Personnel? Other bargaining unit representatives?) play in the shared decision-making structure? What elements are necessary in the creation of an appropriate shared decision-making structure? Who is accountable for decisions made by the shared decision-making group? (Shared Decision-Making Task Force Final Report, 1992)

By 1992, the Geary Board of Education required each school to form a governance team that was representative of the school community. Nelson left the Geary Unified School District in 1993, but the district remained committed to restructuring during the tenure of his successor, Ellen Temple. In 1994, Temple issued the Superintendent's Statement on Shared Decision-Making, which provided a brief outline of the history of shared decision-making in the Geary Unified School district. The document began by linking restructuring to Goals 2000—the Clinton administration's education reform effort—yet it also noted that the process of restructuring in Geary Unified School District had begun as early as 1987. A subsequent district document reported that shared decision-making language was incorporated into the teachers' contract in 1996,[1] and a *Shared Decision Making Handbook* was created in 1997. Finally, the school board adopted a set of procedures for shared decision-making in March of 1998 (*Shared Decision Making Handbook* draft, June 2000, 2).

The explicit link between Goals 2000, a federal reform effort, and the district's own (and earlier) efforts at restructuring suggests that clear and linear relationships between different policy contexts—or for that matter different iterations of policy talk—are often difficult to discern. Reforms overlap in complicated ways across national, state, and local policy contexts. For example, national foundations convened meetings of districts undertaking similar reform efforts. One grant from a major foundation provided the basis for collaboration with other urban school districts in the Southwest around the issue of high school dropouts and the needs of Hispanic students. Another foundation funded site-based decision-making efforts in Geary Unified and other school districts across the country and created a "partnership network" linking these districts. In addition, local foundations such as the Geary Community Foundation participated in national-level coalitions of foundations. Finally, the Geary Unified School District participated in national education reform initiatives, notably the New Standards Project of the National Alliance for Restructuring Education, a New American Schools Development Corporation (NASDC) reform model.[2] Hilltop Charter School was one of five Geary schools chosen to participate in the program. Finally, as the discussion of SB 1274 in chapter 2 suggested, restructuring was also a prominent component of state level reform efforts.

What the account above suggests is that the local, state, and national policy contexts provided a fertile ground for the creation of Hilltop Charter School. However, an even deeper analysis of the history of Hilltop Charter School suggests that, by drawing upon key themes of this policy talk and engaging important organizational actors in his project, an institutional entrepreneur was able to create a school that he hoped would be the new face of public education.

Founding Hilltop Charter School: The Organizational Foundations of School Reform

During its earliest stages as the brainchild of a local businessman and entrepreneur named Tom Jensen—who was described by one of the school's original staff members as the "father" of the school—Hilltop Charter School was explicitly framed as a product of the school restructuring movement. Jensen's goal was to create a school that would be a "catalyst" for radical education reform that would have a ripple effect across the district and beyond. In May 1991, Jensen committed his idea to paper and began to enlist district officials and community members in his project. In his initial memorandum proposing the school, Jensen wrote that the first step in the process was to "get a conceptual buy-off on this proposal from all the organizations that have a substantial stake in the present and who must rebut the critics of change" (Jensen, 1991a, 3).

At the behest of Superintendent Carl Nelson, Jensen conducted a series of interviews with the two members of the local teachers union, four school district employees, the "Chief Educational Officer" of a school that was widely considered one of the most innovative in the district, and the President of the Board of Education. Subsequent interviews included officials from other school employee unions (administrators and noncredentialed staff), the President-elect of Geary's PTA, and additional district and county education officials. Three months later, Jensen had formally interviewed seventeen people and spoke to many others informally. Most, if not all, of the interviewees expressed support for Jensen's idea. Their responses ranged from agreeing that the idea was at least feasible to highly enthusiastic.

Jensen compiled this information into two reports to Nelson, and ultimately a memorandum proposing a summit to "[set] up a one-of-a-kind educational enterprise...a public school where nonstudent stakeholders surrender something of high value, a measure of authority, in advance of gaining something of higher value, a superior education benefiting students, parents, staff and taxpayers" (Jensen, 1991b, 1). While the form of the school was relatively undefined, Jensen argued that a key component of the process was to "suspend [the] traditional rules" that schools were required to follow (Jensen, 1991b, 4).[3] In particular, participants needed the freedom to create new rules and new relationships among themselves that would better serve students. Initially, seven representatives of the following organizations were invited to participate in a planning meeting: the Administrators Association, the Classified Employees Association, the California School Employees Association, the Parent Teachers Association, the school board, the local chapter of the teachers union, and the superintendent's office.[4] All of the participants had to have the "authority to speak for his or her constituents" (Jensen, 1991b, 2). Clearly the participants' organizational affiliations were important to Jensen. As Mehan (1997) aptly noted, "organizations speak through individuals" (253).

Immediately after the meeting, Jensen began drafting an agreement, which was finalized in January 1992, after a long process of negotiation among the participants. While not legally binding, the agreement signaled the group's collective intentions to develop and launch the new school. A seven-person committee was created to oversee the process, designated the "Hilltop Charter School Committee," which retained the representation of the groups initially invited to the planning meeting. The group's first task was to hire a school principal. The principal and the corresponding representative of the "Hilltop Charter School Committee" would then work together to hire the "leadership team," which was comprised of four teachers, four community members, and one secretary, one paraprofessional, and one custodian. One of the four teachers on the leadership team would be the teachers union representative for the site. The leadership team would be charged with creating a school that would: (1) "accelerate" student achievement; (2) facilitate staff development; and (3) serve as a demonstration site for school reform (Hilltop Charter School Agreement, 1992).

Earlier drafts of the memorandum suggest that the parties generally agreed on the broad goals for the school. However, the nuts and bolts of school governance required additional negotiation among the participants. One point of disagreement throughout the process was determining the balance of power between the principal and the staff. For example, in the initial draft of the memorandum, Jensen envisioned the principal as having broad power to select the "leadership team," which would create job descriptions and the school's education plan, and negotiate and oversee the budget. While Jensen saw the principal as both "part of the team" and also primarily responsible for these tasks, the representatives of the teachers union thought this arrangement gave the principal too much power and advocated for shared decision-making among the leadership team.[5]

Ultimately, shared decision-making was coupled to decision-making by consensus; school management was the responsibility of the leadership team. Notably, at the earliest stages of the school's planning, participants agreed that "key decision-makers" at the school site should be empowered to make decisions (Jensen, 1991b, 4). However, the scope and the boundaries of these key decision-makers' roles in shared decision-making were apparently difficult issues to resolve and, as I explain below, remained a source of tension during the school's first two administrations. After the final version of the memorandum outlining the process of establishing the school was approved by the planning group, events proceeded quickly. The principal's job was advertised within a week and a successful candidate, Jack Thomas, was selected a month later. Staff positions were advertised shortly thereafter. Collaboration and staff empowerment were important elements of the formal job descriptions as well as the processes used to interview and hire all staff members. As staff members were hired, they participated in subsequent hiring decisions. These practices were later formalized in the school's bylaws.

Hilltop Charter School reopened in September 1992 at approximately the same time California's charter school legislation was signed by Governor Wilson. A year later Hilltop became the Geary Unified School District's first charter school by converting to charter school status. In its first pre-charter year, participants viewed Hilltop as a de facto charter school. For example, a few months after the school opened, Mr. Thomas wrote an essay in a Q and A format responding to questions frequently asked about the school. One of these was, "Are you one of those charter schools?" Thomas responded, "We are a charter school in the sense that the district has set aside the 'business as usual' label but we are still working within the system." Similarly, in an article published in the local newspaper about six months after the school opened and before the school converted to charter status, Jensen described Hilltop Charter School as "a charter school within the public school system." As staff members described it years later, while the school had been functioning as a de facto charter school, each departure from district policy required that the school apply for a waiver; officially converting to charter status was appealing because the charter would function as a blanket waiver. Hilltop Charter School's 1993 charter described how the applying for the SB 1274 restructuring grant helped the staff develop the vision outlined in its charter. As I noted in chapter 2, in the early years of the charter school movement, a number of conversion charter schools were engaged in restructuring and saw converting to a charter school as the next step in the process of reform. Anecdotal evidence from another study suggests that this trajectory of restructuring school to conversion charter school was not confined to the California context (see the case study of Lamar School in Newmann and Associates, 1996).

Participating in restructuring and charter school reform gave Hilltop Charter School both the funds and the flexibility to achieve some of its early goals. Staff members from that period described the professional development they received under the auspices of the SB 1274 grant as one of the highlights of that period; they also emphasized the school's early reputation as different and on the "cutting edge" of reform.

Sustaining a Culture of Shared Decision-Making over Time:
Leadership and Process

By delegating broad powers to the SSC, Hilltop Charter School's organizational structure disrupted conventional cultural beliefs and norms about authority within public schools, that is, the norm that the school district hires and supervises the principal, who in turn supervises the teachers. Hilltop's reconfigured relationship between the principal and the SSC was succinctly described in a phrase in the original charter that was often repeated by long-term staff members—the principal "serves at the pleasure" of the SSC.[6] Yet in its early history, the school struggled to effectively enact this organizational structure and find leaders who could work within this arrangement.

As the analysis above suggests, Hilltop's planners agreed that "stakeholders" at the school had to be empowered to make decisions (as opposed to parties outside the school). However, determining the balance of power between the different groups within the school was the subject of ongoing negotiation and renegotiation. By the end of the fieldwork, Hilltop Charter School was in the middle of its third administration. The first two were punctuated by periods of crisis. While the events that precipitated each crisis differed, both were conflicts about the scope and boundaries of shared decision-making between the principal and staff members.

Jack Thomas, Hilltop's founding principal, was removed by the Geary Unified School District after members of the teaching staff reported their suspicions about fiscal mismanagement to the district. Years later, the extent of the alleged fiscal mismanagement was unclear—staff members and other involved parties variously characterized the incidents as serious to minor. Yet staff members working at the school at the time agreed that the sense of collegiality and trust among the staff had broken down by the end of the school's third year. One teacher reported that staff members' suspicions about the school's finances and their inability to get accurate information fueled a division within the staff, some of whom went to the district for assistance. Others described a general pattern whereby the principal did not follow the system of governance the school had developed and instead made decisions without consulting the staff.

This volatile situation came to a head when Mr. Thomas tried to disband the SSC and replace SSC meetings with staff meetings, which signaled an effort to establish a more traditional authority structure at the school. While some staff members apparently approved this move, others did not, and wrote a letter to the school board protesting the proposal. The district responded by facilitating a vote among the staff about maintaining the charter. When a majority of the staff voted affirmatively, the district transferred Mr. Thomas out of the school and gave the school a six-month trial period to revise its charter and meet thirteen conditions. A new principal, Mrs. Carmichael, was chosen for the school in a process that was closely supervised by the district. During the trial period the school spent a considerable amount of time and money on consultants to help them restructure their system of governance. The SSC, which was originally a representative body, was reorganized into the direct representational format described in chapter 3. One staff member commented:

> [P]eople felt that their concerns about the administrator may not be heard, because [their] representative on the governance council wasn't voicing their concerns. Or that people were even out-and-out lying. And so we decided the only way to make sure that everyone heard the same thing at the same time in the same way was everybody sits on governance.

After the trial period, the school board voted to continue the school's charter.[7]

Mrs. Carmichael inherited a fractured school. The most obvious divisions among the staff were related to the problems with the previous principal, although the staff was also engaged in pedagogical debates that had in all likelihood increased tensions at the school. Staff members also reported having little influence on the process of selecting Mrs. Carmichael, which they characterized as antithetical to the provisions in their charter. It is hard to assess Mrs. Carmichael's tenure outside of the lens of a second period of political turmoil that culminated in her resignation and the loss of three long-term staff members (three additional long-term staff members left for personal and professional reasons). After a period of ongoing disagreements with the staff, Mrs. Carmichael mandated a policy change related to playground safety that many staff members thought was unnecessary. Mrs. Carmichael saw herself as making a reasonable request of the staff to address an issue that needed to be dealt with. In contrast, staff members saw the new policy as an effort by Mrs. Carmichael to institute a more substantive change in school policy without following the procedures the school had developed for shared decision-making and, as such, exemplified Mrs. Carmichael's disregard for a component of the school's charter that the teachers strongly valued.

At the same time, a group of parents who were dissatisfied with how Mrs. Carmichael handled some concerns they had raised with her individually brought a proposal to the SSC and the school district requesting Mrs. Carmichael's reassignment to another school. However, there were questions about whether or not the proposal was brought before the SSC according to the rules outlined in the school's charter and the SSC bylaws, the Brown Act, which required public notice of meetings, and due process in personnel procedures. Before these issues could be worked out procedurally, Mrs. Carmichael resigned and was reassigned by the school district to lead another elementary school.

In interviews, staff members reported that while Mrs. Carmichael often expressed support for shared decision-making, she often made decisions without consulting the staff. One example they cited was the school's participation in Balanced Literacy, the district's literacy reform. While teachers were not opposed to the reform per se and were even using some of the teaching strategies associated with the reform, they also felt that they should utilize the flexibility they had as a charter school to pick and choose the aspects of the reform they found the most useful. Many viewed Mrs. Carmichael as more committed to the school district and the district reform than the educational vision outlined in their charter.[8] For her part, Mrs. Carmichael saw staff members as so committed to shared decision-making and so opposed to the district's policies they were not making the best educational choices for their students. In addition, Mrs. Carmichael did not see the school as following the principles of shared decision-making outlined in its charter, and instead described it as governed by those who shouted the loudest.

While the events described above were the most obvious manifestations of these tensions, they were also played out in the meetings of the Principal Evaluation Committee, a committee that was charged with designing a site-specific process to evaluate the school leader in addition to the evaluation conducted by district supervisors. The teacher representative to the committee wanted to create a procedure for staff to report problems to the evaluation committee. In contrast, Mrs. Carmichael was concerned about due process; she did not want the committee or the evaluation to become a repository for what she saw as the day-to-day grievances or personality conflicts that arose in the hierarchical relationships between staff members and herself as their supervisor. The important point here is that this committee disrupted cultural norms about the relationship between the principal and staff members, which caused a considerable amount of tension. One teacher attributed the more obvious conflicts between the staff and principal to the existence of this committee:

> I think that the process of [planning] the principal evaluation gave a vehicle that had never been in place before. Even though it wasn't up and running, so to speak. Even though we didn't have that Principal Evaluation Committee evaluating the administrator, I think that it brought the awareness that our administrator was not a good match for the charter and for the vision of this school.

Mrs. Carmichael was replaced by a staff search committee that brought in Tom Jensen (who was working as consultant) to refine the job description and the interview process. With Jensen's assistance, the search committee also collected and vetted resumes in-house—thus bypassing the district's personnel office. Most importantly, the committee changed the name of the position from Principal to Director. Many staff members felt that the title of Principal implied to the school district and the person in the position that there was a hierarchical relationship between the district, the school leader, and the teachers. In contrast, the model they were trying to create was based on a balance of power between the SSC (the governing body dominated by teachers), which was represented by its two co-chairs, and the school's leader. As one teacher noted in her description of the conflicts the school had weathered over the years:

> How the power is laid out at the school is a problem. We shot ourselves in the foot, I think, when we wrote the charter. We put the role of principal in there, and we named it principal. That is giving one person the ultimate authority. Even though [the principal] is supposed to report to the School Site Council, we gave that person the authority.

This comment is interesting because it centered the role of teachers in defining the school's mission and policy and also evoked how powerful the cultural norms around the role of principal can be. Staff members reported that despite their efforts to use the charter to delineate a less hierarchical relationship between the staff and the principal during Mrs. Carmichael's administration, there were strong external constraints working against them: (1) staff members had little substantive input over the selection of Mrs. Carmichael; and (2) the more subtle influence of traditional roles, relationships, and norms, or what one staff member characterized as the "district mindset of what a principal acts like, talks like, walks like." Yet some staff members also suggested that there wasn't a clear vision *within* the school about how this reconfigured relationship should work in practice. Two staff members who became grassroots leaders at the school during these events alluded to the latter in their comments, which were echoed by others:

> I think we were very unclear with Ms. Carmichael [the principal] about what we wanted her role to be. She made up her role as she went along, doing what she had always done as principal.

> For a while site-based management was going on everywhere. And I don't think [the superintendent] believes in it at all. So I think that has been completely taken away as a piece of the program. And [the school district] doesn't know who [on site] to answer to. And again, part of it is our fault. We need to say to [the assistant superintendent], when our SSC co-chairs call, you need to respond to them. They are our leaders as well. So part of it might be our fault. We need to assert ourselves more.

The second teacher's quote also reflected the shift in district policy that occurred when the school district's reform efforts were refocused around systemic reform rather than site-based management; the former was widely characterized as an instance of "top-down" management. As I will elaborate below, as relatively autonomous schools, the charter schools in the Geary Unified School District fit rather uneasily into this reform effort.

Another factor that contributed to the school's apparent inability to translate its vision into practice was staff attrition. According to many staff members, the two periods of political turmoil described above resulted in a high degree of staff turnover at the same time that state-mandated class size reduction in the lower grades expanded the teaching staff. The new teachers who were hired tended to be less experienced. Because Hilltop Charter School was relatively small (twenty-nine teachers in total), the steady loss of original staff members and two waves of hiring, which added at least six newly credentialed teachers to the staff at a time, contributed to this process.

For example, during an interview, one teacher who was hired in the early stages of the Mrs. Carmichael's tenure noted that she was one of a large cohort of teachers hired together, most of whom were first- and second-year teachers. Her comments suggest that it takes time for new staff members—and especially less experienced teachers—to become involved in site governance, because they are so focused on their classrooms. In this context, Mrs. Carmichael was able to exert a lot of informal control despite a formal structure that provided teachers with a great deal of authority:

> There were a few people [names three veteran staff members]. And they knew what was happening.... You know they tried to rally people. And I think a lot of people left. There was a huge turnover when I came. And we started with a new staff. And they [veteran staff members] tried to explain, this is what we are going to do [shared decision-making]. And honestly, I think that there was a sense of people not wanting to take the initiative and to really just sit there and think in their minds, everything will be fine. But it really wasn't. And I think a lot of people actually wanted Ms. Carmichael [the principal] to do all of the work. It takes a lot of effort to have shared decision-making.

In the months leading up to the series of events that precipitated Mrs. Carmichael's resignation, some of these newer staff members—including the teacher above—were taking on activist roles within the school alongside long-term staff members who expended a significant amount of time and energy keeping shared decision-making alive at the school. Thus, teachers new to the school had to be socialized into the culture of shared decision-making. Moreover, newly credentialed teachers may have found it difficult to actively participate in shared decision-making because of the high demands on teacher time, preferring instead to focus their attention on their classrooms. As Eisner (1992) pointed out, empowering teachers often increases the demands on teachers without reducing their classroom responsibilities. Even experienced teachers who are highly committed to site-based management can find it difficult to manage the additional responsibilities it can entail within the confines of recess, lunch, and preparation periods.

Renaming the position from Principal to Director had a powerful symbolic meaning for staff members. More substantively, Mr. Arden, the search committee's choice for the director's position, was a teacher who had experience as a school principal; he had been working as a teacher after making a conscious decision to leave administration to return to teaching. While this latter quality was very appealing to the committee, he was also an attractive candidate because he was a strong advocate for site-based management. Finally, it is not insignificant that the school's decision to choose its own leader was supported by the school district, which many perceived as a departure from the way that Mrs. Carmichael's administration had been constituted.

The Process of Reform: Two Steps Forward, One Step Back

In this section I briefly discuss what was absent at Hilltop Charter School during my visits. In the first years after it reopened, Hilltop Charter School was considered to be on the "cutting edge" of reform. Staff members often commented that during this period the school often hosted visitors who wanted to see its education program in action. Two articles published in the local newspaper the first year Hilltop Charter School reopened described the school in similar terms. This reputation was in part due to the school's participation in high-profile national and state reform initiatives, such as New Standards and the state's restructuring initiative funded by SB 1274.[9] However, did these reform initiatives continue to have an effect on the school after they ended? At the time of the fieldwork, it was difficult, although not impossible, to find evidence of these initiatives in daily school life.

Of the two major programs, the New Standards and the 1274 grant, the latter was more influential; staff members would still mention the grant two years after it ended. However, as staff members that participated in these reforms left the school, the "institutional memory" of each faded. This was particularly true of the New Standards Project, which, according to one founding teacher, provided professional development funds, networking opportunities, and opportunities for teachers to access lesson plans. However, not all of the teachers at the school participated in the program. While this teacher's involvement with the New Standards Project was more limited, it provided her with the opportunity to attend an out-of-state conference. Few teachers had detailed knowledge about the program, which suggests that as staff turnover occurs the effects of a reform initiated at a school site can dissipate over time. As one teacher commented when she was asked to assess the success of the early years of the school:

> I don't really think you can measure things that haven't. [I ask her "It was just too early?"] Yes. Yes. And so maybe you could say none. I mean, unfortunately. I think probably all of the success came with the individual teacher. I think the individuals that were part of it took everything they learned and now are using that in the district, which is great. You have teachers who changed the way they did things, learned new things, and still had that knowledge. But they never pulled it together for the good of the group at [Hilltop Charter School].

In contrast, the 1274 funds paid for computer networking and staff development by "gurus" that was provided directly to teachers at the school site. The grant also funded additional staff positions to work with students. While these activities had a greater impact on the entire school than the New Standards Project, once the five-year granting period ended and the funds were no longer available, the school was less able to maintain these practices. Perhaps the most tangible outcome of this grant was the school's early emphasis on technology; all classrooms were networked and computers were provided for each classroom long before this was a ubiquitous feature of school life.

However, with the constant influx of new staff members and without the on-site professional development, the shared understanding of the school's educational philosophy and how the school worked more generally had, according to some longer-term staff members, gone through a process of erosion and partial reconstitution. The few remaining core staff members worked with newer staff members to recreate these tenets of school life in ways that were at once strikingly similar to the original design yet also altered in the process. One teacher described the school's evolution in these terms:

> So first I had to find the answer to all of the questions. And then we needed to get it written down and put in our gray binder so that everything is clear. Because a lot of things have just been, it is an assumption. Because when the original staff was put together, everyone was of the same mindset. They came here for a particular reason. Now, things have changed. So I have been trying to just get everything on paper, [getting] everything organized. Making sure that everybody is clear about what we are about.... We still have a long way to go, we still have a lot to work towards. Just like with [names a consultant the school worked with on the past] on the phone, right now. I felt like I needed to tell him we are not what we were five years ago when you came. We are much less sure of ourselves and we have a lot

of teachers that need training in multi-age. But if we can keep [the teachers] we have and move forward, I think we will get back on track with the charter.

Hearts and Hands Community School

Like Hilltop Charter School, there were aspects of the policy environment that supported the creation of Hearts and Hands School. California's charter school legislation had recently taken effect when a parent who had contacted the Geary school board with an interest in starting a Waldorf charter school received encouragement from a school board member who was aware of a Waldorf public school operating in inner-city Milwaukee (Research Team, 17).[10] The charter was written and approved in November of 1993 and the school opened the following September. Although the charter had been approved months earlier, school organizers did not have a site until April 1994, when the school board decided to open a previously closed school as an overflow school and agreed to house the charter school at that site. As a result, the school opened its doors for instruction under a very compressed timeline. There was little opportunity for careful planning at a time when charter school legislation was very new and untested. As one of the founding teachers commented:

[Comparing Hearts and Hands Community School to another charter school in the district]...for years they have been planning it. And you take something like that with the years of planning when the laws are far more clear, and they know exactly what population they are going to serve, how they are going to serve, and what they want the end result to be. When our charter was written, I can't guarantee that it was written to be where it is with the children we have and the faculty they have. I am sure [the other charter school] handpicked their teachers over the years, and their director. And I think for charter schools all that legwork must be done before the school opens its doors, because as somebody put the analogy, when you are flying the plane, you sure can't fix it.

In addition, as the first start-up charter school to open in the Geary Unified School District,[11] Hearts and Hands Community School was a novel organizational form as both a charter school and a "*Waldorf-inspired*" charter school.[12] The school's unique status was evoked in the testimony provided by a member of the Geary school board at a Congressional hearing on education reform about a year after the school opened. After describing the district's six charter schools in highly positive terms, he commented:

[Some] of the charter schools that have come into the district may not fit into a public setting. [An] example is the Waldorf Schools, popular in

Germany, and are growing in the United States. The basic premise of the school is that they don't begin teaching reading until the second grade. And yet in a highly mobile inner-city population, it may not work to have that kind of system in an inner-city school. We don't know. We have chartered the petition, but it is one that we will look at.

Perhaps not surprisingly, Hearts and Hands Community School was the target of a series of challenges during the first three years of its operation.

Hearts and Hands Community School: A Novel and Vulnerable Organizational Form

While Geary's school board unanimously approved Hearts and Hands Community School's charter, it did so against the advice of district staff, including the office of the general counsel. The local branches of the state school employees unions—the California School Employees Association (CSEA) and the California Teachers Association (CTA)—also opposed the charter. Thus, while there were some conditions that initially enabled the creation of Hearts and Hands Community School, it was also vulnerable to subsequent challenges. In its first year, two lawsuits were brought against the school by the unions. Both lawsuits challenged the validity of the charter school petition. At the time Hearts and Hands Community School was chartered, California's charter school law required charter school petitions for start-up schools to be signed by 50 percent of the teachers from one school in the district or 10 percent of all teachers in the district. The four teacher signatories of Hearts and Hand's charter school petition were all employed as teachers in the district's home education division. The legal question was whether or not the home education program fit the definition of a school. If the home education program was not a school, then those teachers could not authorize the charter petition.

Based on information available in court documents and contemporaneous newspaper articles, the CSEA's main concern was whether or not the rights of employees at charter schools would be protected. After union members raised this issue at the school board meeting during which the charter was approved, and did not receive a satisfactory response, the union brought the lawsuit. The school district argued that the union was not entitled to be the exclusive bargaining unit at the charter school, noting that when then-Governor Wilson approved SB 1448, he also vetoed another charter school bill (AB 2585) because it contained a provision for teachers union approval of charter schools and "elaborate collective bargaining processes." The court ruled that the school's charter was in compliance with California charter school law but required the charter to be amended so it addressed all of the provisions in the legislation. Ultimately, the collective negotiations contract between the classified employees union and the school district was amended to clarify the rights of union members employed at charter schools.

At the beginning of the school's second year, a separate complaint was brought against the school by a newly hired staff member who alleged that the school violated the separation of church and state. The staff member and some parents objected to the content of a professional development session for teachers, claiming it contained a spiritual component that was inappropriate for a public school. To respond to the complaint, the district's legal department reviewed the broader question of whether or not a Waldorf-inspired public school violated First Amendment provisions for the separation of church and state. The district also conducted an evaluation of the school by an outside agency. During this period, Management and the school's director were also embroiled in a conflict over hiring practices (Research Report, 1996).

The teachers union lawsuit went to trial two years later and revisited all of the issues described above: the validity of signatures on the charter school petition, the legality of the charter petition, and the issue of religion in the curriculum. In addition, the union alleged that because the school served as an overflow school there was a significant proportion of the school's population that was a "captive audience," whereas the state legislation required that parents "affirmatively opt in" to charter schools.[13] Finally, the union contended that the school did not meet statewide performance standards as required by charter school law.

With the exception of ordering that the school's charter must specify the other schools that students could attend in lieu of Hearts and Hands Community School, the court did not accept any of these challenges. This account suggests that at this early stage in charter school reform, Hearts and Hands Community School was a particularly vulnerable organizational form. While perhaps innocuous on their own, in combination, the different elements that comprised the school were viewed as a formidable challenge to traditional conceptions of schooling. To be more specific, teachers from a nontraditional school signed off on a new school that was: (1) subject to fewer regulations than a conventional public school; (2) not required to follow the collective bargaining agreements for school employees and the credentialing requirements for teachers; and (3) implementing a curriculum that was outside the mainstream and had religious overtones.[14]

A comparison between Hearts and Hands Community School with Hilltop Charter School brings this vulnerability into sharper focus. As I detailed above, Hilltop Charter School had broad-based organizational support that was nurtured by an institutional entrepreneur. More specifically, in the case of Hilltop Charter School, the first charter school in the district, representatives from the teachers and classified employees unions were involved in the negotiations to reopen the school. Only after the school was opened—and staffed by credentialed teachers under the terms of the teachers' contract—did the school vote to convert to charter status.[15] At the time of the fieldwork, many Hilltop Charter School teachers belonged to the teachers union and the school had union representatives. Hilltop Charter School's education program also dovetailed with the findings of a district task force on early childhood education, so there was significant policy support for its education program within the district. Hilltop Charter School undoubtedly also benefited from the added legitimacy of participating in high-profile national and state reform efforts, one sponsored by a private organization with ties to the federal government and prominent foundations (NASDC) and the other by state legislation (Rao, 1998).

In contrast, even in its early planning stages, Hearts and Hands Community School faced considerable opposition from school employees unions. In addition, on two occasions the school board voted to support the school against the recommendation of district employees. As a result, Hearts and Hands Community School was the least legitimate charter school among those operating within the district and the most vulnerable to challenges. This conclusion is suggested by an exchange between the judge and the teachers union lawyer during the hearing for the teachers union lawsuit. When the lawyer noted that district staff recommended that the school board reject the charter, the court commented that these concerns, while "genuine," should have been raised long ago. The lawyer responded:

> The reason we weren't here a long time ago, your Honor, there are a number of these charter schools that never become viable. This very defendant [the school district] has authorized 11 charter schools, of which only 7 are now operating. It would be a waste of time and the plaintiff's resources to sue when a school isn't even up and running.

Complicating matters further, the teachers union lawsuit also intersected with the agenda of another grassroots organization, People for Legal and Nonsectarian Schools (PLANS). Founded in the early 1990s by a former—and disillusioned—Waldorf parent to challenge the incorporation of Waldorf educational principles and practices into public education, PLANS viewed the Waldorf school movement as a religious cult. In addition to maintaining a web site critiquing Waldorf education and soliciting supporters, PLANS members picketed Waldorf public school sites

(Mealy, 1997). In the teachers union lawsuit against Hearts and Hands Community School, the founder of PLANS was a witness for the plaintiffs and testified that the Waldorf-inspired education offered at the site was based on the religious doctrine of Anthroposophy. He also asserted that it is impossible to remove the religious components of Anthroposophy from the Waldorf curriculum.

At the time the fieldwork was conducted, PLANS had filed lawsuits in federal court against two Northern California school districts in which they argued that the districts violated the Constitution by providing public funds for schools utilizing a Waldorf curriculum.[16] In interviews, staff members mentioned this organization or its founder, which suggested that it posed a threat to the school's educational vision. One teacher reported that the Curriculum Committee was originally called the College of Teachers, as in private Waldorf schools, but the name was changed so that the school would look less like a private Waldorf school, also highlighting how the school was a vulnerable organizational form.

Between District and Charter

As I suggested in chapter 3, while the Waldorf-related aspects of the school's education program were the most highly visible within the school, another salient feature of the school culture at Hearts and Hands Community School was the idea that the school's curriculum was a combination of the Waldorf education and the "district" educational model,[17] so that it was neither one nor the other. For example, in the charter school submitted to the school board for its renewal in September 1998, the curriculum was described as a blend between a "Waldorf-inspired program" and California state frameworks. In practical terms, both elements were to be integrated in the curriculum through the main lesson format, described in chapter 3. By the time of the fieldwork approximately a year later, in practice the curriculum tended to be described as a blend between Waldorf-inspired and "district," as in this teacher's comments at a Management meeting:

> [Describing a program document that was being developed to provide an overview of the school's curriculum] There is a draft here of the program. It is very, very comprehensive, in a certain sense it is not complete but it is more complete than anything that has ever been brought to this school before. This is a teacher's version... there wouldn't be this much detail that we would hand out in that parent handbook. This is so that a new teacher coming on board can have tremendous clarity of what they would be teaching and how they should be teaching it, what the objectives would be, how they would present it, and the standards it would address. And

that is partly what has taken so long, because we are creating something that has never existed before, this is not just a Waldorf curriculum and it is not just a district curriculum, this is the first time in history that this has [been created].

This statement also referenced some of the ongoing tensions at the school. Over the years the school had developed program documents that outlined its curriculum. During the fieldwork the Curriculum Committee had spent most of the school year trying to blend the Waldorf curriculum with district and state curriculum frameworks to create the Hearts and Hands Community School curriculum in a new and more detailed program document that this teacher was referencing to in her comments. As I explain in more detail below, many staff members felt that the revised program document was needed because prior versions were not detailed enough for teachers or parents. While this effort was underway, the two components would commonly be described as separate entities; some parts of the school's education program would be characterized as "Waldorf" and some parts of the program as "district." "District" encompassed not just the curriculum per se but also the teaching techniques taught in district-sponsored professional development workshops.

Yet the blend of Waldorf and non-Waldorf—and in particular the Geary Unified School District's reform based on the Balanced Literacy approach—was not always a happy marriage. One teacher noted that, on the one hand, participating in district trainings made her more self-conscious as a teacher about what she was doing in the classroom, which she found helpful. On the other hand, she also felt that if the district's focus on literacy was too rigidly applied, it would exclude aspects of the Waldorf curriculum that she felt enriched children's educational experiences and supported their literacy development:

> We were on the last two chapters of this book called *By the Greyhorn Spoon*, which is a book about the Gold Rush and we are teaching the Gold Rush in Main Lesson. [In] language studies they do that, use historical fiction to teach [the] curriculum. That is what you do [in Waldorf education], only you do it through oral storytelling, basically. But [the students] had to write what they thought was going to happen in the last two chapters. And there were really some big surprises. And I said [to the students] there are going to be some surprises. And someone asked, "Can I make a really silly surprise?" I said, "Go ahead. You can predict something that is not serious but I want some serious predictions as well." He wrote this whole thing, I said OK, who knows what genre we are reading. It is historical fiction, Ms. Johnson. Great. Who can tell me what he was predicting? Oh, that was fantasy, or oh, that was science fiction. And they argued for it, and it was done in a very fun way. So the Norse myths, we talked about myths and

legends. "Why were there frost giants? Well, Norway—it is very cold there. Why would you make that your enemy? Because a lot of people would die in that kind of weather."...So I know the [district reform] has done that for me, whether it would have happened anyway as a teacher, I don't know. And my vocabulary, I am more likely to say "genre." I never would have said that before, because it is such a funny word. Those kinds of things. But to take that block and say I can only teach reading from 8:45 until 11:45 and I can't do Main Lesson is saying that Main Lesson isn't reading. And I would argue that it is. I have children here that can decode well, and I can read in Spanish, but I don't understand what I am reading.

Two features of this description are worth highlighting. First, this teacher describes the professional development she has received as a result of the literacy reform in positive terms, suggesting it has allowed her to hone her teaching techniques. Yet her comments also suggest that, as she understood it, the Literacy Block entailed a fairly rigid set of activities that did not include the range of activities associated with the Main Lesson. She also cited some instances where the two approaches were incompatible. For example, in the circle activities described in chapter 3, students often had to work together to sustain complicated rhythmic patterns. To make her schedule work, she often had to schedule Independent Reading—a solitary activity—after the group-oriented circle activity, which did not make pedagogical sense to her. Likewise, fully implementing the Balanced Literacy approach would squeeze some of the arts activities, which were a fundamental part of the Waldorf educational model, out of the class schedule.

The often uneasy blend between the Waldorf-inspired and "district" educational models also had an influence on school culture. While in any organization there are likely to be disagreements among its members, the fault lines at Hearts and Hands Community School crystallized around the extent to which the school was a Waldorf-inspired school and to what extent does the school follow district policies. One teacher commented on the division within the staff directly.

You have two kinds of groups here at this school. You have the groups that came here because it was a Waldorf school, whether certified or not. And then you have the groups that came because they liked the feel of the school, or they fell into the job. And for that group of people, I think that they truly believe that our first responsibility is to implement what the district is telling us to implement. And second, if they have time, they will do watercolor painting or some of the frilly things. I don't think that is going to be successful.

This teacher's remarks (and some of the others above) also tap into another component of the tensions embedded in this effort to blend the two approaches. In the Waldorf approach, artistic practice is a central component of the pedagogy. For example, a leading proponent of the Waldorf education writes:

> To ensure that education does not produce one-sided individuals, crippled in emotional health and volition, these less conscious aspects of our human nature must constantly be exercised, nourished and guided. Here the arts and practical skills make their essential contribution, educating not only heart and hand, but in very real ways, the brain as well. (Barnes, n.d.)

As I described in chapter 3, teachers and parents at Hearts and Hands Community School would express similar understandings of the arts as a central and meaningful component of the educational experience offered by the school.

However, in the district's literacy reform, there was a sharper division between the arts and academic lessons. The differences between the two approaches were reflected in an administrator's description of the two programs as a "strong instructional program" (the Geary Unified School District's reform) and the Waldorf philosophy, which he characterized as child-centered, developmental, and not a strong fit with the district's "high powered academic program."[18] The mismatch between the two approaches can be illustrated by a comparison between the district's goals for kindergarten and those of a conventional Waldorf school. According to the Geary Unified School District's guidelines for a reading assessment all schools were required to utilize,[19] kindergarten students were considered at grade level if they were reading simple texts by the end of the school year. In Waldorf schools, students do not learn letters until the first grade. One teacher commented that over time the school had shifted away from the conventional Waldorf model as a result of this external pressure:

> The first year that I was here [a year before the district's systemic reform initiative began], the administrator that was in charge of the kindergarten program flatly stated to me that we would be teaching letters to the children at this school over her dead body. We are teaching letters to the children in kindergarten and she is not here. I think that is huge. That first year I was here, my estimation was that we needed to take the Waldorf curriculum and downturn it one full year. And I was treated like I was kind of a crazy woman with a... I was going to damage students by pushing them too fast, and really that was slow compared to other early childhood educators' ideas. And this year I heard one of the kindergarten teachers say, well, if we just put the kindergarten curriculum back one full year then we will meet the district standards.

This teacher also noted that she viewed this evolution as positive:

> It really shows a shift in the way we are approaching education in this school. Paying attention to the outside demands for upgraded standards.

In contrast, another teacher with extensive Waldorf training suggested that Hearts and Hands Community School needed to emulate other Waldorf-inspired schools and be more proactive in educating parents and the district about the differences between a Waldorf-inspired program and the education programs offered by conventional public schools:

> The challenges happen because [when Waldorf-inspired schools try] to follow this curriculum that is trying to meet the needs of the child they don't score well on testing in second and third grades. But [other Waldorf-inspired] schools have worked very hard with the parents and with the districts that are sponsoring them to educating them as to why that is. And then their scores are very good in the upper grades, which is when testing is more appropriate when you look developmentally. And because of that, because of the education, because the scores are better if not exceeding what they had hoped for, or [those of] children in like schools, they have been supported by their districts.

The school's apparent inability to clearly define its education program and provide staff with training in the Waldorf educational philosophy and pedagogical approach created a Catch-22. New teachers were hired (some reportedly to fill last-minute vacancies) and were expected to follow the school's educational philosophy. Yet if these teachers did not have Waldorf training, or if they were not provided with a detailed description of the school's education program and philosophy (i.e., the program document described above) and training, they were less likely to teach the Waldorf-inspired curriculum. The teachers steeped in Waldorf pedagogy interpreted this as a dilution of the school's educational philosophy, which exacerbated the tensions around the school's mission and pedagogy.

Likewise, although there was broad agreement that the lack of site-sponsored training and mentoring was a problem at the school, teachers who were strongly committed to the Waldorf philosophy would get Waldorf training on their own time and at their expense, or in some cases, already had extensive Waldorf training before being hired by Hearts and Hands Community School. As a result, these teachers needed relatively less guidance in how to teach a "Waldorf-inspired" curriculum. One of these teachers noted that her training allowed her to take the skeletal outline of the curriculum provided in past program documents and create detailed lesson plans. This teacher also felt that she was also better able to integrate aspects of the Waldorf curriculum with more traditional teaching approaches than some of her peers, commenting:

> [I]t really is a balance and I think that is where a lot of people struggle here, understanding that you can do both. I think that a lot of people think it is an either/or situation, but Waldorf education isn't separate from skills. It isn't. It really is economy of teaching. You just have to be smart about how you plan and you have to put a lot of time in.

However, some staff members—in particular those most involved with articulating the curriculum—also saw this situation as the outcome of a leadership problem within the school.

> We are in the business of educating and if we have lax administration and weak leadership, and fractions of people here doing this and not following the philosophy because philosophy is not being, the vision is not being, someone is not out there carrying the flag. We need a person out there to carry the flag, and say this is Waldorf-inspired education, this is Hearts and Hands Community School, and this is what we do here. From the new teachers that are hired to the custodian that cleans up at night, everybody needs to know that this is the vision of this school. We are all stakeholders in this thing.

Yet the call for strong leadership at the school that would require teachers to teach using the Waldolf-inspired model was itself riddled with contradictions. Because the school was organized around a site-based management model, the responsibilities for school management were distributed widely. In this case, the teachers on the Curriculum Committee were charged with the task of clearly articulating the school's "Waldorf-inspired" education program. Yet the committee took about a year to produce a draft.[20] Moreover, if the program document was to be the definitive statement of the educational vision, then the school's management team was expected to rally the school around a vision that was not fully articulated. One parent member of Management attributed a wide range of problems to the *absence* of this document.

> In reviewing past staff reports, governance reports, and parent complaints, it is clear that the prevailing and most significant unresolved issue is the establishment of a comprehensive Hearts and Hands Community School Program. While it is alluded to in staff meetings, Finance Committee Meetings, at the district level, and from our Curriculum Committee, no comprehensive document has been submitted, accepted, or adhered to. Its lack has caused faculty/staff turnover, employee dissension and massive personal attacks, finger pointing, and low school-wide morale.... The entire school life revolves around the implementation and adherence to a

site program. The documentation drives the frameworks for which ALL other school activities respond to. Its completion will create unity in the teaching methods and create a clear understanding of the focus, mission, and vision of our charter.

The discussion above suggests that this conflict was tightly linked to other salient issues at the school, most importantly teacher training and the degree to which members of the teaching staff were committed to implementing a Waldorf-inspired program. For example, one teacher commented that, as teacher turnover occurred, the empty positions were filled with people who were not sufficiently committed to implementing the Waldorf-inspired model. Like other Waldorf-inspired charter schools, Hearts and Hands Community School posted employment advertisements for teaching positions at the school on a web site devoted to Waldorf education. While other Waldorf-inspired charter schools tended to specifically seek applicants with Waldorf training that were either credentialed or willing to pursue a teaching credential, at Hearts and Hands Community School, Waldorf experience was not an absolute condition for employment. Teachers with a strong arts background were also encouraged to apply for teaching positions. Some teachers felt that other than peer pressure there was no way to require teachers to use the Waldorf curriculum in their classrooms. In addition, teachers had not been formally evaluated for some time, which fueled the perception of a breakdown in school leadership among some members of the staff.

At the same time, the Geary Unified School District's reform was unfolding rapidly. While some of the tensions described above were attributable to internal issues of school organization, they were exacerbated by a contextual factor—the increasingly well-articulated vision about what "good teaching" looked like in the district. Staff members repeatedly alluded to this conundrum at Management meetings:

> We have struggled in the past with a dualistic approach, between this district and Waldorf, we have struggled to make a unified program since October, with teachers putting this thing together, and we have called in facilitation to amalgamate. We have got to have an addendum on [the teacher's contract] this year, before people sign their contracts that they are going to be committed to not just doing what they were taught at Geary or not just doing what they were taught at Rudolf Steiner Institute.

Apparently a long-term subject of debate at the school,[21] this issue gained particular salience as the district's efforts at systemic reform ramped up in March of 2000. As I noted in the Introduction, the Geary school board passed *The Plan for Student Learning*, a reform effort aimed at ending social promotion at all levels of the school system, from elementary school to high school. *The Plan for Student Learning* reallocated Title I funds for all schools in the district toward the efforts outlined in the plan. The school's director reported to Management that this budgetary shift would have a substantial impact on Hearts and Hands Community School's education program because Title I funds paid for positions that were a key component of the Waldorf curriculum, such as the gardening and the handwork teachers.

By the end of the year, in an effort to maintain the Waldorf-inspired components of its program, and a year earlier than planned, Management elected to switch to the direct funding model described in chapter 2, which gave charter schools more control over their funding than the revenue-limit funding model. At the same time, some of the staff members promoting the Waldorf-inspired component of the curriculum began using the Personnel Committee to create a standardized process for hiring teachers in an effort to ensure that new staff members would be trained in the Waldorf model. One of these teachers described this process as having a broader effect on the school community:

> *Teacher*: [T]his work with the hiring committee and raising a higher standard for hiring has trickled down into criteria for rehire. So we have been able to demand that people go get training and some people have decided to resign because of that. So it has been a process where we could actually find who really is committed to the program.
>
> *Jeanne*: As I understand it...there wasn't a similar level commitment to Waldorf education [across the school].
>
> *Teacher*: Right, and unfortunately when you have even one or two people who are in that category, it sours the rest of the barrel, because people react and feel undermined, even though the majority are right there. So we have been painstaking in making sure that everybody was on board with this.

Inspiration School

In contrast to the other schools in this study, by virtue of its ties to Educational Enterprise Corporation, Inspiration School brings another aspect of the charter school movement into focus—the dynamic relationship between charter schools and the voucher movement. Indeed, members of Educational Enterprise Corporation's management team were activists in the voucher movement prior to becoming involved in charter school reform. For example, testifying before Congress in 1998, an Educational

Enterprise Corporation administrator described charter schools and vouchers as two sides of the same coin:

> [W]e believe that operationally independent charter schools and educational opportunity scholarships (funded publicly and privately) are simply means to the same end, namely, the granting to parents, especially low income families, of the fiscal reality of their constitutional right to choose the best school for their child.

While Educational Enterprise Corporation was a nonprofit organization whose main mission was to develop charter schools, in its formative stages it was an organization that was actively promoting school voucher initiatives, primarily through research. Educational Enterprise Corporation and another organization, the Council for School Change, were both incorporated a few months apart in 1994.[22] Both organizations were initially sponsored by a prominent local businessman, the heir to a well-known Fortune 500 company and a generous donor to private voucher programs. In its early years, the Council for School Change was headed by a former business executive who subsequently became the primary executive officer of Educational Enterprise Corporation. Although its promotional literature dated its founding to 1994, and one of its administrators reported at a conference that the organization had been focused on research until 1996, newspaper accounts suggest that Educational Enterprise Corporation was not politically active until 1997.

The Council for School Change was actively promoting school vouchers; it had planned to place a voucher referendum on California's November 1996 statewide ballot. After a poll commissioned by the organization found that there was not widespread support for another voucher referendum in California, the organization revised its strategy. By August of 1996, the organization's president was promoting charter schools in an editorial article written for the local newspaper. In 1997, the Council for School Change moved to Indianapolis where it operated for about a year and advocated tax credits for families with school-age children (Mendel, 1997). The organization subsequently moved to Milwaukee. Notably, both of these cities are "ground zero" for private voucher programs. The Educational Choice Charitable Trust (CHOICE), established in 1991 in Indianapolis, is among the earliest privately funded voucher programs (Moe, 1995; Heise, Colburn, and Lamberti, 1995). The CHOICE program has since served as a model for subsequent privately funded voucher programs such as CEO San Antonio and the Milwaukee PAVE Program (Martinez, Godwin, and Kemerer, 1995; Beales and Wahl, 1995). Milwaukee has the additional distinction of having the first and longest running publicly funded voucher program.

These complex ties between Inspiration School's parent corporation and organizations associated with school vouchers and market-driven forms of school organization highlight the important differences between Inspiration School and restructuring charter schools, as represented in this study by Hilltop Charter School. The latter are grounded in the first wave of school reform after *A Nation at Risk*, discussed in chapter 2, during which restructuring was most often framed as a way to promote teacher empowerment. Inspiration School fits more squarely in what some analysts have described as the "third wave" of school restructuring, which invoked market principles as a rationale for school reform. Indeed, the Educational Enterprise Corporation's self-conscious discussion of the market potential for its services on its web site placed it squarely in this tradition of school reform. It argues that in the context of a failing educational system:

[C]harters, vouchers, and tax incentives are methods of providing choice and competition that are becoming popular. Policy shifts that expand the above and create equity in financing create instant markets.

These links to the voucher movement suggest the elasticity of the charter school movement. Rather than serving as a "firewall" against vouchers, as State Senator Gary Hart and other early proponents of charter schools in California intended, charter school legislation and the charter school movement it has generated has instead provided an opening within the education system for new types of actors, such as educational management organizations (EMOs), to become important players in efforts at education reform.[23]

While a skeptic could argue that Educational Enterprise Corporation was a nonprofit organization, and thus different from for-profit EMOs such as the Edison Project, in practice and perception, these organizations were quite similar. For example, when it reported that a neighboring school district had approved two charter schools, one proposed by a prominent national for-profit EMO and the other by Educational Enterprise Corporation, a local newspaper article characterized both organizations as "private groups" that were coming into the district to run their respective schools. This perspective is consistent with other newspaper reports across the country on the two organizations. For example, one article discussed both the Edison Project and Education Enterprise Corporation as "private management companies." A key similarity between the two organizations was that both explicitly emphasized business models of school management. The major difference between the two was the latter's nonprofit status.

Finally, to lend further weight to this interpretation, both in an interview in a national business magazine and a letter on the organization's web site, one of Educational Enterprise Corporation's major donors suggested that as part of an effort to expand its operations, the organization had been exploring the possibility of converting to a for-profit EMO. While the documents also suggest that this strategy was unfeasible, that it was a serious option speaks volumes about the complex relationship between charter schooling and other types of school organizations that have come to be considered forms of privatization. I return to this issue in more detail in the section below.

The preceding discussion also suggests something distinctive about the school's context. Unlike the other two schools in this study, at the time of the fieldwork, Inspiration School had politically influential supporters. Educational Enterprise Corporation's principle benefactor was a politically prominent businessman who supported a wide range of educational causes. In addition, other prominent local citizens served on the corporation's board of directors. Educational Enterprise Corporation was also at least a nominal member of an influential group comprised of prominent local businesses that actively promoted education reforms that they viewed as compatible with business models. While this latter group was an early supporter of charter schools, it also played a crucial role in hiring Superintendent John Tower, and was a prominent supporter of Geary's systemic reform initiative. Perhaps not surprising, then, observers of charter schools often cited Inspiration School as one of the relatively successful charter schools in the area.

In many ways, Inspiration School represented what some critics of school choice most feared. The involvement of a nonprofit organization with strong ties to the voucher movement raised the specter of the privatization of public education. Similarly, with the majority of its student population drawn from a single "underrepresented" minority group, Inspiration School could also portend the balkanization of ethnic groups within niches of the public school system.[24] Thus, the school enacted some of the tensions at the heart of the charter school movement. On one hand, we might be uneasy about Educational Enterprise Corporation's involvement with the school. In particular, the corporation's efforts at rapid expansion and the highly centralized organizational model it created, which, contrary to the intent of charter school law, gave teachers and parents little substantive influence over school policy, raises red flags.

On the other hand, given the persistent achievement gap between minority students and white students, and the well-documented and apparent intractability of racism in many public institutions, including the education system (see, for example, Lewis, 2003), Inspiration School would seem to represent an important choice for these parents and students. Indeed, overall, the school provided a positive environment for its students, due in no small part to the adults working at the site and who cared deeply for the students at their school. Yet this begs the question: why should these and similar parents have to choose between what are often substandard public schools and other relatively privatized options, such as corporate model charter schools (for a similar argument in the context of the Milwaukee Parental Choice Program, see Lowe and Whipp, 2002).

Charter Schools: Marketization Not Privatization

Some analysts have argued that the emergence and expansion of charter schools should be seen as one component of a broader process, the privatization of public education (see, for example Wells, Artiles, Carnochan, Cooper, Grutzik, Holme, Lopez, Scott, Slayton, and Vasudeva, 1998; Wells and Oakes, 1998). These critics view charter schools as one of an array of forces that are blurring the boundaries between public and private schooling. However, as I suggest below, this phenomenon is best described as marketization rather than privatization. In the sections that follow, I define marketization and then examine what Wells and Oakes (1998) described as the "micro-politics" of marketization at the three schools.

Defining Marketization

In general, analysts and policymakers engaged in debates around privatization are concerned with how public goods and services such as education are provided. Most analysts agree that privatization entails a shift in the principal site of an activity from the public sector or the state to the private sector (Starr, 1989; Butler, 1991; Feigenbaum and Henig, 1994, 1997). Feigenbaum and Henig (1994) also noted that privatization can also entail an expanded use of market dynamics in the provision of social goods (see also Starr, 1991). Using these definitions as a starting point, I argue that while some of contemporary efforts at education reform involve processes associated with privatization—deregulation, contracting, and the use of vouchers—they are best described as marketization rather than privatization (Pierre, 1995).

There are three important differences between the "education market" and the commodities market (Cookson and Berger, 2002). First, public education is for the most part publicly provided. Second, families consume education differently than they consume other commodities. In theory, students in market-driven schools can take advantage of the "exit option" if they are dissatisfied with their schools (Chubb and Moe, 1990). In practice, unless there is a large disparity in the quality of their old schools compared to their new schools, switching schools is not cost-effective for students. As Pierre (1995) noted "exit...will probably inflict more damage on the customer than the provider" (72). Third, education is "produced" differently than other types of commodities. While some critics claim that the United States' system of public education is a "monopoly," the American education system is fundamentally a decentralized system based on a patchwork of local, state, and federal control.[25] In contrast, the formal definition of a monopoly is the exclusive control over the production of a manufactured good or service by a single provider.

While both marketization and privatization entail a shift from the predominance of the public sector in service provision to the increasing involvement of the private sector, as the analysis of state policy dynamics in chapter 2 has suggested, debates around education reform have fairly clear boundaries that stop far short of advocating a wholesale shift to the private sector (see also Cookson, 1999). There are few, if any, calls for radical privatization via the sale of public schools as one might sell other government-owned enterprises. Likewise, while the roles of for-profit companies in the public education sector have expanded considerably, the public support for this type of business activity is uneven at best. As a result, marketization is best conceptualized as a continuum between public and private sector forms of school management, as illustrated by figure 4.1.

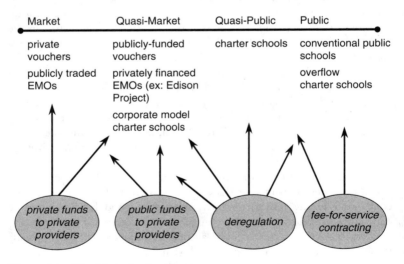

Figure 4.1   The Marketization Continuum
Source: Adapted from Powers and Cookson (August 1999).

The Local Dynamics of Marketization

Evidence from these charter schools suggests that the process of marketization "on the ground" was complex and uneven. As I discussed in chapter 3, Educational Enterprise Corporation's goal was to promote the market model of education reform. However, many teachers at Inspiration School were critical of the market model as they were experiencing it, and noted the gaps between market rhetoric and market reality. Moreover, staff members, particularly those who were affiliated with the school's other partner, a faith-based organization, tended to describe the school as a community-based institution rather than a demonstration site for market principles:

> *Teacher*: But I think that [the faith-based organization] has really touched on a promising idea, I will put it that way. Because even though church and state need to be separated in the educational process, that is an area [of reform] that a lot of people still believe should happen. And if an opportunity is there for them to accept a school that is in their neighborhood, at a facility that is near their church, they are all the more for it. We get tons of calls every single day and we do not have the space to accommodate them. So if the [the faith-based organization] has a building, if the [the faith-based organization] has a facility or some land in conjunction with starting a school or facilitating that idea, then they should do it.
>
> *Jeanne*: So it fills a need within the community? And also fills a need in terms of [the faith-based organization's] mission?
>
> *Teacher*: Absolutely. Absolutely. The [the faith-based organization's] mission was to have a private school here. But it costs a lot of money. Money that we don't have. So, it worked.

This exchange highlights a number of relevant issues. First, this teacher saw the school as primarily associated with its other partner, a faith-based institution, rather than Educational Enterprise Corporation (which she rather criticized). Second, the charter school was a more financially viable alternative to the faith-based organization's original goal to start a private school. Other interviewees described Inspiration School as analogous to a private school:

> I think the public school system has to focus on so many kids and so many schools that I think it is a very overwhelming task. I think charter schools are good—they are almost like private schools—they are just real small and they are just focused on the children that they have on the school with them and they are not so concerned with what is going on in the district.

On the other end of the continuum, teachers and administrators working at Hilltop Charter School voiced a strong belief in the democratic mission of public education and tended to emphasize that charter schools fundamentally are public schools. Some also noted that public schools, and particularly those serving inner-city students, often did not fulfill that promise.

> Well, they give a little more leeway, a little more freedom. And are better able to meet the needs of special populations, give teachers more input into meeting the needs of the students that they have. So I think it is a good direction for public education to go. Because [being a charter school] gives you that compromise. You are still a public school and yet you have more freedom and more leeway. So I think the charter movement is very, very important in that whole idea of preserving public education and regaining public trust.

Finally, Hearts and Hands Community School fell somewhere in the middle because it was a public school implementing what has largely been a private school educational model. Much like it has facilitated the expansion of EMOs and corporate model charter schools, charter school legislation seems to have facilitated the spread of the Waldorf model to the public sector, particularly in California. Corporate model charters and Waldorf charters are similar in the sense that charter school legislation has provided the opening for these new organizational forms. However, in general, corporate model charters tend to have more resources available for expansion whereas Waldorf charters tended to be founded by local activists. Moreover, private Waldorf schools are independent schools. For example, one teacher who had many years of experience teaching in private Waldorf schools made the following distinction:

> I don't call [a private Waldorf school] a private school because it is only private in the sense that it is seeking freedom of curriculum, freedom from the state's constraints by being based on tuition. So it is not private in the sense of wanting to be exclusive, it is basically independent.

However, an unintended consequence of some of the changes in charter school legislation that were unfolding during the fieldwork may have been the acceleration of marketization, even within less explicitly "market-driven" charter schools. After 1999, charter school funding was more concretely tied to enrollment and daily student attendance than it had been under the revenue limit funding model. Thus, any decline in a school's enrollment had a much greater budgetary impact than in the past. This shift was reflected in a discussion about the implications of the new funding model during a Management meeting at Hearts and Hands Community School:

> *Mgmt1*: [discussing changes in enrollment over the course of the school year]. But with the new funding model, every day are dollars that we

miss. You lose a student you've lost bucks. And hopefully you don't lose them at the beginning of the year.

Mgmt2: Well, this brings up a question for me about looking at size, because I am wondering if there has been an optimal size and perhaps students' satisfaction, families' satisfaction might have to do with the size of the classes. And if you go too high, you may be bringing in more bodies, but it may be counterproductive.

Mgmt3: I think it would be really interesting to ask the Finance Committee to come up with an optimal number of students for the average teacher's salary. That might be a piece of information that would be really nice to have.

At Inspiration School, teachers and staff were a critical of the idea that schools should be run as a business. Likewise, at both Hilltop Charter School and Hearts and Hands Community School, there was an uneasy tension around the market model and its relevance for schools. Participants at both schools acknowledged the need for fiscal responsibility and were aware that fiscal impropriety could trigger the revocation of a school's charter. However, the school as an educational organization and the school as a business did not always fit together seamlessly. There was often a tension between what participants envisioned as the ideal education program, budgetary limitations, and a wariness of having financial considerations drive their respective school's education program. However, the changes in the funding formula may have had the effect of pulling these schools more squarely into the business model. Thus, charter schools, regardless of type, are not unambiguously "privatization" or "grassroots."

Decentralization Meets Systemic Reform

In this section I discuss how the schools responded to the Geary Unified School Districts systemic reform. As I noted in the Introduction, the Geary Unified School District was in the process of rolling out a massive reform effort. While the Geary reform started with literacy reform in the elementary grades, over time the administration "scaled up" the reform to include other grades and subject areas. All schools were expected to implement the Balanced Literacy approach, including charter schools. The pressure was particularly salient at Hilltop Charter School and Hearts and Hands Community School because, as overflow schools located in district buildings, they perceived themselves as less independent from the district than other charter schools. In both cases, decisions made when the schools were founded had unanticipated long-term implications for the schools' abilities to maintain the education programs outlined in their respective charters.

While I discussed the impact of the reform on Hearts and Hands Community School in more detail above, at all three schools teachers were critical of having to participate in the district's reform. Yet there was a wide range in implementation both within and across the three schools. For example, at Hilltop Charter School there was broad support for the components of the Balanced Literacy approach—many teachers at the site had been trained in and utilized some of the techniques described in the Introduction. At the same time, Hilltop Charter School teachers were critical of what they perceived as the "top-down" implementation of the reform, which conflicted with the culture of shared decision-making at the school.

At Inspiration School, the aspect of the reform that was most widely implemented school-wide was the requirement that literacy be taught in a three-hour block in the morning, although there was variation across classrooms. Finally, as I described above, at Hearts and Hands Community School, the district reform was described by many teachers as being in tension with the schools' secularized version of Waldorf education, yet implementation also varied widely. Despite the unevenness of implementation, teachers and other staff members at all three schools tended to perceive the reform as at odds with their goals and mission as *charter* schools. School administrators had to walk the fine line between staying abreast of the district's efforts and sharing "best practices" with their staffs and not appearing co-opted.

The apparent conflict between the Geary Unified School District's literacy-based reform and the charter schools' educational goals can be interpreted as the result of the tension between a reform aimed at creating a technical environment versus a reform aimed at creating an institutional environment. Organizations operating in technical environments are expected to provide efficiently produced goods and services for clients (Scott and Meyer, 1991). Organizations operating in institutional environments must comply with legal or social rules to receive legitimacy and support. Scott and Meyer argue that these two types of environments can be conceptualized as dimensions along which different types of organizations can be arrayed. In general, schools are organizations with a weak technical environment and a strong institutional environment because they are subject to legal mandates via regulations, rather than requirements to follow specific practices to produce a "product." As Cuban (1995) noted:

> [W]ith schools, defining what they ought to "produce" in their graduates is eventually contested. How "good teaching" and "effective learning" occurs is ardently debated. Moreover, school board members and their appointed

administrators cannot observe directly what teachers do in their classrooms (except when principals occasionally visit) or what students learn (except by monitoring standardized tests). Thus the technology of schooling (i.e., teaching) is divorced from common managerial controls used to monitor production elsewhere. (6)

Viewed in these terms, because charter school reform aims to reduce the amount of regulations schools must comply with, it is an effort to create a weaker institutional environment. As I argued at the beginning of this chapter, charter school reform is conceptually empty. That is, charter school legislation says nothing about the core technology (curriculum and instruction) these schools should utilize in educating their students. However, the Geary reform was comprised of a distinct set of teaching practices. Thus, it was an effort to change the technical environment of teaching, because good teaching within the district was defined by the use of these techniques. Thus the two types of reforms created competing environmental pressures for these schools.[26]

Yet these competing environmental pressures were mediated by another factor, the revisions to California's charter school law, described in chapter two, that changed how charter schools were funded by the state. By the time the district reform effort was ramping up, Inspiration School had already switched to the direct funding model, which gave the school more control over its funding. At Hearts and Hands Community School, the reallocation of Title I funds to support the *The Plan for Student Learning* affected the staffing associated with the Waldorf educational model. As a result, to avoid the reapportionment of the school's funds, the school switched from the revenue-limit funding model to the direct funding model a year earlier than the school had planned. Finally, Hilltop Charter School opted to remain under the revenue-limit funding model and participated in the reform initiative, although they used the flexibility they had over their site funds to avoid some of the consequences of the reallocation that other schools in the district were experiencing.[27]

On the one hand, at all three schools staff members were wary of following district policies too closely. On the other hand, their resistance primarily focused on district *mandates*, such as the extent to which the schools are required to have—and fund—positions associated with the literacy-based reform. The schools participated in programs made available to them by the district, such as an after-school reading program, or professional development opportunities for teachers. Of the three schools, Hilltop Charter School most consciously tried to walk the finest line between "district" and "not-district;" the school's administrators described the school as open to adopting district practices when possible and feasible. In one teacher's words, Hilltop Charter School wanted to have a "symbiotic relationship with the district, but at the same time not be poisoned by it." Likewise, when discussing the implications of the switch to direct funding for governance at the school, the administrator of Hearts and Hands Community School argued at a meeting:

I am going to get on my soapbox right now, because the ball has gone from being this kind of hybrid [under the revenue limit funding model] and when one argument or when one camp seemed to work best for us we would live in that one, and when we want to live in the other one we would move into that one. No camps now [under the direct funding model]. It is sitting right here, this body is incredibly responsible for the survival of this school.

The Meaning of Charter: National and State Discourses, Local Context and Actions

While much of analysis in this chapter and chapter 3 has focused on the differences between the three schools, there were also some important similarities between them that are worth noting. As Wells and her colleagues pointed out in their study of seventeen charter schools in ten California school districts (1998), teachers in charter schools developed what they described as a distinctive esprit de corps (see also Lopez, Wells, and Holme, 2002). In general, the teachers, administrators, and other activists I came into contact with throughout the fieldwork saw charter schools as something distinct from traditional public schools in various ways. Perhaps not surprisingly, then, "charter" was a salient feature of school life for participants. For example, in the context of a discussion about a different topic, a teacher referred to "charter stuff." When I asked her what "charter stuff" meant, she replied:

Finding ways to keep us different. Staff developments like retreats. Things that keep teachers from feeling overwhelmed. Keeping us like a unit. Making sure that everything is on the same page when it comes to governance, when it comes to budget. When it comes to charter things. Going out there and making the connections from other charter schools and coming back.

Participants also often drew a sharp distinction between charter schools and other schools by using the term "district" as a generic term to denote conventional public schools. This could have been because the vast majority of schools are sponsored by school districts and as such are the entities that have the most proximate control over charter schools. Here a teacher described the impact of new "regulations"—the state charter school legislation that took effect in 1999.

> They are giving them deadlines to pass the CBEST and the test and they are saying everyone has to be credentialed. And they are just falling right into the district pattern. And this was one of the exciting things I heard when I started at the school, that they would have alternatives to teachers teaching classes, that they would have these innovative things going on. But now they have regulated the teachers to be exactly just like district teachers.

Although these new requirements originated with the state legislature, this teacher characterized the changes in policy as "district." Thus "district" seemed to be a generic term that denoted governmental regulation. This invidious distinction may have had particular salience in the Geary Unified School District because it was rolling out the ambitious systemic reform initiative described above. In addition, some of the staff members at Hilltop Charter School and Hearts and Hands Community School held charter employment contracts while others were employed through the school district, which also tended to highlight this distinction.

As a result, most participants saw this distinction between "charter" and "district" meaningful. Two themes recurred across the three organizational settings that mapped onto themes from the charter school policy talk described in the Introduction. First, staff members were critical of what they saw as the bureaucracy of district schools. The second theme was related to the first. Participants believed that charter schools had—or should have—the freedom and flexibility to be "different" or "innovative." While overall there were similarities in the ways participants across the three schools invoked these themes, teachers' descriptions were also shaped by their respective school's organizational structure and school culture.

Charter Schools as an Anti-Bureaucratic Reform

Charter school participants shared an understanding of the public school system as an intensely bureaucratic environment and in dire need of change. In this context, a charter school was a site of freedom and of flexibility. As I suggested in the Introduction, this theme maps onto state and national policy talk about charter schools. For example, a former state department of education official who was working for a state charter school organization made the following comment on an e-mail discussion list:

> Many of you have heard me state that charter schools are not an educational innovation, but an organizational one. Another way of saying it is that charter schools are an anti-bureaucracy and school-empowering innovation.

What I mean is twofold. As it relates to bureaucracy, charter school law gives a charter school the authority to wipe away thousands of pages of education code and rules, the accumulation of years of "this is the way we must do it." As it relates to power, the charter school is in charge! They have switched position from being on the bottom of the power structure, to being on top. They are not subordinate to the rules and policies of the district office or state bureaucracy. The charter school gets to decide almost everything based on what those at the school—staff, parents and students—think is best. In return for all this freedom, charter schools are responsible for achieving a level of student achievement. If the school is successful, its reward is that it is allowed to continue. If it fails to adequately educate students, its right to exist is revoked. A systems way of saying this is that charter schools are part of a performance-based system, and not the current rule-based system that controls public education in California today.

Similarly, many of the participants in these schools described charter schools as an antidote to an overly bureaucratic education system. For example, one teacher at Hilltop Charter School noted that the charter school movement was complicated. While she saw one part of the charter school movement as about privatization per the discussion above, she also argued that charter schools were about changing bureaucracy:

[T]hen you've got this other faction that are interested [in charter schools] because they want to get out from under the educational bureaucracy that we have and try some new and different things, some new ideas, new ways of teaching, new ways of educati[ng]. Charters are really the answer to trying out new ideas in the hope of reforming public education.... I made up my mind... that if I continued on in this career... I didn't want to be just part of that same old system. I want to be part of the solution.

Similarly, a teacher at Hearts and Hands Community School used the term "red tape" and noted that, in contrast, a charter school had more flexibility:

I see charter schools as alleviating some of that—red tape if you want to call it—red tape. Instantly we can change. If something is not working, we can change. I see that as the benefit of being in a charter school.

Other terms commonly used by teachers and other participants to express similar sentiments were "top-down" and "hierarchical"; they also described the district as "mandating" particular policies. The most striking metaphor used by a participant, also a teacher at Hearts and Hands Community School, referred to public education as a dinosaur:

It is one way to get those innovations going, because the big dinosaur, we have this long-necked dinosaur of public education, and one way that there can be a few raptors to come in and take a few bites out of it is to have charter schools....Everybody uses dinosaur to indicate something that is slow-moving and stupid. So the raptors are the small, swift-moving, voracious creatures of the dinosaur age. So I see charters as raptors. [T]hey are going to damage the dinosaur a lot. There is going to be some bloodletting. But hopefully, though, they will create a whole new population of schools. There are some good successes out there with it. I am hearing a lot of good stuff.

On one hand, charter school policy talk suggests that, compared to conventional public schools, staff and parents in charter schools will have more opportunities to make decisions about school policy. In the case of Inspiration School, decision-making was concentrated at the corporate level, which in turn delegated at least some authority to the principal; teachers reported being unsure about the balance of power between the principal and the corporation, or how decisions were made. Teachers also felt that they had little influence over decisions at the school site. According to one teacher, the teachers were able to speak their minds—and many did—but they were not listened to. Parents also had little formal influence over school policy, as the school's parent organization served as an advisory group.

The teachers at Inspiration School who were familiar with other charter schools believed that teachers and parents should have more formal voice in school policy, in part because they expected to find a more diffuse system of authority at a charter school:

How [charter schools] are supposed to be run, the teachers are supposed to have a lot of say as to what goes on, the community, the parents are supposed to have a lot of say. So it is not like this top-heavy institution....This school is run very much like a regular elementary school and I taught in a regular elementary school already.

Tinkering Toward Bureaucracy?
In contrast to Inspiration School, teachers and parents at Hilltop Charter School and Hearts and Hands Community School had considerably more influence over school life through formally organized systems of governance. At both schools, site-based governance or shared decision-making was highly valued. However, staff members at the two schools also devoted a considerable amount of time and energy creating and recreating effective systems for self-governance.

As the descriptions in chapter 3 suggested, the two systems of governance at Hilltop Charter School and Hearts and Hands Community School were very different in their formal features. However, underneath these differences, both resembled what Cohen, March, and Olsen (1972) described as "organized anarchies" (1). There are three properties of organized anarchies. First, preferences are unclear and are often discovered by the organization in the process of acting. School governance often consisted of crisis management, particularly at Hearts and Hands Community School. The second feature of organized anarchies is unclear technologies where participants lack a clear understanding of the organization's policies and procedures. At both schools, participants often commented that policies and procedures were not sufficiently documented, which prevented consistent understanding and application of school policies. At both sites there were moments when the decision-making procedures the schools had developed broke down; situations would arise that could not be clearly resolved by the processes outlined in the schools' charters and/or governance bylaws. In addition, responsibilities were delegated to committee systems with frequent turnover, which contributed to the gaps between formal procedures and daily practice that often occur within organizations.

The third characteristic of organized anarchies is "fluid participation," which took different forms at each school (Cohen et al., 1972, 1). At Hilltop Charter School, participation in decision-making was somewhat dynamic because the SSC consisted of all full-time staff members. There was no formal roll call. Instead, a sign-up sheet was circulated and incorporated into the official minutes. Although all staff members were expected to attend SSC meetings, their absence was only visible if they had to give a report. Few decisions required a quorum for a formal vote. Only the most controversial decisions were voted on; most proposals reached consensus or were tabled. At Hearts and Hands Community School, there was a formal roster of Management members compiled at the beginning of the year. However, toward the end of the school year, participation in the governing board was relatively loose for a combination of reasons: staff members left the school, personal reasons, and the parent-chair resigned after a controversy around a school-wide retreat. Indeed, the membership of Management had been so fluid that in more than one instance the official members had to be determined before the group could take a vote. In addition, staff members and parents who were not members of Management started to attend meetings and participate in discussions. While they could not formally vote on decisions, these observers could influence the decision-making process.

Yet there were also some important differences in the two schools' systems of school governance. At Hilltop Charter School, after Jack Thomas left the school, the school worked with a consultant for about a year to create the consensus-based model of governance described in chapter 3. In contrast, at Hearts and Hands Community School, Management was supposed to follow the procedures outlined in Robert's Rules of Order. In practice, the group implemented a rather loose approximation of parliamentary procedure. A quorum of members had to be present for the meeting to begin; items for discussion and/or a vote would be allotted a specific time on a set agenda, although discussions often exceeded the times specified on agendas. Finally, motions would be brought to the group and voted on based on majority rule, or tabled for further consideration.

Thus decision-making at Hilltop Charter School tended to follow a more "organic" or site-generated model of decision-making based on large-scale participation, with ritualized repetition to keep it working (relatively) smoothly. On the whole, teachers and staff members were well-informed about school affairs. In comparison, the much smaller representative and majoritarian model adopted by Hearts and Hands Community School seemed to produce more dissent, particularly as the school was embroiled in a debate about the direction of its education program. Some staff members felt that Management was not working effectively and not promoting the interests of the entire school. For example, in one debate about creating a process for staff evaluations, a parent-observer repeatedly asked how Management was being evaluated. Some members of Management attributed this perception to the unwillingness of members of the school community who were not part of Management to stay informed about the issues that were being considered by the group. Yet Management was not providing formal minutes to communicate its decisions to the rest of the school community in a timely manner, which exacerbated these tensions. By the end of the year, as the school worked with a consultant to "rebuild" the school, some staff members advocated reconfiguring Management by seeking new members with particular skills and/or expertise. One teacher who emerged as a grassroots leader proposed moving toward a consensus-based structure of governance to address some of these issues.

While charter school policy talk argues that schools should be subject to fewer rules, the rules in question are *external* rules. Yet, as the experiences of the two schools with more diffuse authority structures suggest, in order for decentralization to work effectively, organizations need clear *internal* rules. As Tom Jensen, Hilltop Charter School's institutional entrepreneur commented:

> It was a systems problem. Too many good teachers who had their heart in it, who were smart, who were hardworking, who were not effective because of everything they had to deal with. The mistake was if you clear the brush, give them the latitude to work, that they wouldn't have organizational issues that were entirely new to them. Because, by the way, you need some rules. Anarchy won't work. You need [to have] some authority in some people.

And to the extent that charter schools have had problems, it has seldom been in curriculum and instruction.

What Jensen described as crucial to the process of site-based management is similar to what Sarason (1998) has called the "governing rules [which] put flesh on the bones of the abstraction contained in its distinctive mission" (34; see also Johnson and Landman, 2000). As one of the first teachers at Hilltop Charter School commented:

> We have grown light years in how to do shared decision-making. At the beginning, I very clearly remember being here until 6:00 where nothing, literally nothing was accomplished. We just kind of went into it very naively thinking that if we just sit down, we will get everything all figured out and organized. Some people now go crazy, saying "the process, the process, we have to follow the process." It is crucial. We didn't have a process back then. And it was an incredible time-waster, to not have a process. I would say that we made a lot of good faith efforts to get things done.

Finally, at both Hilltop Charter School and Hearts and Hand Community School the "informal" kept creeping into organizational life. Staff members would make explicit efforts to create positions and/or policies that were independent of the people associated with them. A familiar refrain at both schools was that issues should be discussed in terms of the "position, not the person." For example, one staff member at Hearts and Hands Community School described an experience with a personnel committee:

> We had a situation where we found a candidate for a position that we wanted to hire for. And several of us knew this person. And one member was eagerly saying, well, look, it is obvious, we should just hire this person. Of course we were all tired. But no, we have a procedure to go through. And other members were saying, yes, but now we have to forget that we know this person, and we are going to go through the screening and then the interview and then the observation and then we will decide. And we won't regret it because we will have it on paper and that person will have gone through the same procedure as everybody else.

As one of Johnson and Landman's (2000) respondents observed, "Sometimes bureaucracies have their charms" (112).

Giving Schools "Freedom" To Be "Different"

Another shared feature of participants' descriptions of charter school reform is related to the first. If participants saw conventional public schools as slow-moving and bureaucratic, participants tended to describe charter schools as having the freedom and flexibility to do things differently. Teachers and staff members also tended to contrast charter school difference with what they saw as the sameness of conventional public schools. As one Hilltop teacher noted:

> I think that probably, the whole movement stemmed from people who wanted to do things in a different way, who thought they could use the funding from the state and design programs that would better meet the needs of kids in a diverse society rather than have a cookie-cutter mold, one curriculum, one way to do it for all, which I don't think is the answer for a place like California that has such a diverse population. The focus needs to be on achievement and I think that has been made real clear to us. And something that we are real concerned about too is that our kids achieve. But being able to do it in a different way.

Likewise, when she was asked in an interview how working in a charter school influenced how she saw school reform, another teacher from Hilltop Charter School articulated this idea of charter schools as different quite clearly. She also tied her discussion of difference to specific features of the school's education program.

> [P]eople would ask me, what is the difference? What makes your school different? And I honestly could not tell them. I used to say, "oh, we are developmental. We believe that children learn in a variety of settings." Well, there are district schools that are developmental now. And so that no longer qualifies us to be different. [Now] the things that make us different. Families. Teaching children how to problem-solve. Doing the role-playing. Having the ability to teach children language arts in the afternoon and math is different. I think those things make us different. But Ms. Carmichael, I think she was trying to fit us into the square peg of the district. And I don't think that this is wrong. I think that is all that she knew. And I think she thought that she was doing the children the best she could. I think once we started fighting it and realizing, hey, this isn't what we want to be, and now we have so many new teachers, we are kind of like this oblong shape. We are not a square peg, we are not a round, we are this funky shape of our own.

Yet this teacher also implicitly highlighted the ambiguous nature of charter school difference, which often did not entail radically different educational practices. Rather, Hilltop Charter School was different compared to its immediate context—other schools in the district. Another teacher noted that charter schools often implemented programs school wide that were often used on a smaller scale at other schools.

Teachers and staff members at Inspiration School expressed a similar sentiment. In this case "difference" for many meant being able to utilize a curricular program that many of the teachers and staff felt would best meet the needs of the children at the school but was not among the district's textbook adoptions. Some teachers also reported that the district curricular materials (some of which the school was using) were not rigorous enough for their students.

> We are using Grand Heritage for our curriculum. Well that is a charter-like thing, in this situation. In Florida, a district has adopted it; the whole district uses it. But at this school, we are using the Grand Heritage curriculum. So we use that as our theoretical approach, the basis for everything we do. However, we have this Daily Math kit and those social studies books, which are district materials. These two materials, in comparing them to the Grand Heritage, they don't match. This stuff seems really babyish, very, very primary. The stuff that is in Grand Heritage books takes the kids to a whole other level.

Likewise, one respondent, who had experience working at another charter school prior to working at Inspiration School, referenced being different as an expectation when describing her experience at the first school. However, unlike the teacher above, she was more focused on her classroom.

> I really thought that the charter would be a way that we could do things differently. I would have a voice in the program that I want to teach in my classroom. I wouldn't have to go by the basic district program. If I want to teach Direct Instruction, I can do that. If I want to implement, just restructure the whole curriculum, I could do that. As a charter, we could do that. Whereas in the district, you have to go by district guidelines. You just can't walk in and do that. [In a charter] we can meet the needs of our kids, we would have a choice as far as choosing programs that would benefit our kids. Reading program, language arts programs, things like that. I really wanted to be involved in that way, in restructuring our curriculum. Especially that would meet the needs of [minority] children in this community.

In the case of Inspiration School, then, difference came not necessarily from being outside the box, as some charter school advocates have suggested, but being able to choose another box that participants saw as more effective (Lubienski, 2003). In a similar vein, teachers at Hearts and Hands Community School saw participating in charter school reform as a way to provide public school students access to what they saw as an effective educational model that was primarily available to students with the familial resources to attend private school.

> I have a philosophical ideal about democracy. And the cost of tuition was skyrocketing in my old school. I was very happy there. I had no particular

reason to move other than I wanted another challenge and an opportunity to share this wonderful curriculum with students who would never otherwise have access to it because of their income level.

Across all three contexts, charter school participants articulated this notion of difference as a strong expectation, particularly when they perceived that their school was not as unique or as distinctive as they felt it should or could be. "Charter schools are different," then, was a normative construct within the charter community.

Discussion

In this chapter I analyzed the influence of policy contexts on charter school implementation. Hilltop Charter School was deeply grounded in the first "wave" of restructuring, which was aimed at empowering teachers to be key decision-makers at their schools. The initial vision of the school's first proponent, Tom Jensen, was congruent with the restructuring reform underway in the Geary Unified School District. Jensen wanted to "clear the brush" of bureaucracy to allow teachers to invent a school. The teacher's union was also advocating shared decision-making. These more local efforts mapped on to state and national efforts at restructuring.

In comparison, Hearts and Hands Community School's early proponents took the opportunity offered by charter school reform seriously and proposed a school that was based around an alternative educational model, which had made few inroads into public education. Yet there was a "real-world" example of a public school of this type, which provided an important initial model and remained significant as an example of the education program the staff was striving to implement. While the existence of a Waldorf public school facilitated the school's creation, the school was not buffered from external challenges. As the first "start-up" charter school in the district that was also based on an alternative educational model, Hearts and Hands Community School was a particularly vulnerable organizational form. Without the much broader legitimacy that comes from congruence with the wider policy environment, the school's education program was challenged. As a result, the school's early history was punctuated with periods of instability. During my fieldwork, participants would often discuss the problems the school was experiencing as having deep historical roots. These challenges created internal instability and a considerable amount of staff turnover. In particular, teachers came into the school without Waldorf training, and the school was unable to provide it—in part because of the challenges to its education program. In addition, the apparently long-standing tension between "Waldorf-inspired" and "district," which was embedded in the school culture, gained particular force as the district's systemic reform initiative accelerated in pace. However, a grassroots movement among activist staff members to move the school more squarely toward the Waldorf model also suggests the importance of agency.

Inspiration School highlights some of the tensions within the charter school movement. The organizations affiliated with Educational Enterprise Company suggest that some of the market-oriented policy goals that shaped Arizona's charter school legislation had some traction in California through the activities of EMOs. While Inspiration School was the most explicitly market-oriented charter school of the three described here, there was evidence that all three schools were shaped by the micropolitics of marketization to some degree. Another more local influence on the schools' policy context was the Geary Unified School District's systemic reform initiative. While charter school reform is an effort to decentralize teaching and school governance, the Geary reform was an effort to harness the work of schools and teachers around a specific technology of teaching. As a result, the schools experienced competing environmental pressures. The final section of this chapter highlighted how the charter school policy talk I described in the Introduction shaped how teachers and other staff members at the three schools understood charter school reform. In the next chapter I expand on some of these themes by examining how policy contexts evolve over time and how this process shaped the trajectories of Hilltop Charter School and Inspiration School.

CHAPTER FIVE

POLICY DYNAMICS—SCHOOLS AND ACCOUNTABILITY POLICIES

> *When applied to schooling, the vision that sees things big brings us in close contact with details and particularities that cannot be reduced to statistics or even to the measurable.*
>
> —Maxine Greene (1995, 10)

As I suggested in chapter 1, statements of legislative intent provide a window into lawmakers' goals for charter school reform. The original statement of legislative intent framing California's 1992 charter school law outlined six purposes for charter schools, some of which overlap. Charter schools are a means to: (1) improve student learning; (2) expand the learning opportunities for all students and in particular low-achieving students; (3) promote the utilization of different and innovative teaching methods; (4) provide new professional opportunities for teachers; (5) provide increased educational choices for parents and students; and (6) make schools "accountable for meeting measurable pupil outcomes" and thus shift from "rule-based to performance-based accountability" (California Education Code, §47601). In 1998, this statement of legislative intent was expanded to include a seventh clause stating that charter schools are intended to increase competition within the public school system as a means of improving all public schools.

As I noted in the Introduction, this statement and other instances of policy talk related to charter school reform imagines that once the formal external controls on schools are relaxed, teachers will be able to more effectively promote student achievement. Also implicit in this policy talk is the assumption charter schools will be founded—and ideally thrive— in stable policy contexts. Yet since California's Charter School Act became law, sweeping changes in state and federal education policies related to accountability, testing, and curriculum standards have taken place.

In this chapter I explore the consequences of these policy shifts in the daily lives of Hilltop Charter School and Inspiration School. I focus on school practices not to explain variability in performance outcomes but to examine how the policy context enables or constrains processes that occur in schools. Despite a large body of research suggesting that there is a great degree of "loose coupling" between school processes and measures of school performance, standardized testing policies have important *political* implications for schools. Since the late 1990s, in California all public schools and districts could be targeted for intervention or rewards by the state on the basis of their students' performance on the state-administered standardized tests. California's system of accountability predates No Child Left Behind (NCLB) by about three years. Under NCLB, states were required to develop accountability systems that assess whether or not public schools and districts are making adequate yearly progress (AYP) toward academic achievement. Schools receiving Title I funds that do not make AYP for two consecutive years are subject to a series of interventions, which can culminate in restructuring of the school by the fifth year should it continue to miss its AYP targets. Prior to NCLB, which has increased accountability requirements for all public schools, charter schools were viewed as particularly vulnerable to intervention if their test scores declined; a common rationale for charter school reform is that the schools will be held accountable for the student outcomes identified in their charters.[1]

I analyze the distinct theories of teaching and learning at Hilltop Charter School and Inspiration School to raise some broader questions about how different types of education policies interact. I use the term theories of teaching and learning to refer to a particular aspect of school culture—the often implicit norms and beliefs embedded in school practices about what "good teaching" looks like and what comprises learning in schools. I situate this analysis within a brief history of California's policies around standardized testing, state standards, and elementary education. Before turning to the analysis, a caveat is in order. In this age of increased accountability for all public schools, it is tempting to pit one model of teaching and learning against the other to determine which model is "better" than the other. Here, I am asking a different question in an effort to reframe these and similar debates in a way that captures the dynamism in the cultural and political environments that shape how implementation unfolds: under what conditions can schools take advantage of the decentralization embedded in charter school reform? In chapter 4 I have suggested that charter schools are conceptually empty. In this chapter I elaborate on my argument that one of the unanticipated consequences of this openness in the context of a dynamic policy environment is that, as organizations, charter schools may be more susceptible to environmental imprinting than conventional public schools.

Dynamism in the Policy Context: Changes in State Policy

While the changes in California's testing and accountability policies were among the most high-profile state efforts at education reform, state policies around curricula and standards and elementary education were also in flux during this same period. As the accounts below suggest, these policy shifts were intertwined; I separate them here for analytical purposes and discuss each in turn briefly. I also highlight how these policies intersected with charter school reform where relevant.

Accountability and Testing

The most recent chapter in the history of state testing in California began during the administration of Governor Pete Wilson, who promised in his 1990 gubernatorial campaign to institute a statewide testing program. An earlier testing program, the California Assessment Program (CAP),[2] was cancelled in 1990 by Governor George Deukmejian when he vetoed the testing funds (Merl, 1992). The CAP testing program assessed only school and district performance. In contrast, Wilson campaigned on an assessment system that provided information on individual student performance (Connor and Melendez, 1994). The first effort at establishing such a program, the California Learning Assessment System (CLAS), was administered in 1993 and 1994 and tested fourth-, eighth-, and tenth-grade students. The CLAS received national attention as a performance-based assessment because it was structured around open-ended rather than multiple-choice questions (Merl and Ingram, 1994).

In her analysis of the politics of state testing policies, McDonnell (1997) argued that the CLAS resulted from a "rare consensus" between Governor Wilson, Gary Hart, the chair of the Senate Education Committee in the California Legislature, and Bill Honig, the state superintendent of instruction (6). McDonnell's analysis also indicated that while the three policymakers agreed on the need for a testing program, they diverged on the primary policy goals each saw the program as furthering. Wilson wanted the program to generate test results for individual students as a way to move toward a merit-based pay scale for teachers. For Hart, the program was a mechanism for creating the school accountability that he saw as a precondition for site-based management. Honig wanted a performance-oriented assessment that would reflect curriculum standards and could also be used to shape teaching practices. According to McDonnell (1997), the practical consequence of these discrepant goals for the testing program was that the California Department of Education (CDE) agreed to produce individual level scores on a performance-based assessment under a highly compressed timeline without adequate funding or technical capacity.

Because of a short timeline—the legislation specified that the program would end after three years—the CDE focused on creating a test-centered accountability program at the expense of creating materials for ongoing assessment that would be more tightly connected to classroom teaching.

Complicating matters further was the public and the testing community's respective responses to the CLAS after the first administration of the test. The CLAS generated a considerable amount of public controversy because some questions in the upper-grade tests asked students to respond to literature that dealt with religion, racism, death, and family conflict. The test was challenged in the courts on the grounds that the questions constituted an invasion of students' privacy; many parents and a few school districts refused to participate in the testing program.[3] The reliability of the sampling and scoring procedures used to administer the CLAS was also criticized by a panel of experts convened to review the program after the first year, although the panel did not recommend scrapping the test entirely (Cronbach, 1995; Merl, 1994). Under the guidance of the expert panel, the CDE changed the test questions and scoring to increase the reliability of the results, which meant that the 1993 results could not be compared to the 1994 results (Colvin, 1995a). Even more problematic in light of the political context described above, the expert panel recommended that the CDE focus on using the CLAS to create accurate school-level scores and only generate individual level scores on a trial basis.

As this drama unfolded, Governor Wilson withheld funding for the program in the spring of 1994. The bill's original sponsor, State Senator Gary Hart, rewrote the legislation to address some of the concerns raised about the program (Asimov, 1994), but Wilson vetoed the revised bill in September of 1994. After a protracted negotiation, in October 1995 Wilson signed Assembly Bill 265 that created a new two-part testing system. Students in grades two through ten would take nationally normed standardized tests chosen and administered by their school districts; the bill also authorized funds for the creation of statewide tests that would be administered in 1999. In May of 1997, Wilson announced a new plan of his own. Students in grades two through eleven would be tested using a commercially available test that focused on basic skills (Colvin, 1997a). Wilson's plan conflicted with the work of a state panel that was charged with recommending a set of standards to be adopted the following year that was to serve as the foundation for a customized state testing program. By using his power to line-item veto part of the education budget, Wilson pressured the state legislature into passing Senate Bill (SB) 376, a statewide testing bill, in September 1997. The legislation passed despite the objections of the State Superintendent of Instruction, Delaine Eastin, who recommended waiting to institute a large-scale testing program until a test could be created based on the state standards that were in the process of being revised and approved (Colvin, 1997b).

Under the provisions of SB 376, Eastin was required to recommend a test for approval by the State Board of Education on an extremely short timeline. Testing companies had just over a week to submit tests for consideration; Eastin had to make her decision within the two weeks that followed (California Department of Education, 1997). After soliciting the input of a seventy-one-member task force of superintendents, teachers, and curriculum specialists that reviewed bids from three test publishers, Eastin reluctantly recommended the CTBS/Terra Nova by McGraw-Hill in October of 1997:

> When the tests submitted for consideration are examined against the recommended state standards and California's curriculum, all of them are seriously flawed, with the level of test content falling years below grade-level expectations.... The middle school and high school tests have too few items that align with the grade-level standards. Although these tests provide nationally normed information, none of them has the rigor, nor the breadth and depth of content, that California needs. These tests are simply not world class. (California Department of Education, 1997)

Eastin also advocated using the "off-the-shelf" test until the tests based on the state standards were created. Without providing a rationale for its decision, the State Board of Education chose the SAT 9 test produced by Harcourt Brace, the lowest bidder of the three companies that submitted bids (Mendel, 1997). Experts reviewing the tests considered the SAT 9 to be more traditional than the Terra Nova (Colvin, 1997b, 1997c). The SAT 9 was used from 1998 to 2003 to test students in grades two through eleven. Starting in 1999, the SAT 9 was augmented with the California Standards Tests (CST).

California's testing program was further elaborated by the Public Schools Accountability Act (PSAA) in 1999. The PSAA mandated an annual ranking of all California public schools based on their Academic Performance Index (API), a summary score for each school ranging from 200 to 1000 that was constructed by weighting student scores on the SAT 9 by their national percentile ranking (NPR) (California Department of Education, 2000). Once the API score is calculated, schools are ranked based on their API in two additional ways. First, all schools are ranked statewide solely by their API and then divided into deciles and assigned a number on that basis. Second, schools are grouped within cohorts of 100 schools that share similar characteristics and divided into deciles. This latter score is called the Similar Schools Index (SSI). Thus there are three possible ways to compare schools: (1) the API score, which ranges from 200 to 1000; (2) the score of

1 to 10 a school is assigned based on its API score; and (3) the score of 1 to 10 a school is assigned based on its performance compared to its cohort of similar schools.

In the first two years of the program, 1999 and 2000, school API scores were calculated using only the results of the SAT 9 test; the augmented tests linked to the state standards (the CST) were not incorporated into the API rankings. As I suggested in chapter 1, PSAA ushered in an unprecedented era of accountability for *all* public schools in California—including charter schools—well before NCLB took effect.

State Standards and Curriculum Frameworks

As noted above, in the period between the end of the CLAS testing program and the statewide adoption of the SAT 9 test, state content and teaching standards were being revised for all major subjects. California's subject matter standards or "curriculum frameworks" had been revised in the late 1980s and early 1990s as part of the broader array reforms initiated in the wake of the publication of *A Nation at Risk* (Ravich, 1993). By 1995, the controversy around the California Learning Assessment (CLAS), and the state's poor performance on the National Assessment of Educational Progress (NAEP), initiated another round of revisions to the curriculum frameworks (Gardner, 1997, 2001). The Reading/Language Framework received approval from the State Board of Education in December of 1998 and a mathematics framework was approved soon after (Helfand, 1998; California Department of Education, 2002). The process of revising the frameworks tended to be characterized in newspaper accounts as a shift toward back to basics instruction (e.g., Colvin, 1995b; Stein, 1995; see also Coburn, 2001; Jacob, 2001; Lemann, 1997).

California's charter school law was enacted in the early stages of this policy shift; by the end of the 1997–1998 school year, there were 126 charter schools in operation.[4] The original charter school legislation that was passed in 1992 required charter schools to identify "measurable outcomes" for their students based on the goals of the education program outlined in the schools' charters and also identify how these outcomes would be measured. The 1992 law also required charter schools to meet "the statewide performance standards" and administer state-mandated assessments (California Education Code, §47605). These seemingly straightforward charges are more complicated when considered in light of the changes in testing policy and curriculum standards described above. For example, an early Department of Education document interpreting charter school law commented that the emphasis in the legislation was on "accountability"– through the statewide student assessments rather than "requiring a curriculum" (California State Board, 1993). Yet in the spring of 1994 the statewide testing program had been discontinued. Commenting on these requirements in charter school law, an influential charter school policy and advisory organization noted in 1997 that the relationship between the existing standards and the curriculum standards that were under development was unclear and that state officials recommended that charter schools "pay attention" to the new standards and assessment (Gardner, 1997, 6). In 1998, California's charter school legislation was revised and charter schools were required to meet all state standards and administer the student assessments required by state law.

Elementary Education

During this period there was a shift in state policy related to elementary education, which also reflected the broader changes in testing policy described above. To illustrate this dynamism in the policy context, I analyze the policy statements issued in 1992 and 2000 by two different Elementary Grades Task Forces. The 1992 task force was convened by State Superintendent of Instruction Bill Honig; its report, entitled *It's Elementary* outlined "what an outstanding California elementary school of the 1990s might look like" and a series of recommendations for implementing this vision (Elementary Grades Task Force, 1992, xi). The report was described in a *Los Angeles Times* front page headline announcing its release as a "Bold Blueprint" for elementary education and was distributed to all elementary school teachers in California (Asimov, 1992, A1). The opening chapter of *It's Elementary* noted that the performance gains made by California school children on the CAP testing had begun to "plateau" by the late 1980s. More telling was the conclusion that

> many standardized tests do not tell whether schools are providing the education our students need to succeed in the twenty-first century. Rather, such tests tend to assess what most elementary schools have concentrated on in the past: teaching basic skills in the three Rs. (Elementary Grades Task Force, 1992, 1)

Instead of emphasizing "basic skills," *It's Elementary* proposed a "thinking curriculum" (Elementary Grades Task Force, 1992, 3). While not eschewing basic or "traditional academic skills," the task force argued that students will most effectively learn these and other skills if teachers employ a "hands-on, student centered, experiential" pedagogy rather than a "skills-based pedagogy" (Elementary Grades Task Force, 1992, 3). The rest of the first chapter consisted of specific subject matter recommendations consistent with this vision of teaching. For example, in the section on Language Arts, the task force criticized the use of basal readers with matching workbooks and skill sheets, arguing that these overemphasized basic and unconnected skills. Instead, the Task Force advocated literature-based activities that integrated subject areas (e.g., math, science) and language development skills (reading, writing, listening, and speaking) with the goal of teaching children how to "read for meaning" (Elementary Grades Task Force, 1992, 4).

To implement this "thinking curriculum," the task force made no less than thirty-one additional recommendations targeted at classroom teachers, schools, districts, and the state (Elementary Grades Task Force, 1992, 3). The task force advocated that classroom teachers use a variety of strategies for grouping students and provide students with cooperative learning activities. In turn, schools should utilize mixed age and nongraded classes, avoid grade retention, and provide teachers with opportunities to collaborate. Districts should allow schools more autonomy to set goals. The state should expand the use of authentic assessments, create performance standards based on a scale or continuum, and assess English-language learners in their home language. Finally, the report advocated the use of performance scales to report student learning in the primary years rather than grades because grades "label" and "sort" rather than provide parents and teachers with useful information about student progress (Elementary Grades Task Force, 1992, 73).

Finally, *It's Elementary* advocated the California Learning Record (CLR) as a model for reporting student progress in language arts. Developed in California in the late 1980s and early 1990s, the CLR was used to report students' language skills using narrative and performance scales with the goal of highlighting students' abilities rather than deficits. Student records compiled by individual teachers are moderated or read as group until the teachers reach a common understanding of the performance scales. The CLR was modeled on an evaluation tool developed in London, which was brought to California under the auspices of the California Literature Project, a statewide professional development program for K-12 teachers administered by the University of California, which assembled a working group to develop the CLR (Syverson, n.d.). The Geary Unified School District was one of the districts participating in the development of the CLR through pilot schools, one of which was Hilltop Charter School, which participated in the program until 1995. Hilltop Charter School teachers served on the statewide committee developing the CLR in 1992.

Eight years later, the vision for elementary education outlined in *It's Elementary* was revised by a new Elementary Grades Task Force under State Superintendent of Instruction Delaine Eastin's guidance. The new document,

Elementary Makes the Grade, began by noting that *It's Elementary* provided an important—albeit incomplete—foundation for "standards-based reform." Where the focus in *It's Elementary* was the curriculum and the technology of teaching, *Elementary Makes the Grade* described the focal point of the first report as "but one of several components of the state's larger, *more rigorous, standards-based education system*" (Elementary Grades Task Force, 2000, 2; italics added). Changes in curriculum and instruction were one component in a process of systemic reform focused primarily on schools that also included assessment and accountability, content and performance standards, and professional development. School districts should provide leadership and support for the reform process. Ideally, all of these should be the components of a "continuous cycle" starting with standards (Elementary Grades Task Force, 2000, 38). The content standards adopted at the district should drive the construction of the curriculum at the school and in the classroom, which should subsequently be revised using the results of student assessments based on performance standards, and so on. Professional development and district-level leadership should support implementation of the first three components.

In the discussion of assessment and accountability, *Elementary Makes the Grade* recommended using entry level and ongoing assessments to monitor student progress during the academic year. "Summative assessments" such as the SAT 9 should be used at the end of the year to ascertain whether or not students met the goals outlined in the standards (Elementary Grades Task Force, 2000, 22). The report further noted that the main mechanisms at the state level for holding schools and districts accountable were the API and a high-school exit examination required for all students starting with the class of 2004. Thus the SAT 9 and the API, which is derived from it, were framed as the centerpiece of assessment in California—which ideally would be integrated with local accountability systems to provide teachers and schools with multiple measures of student performance. Yet at the time *Elementary Makes the Grade* was released, the California Standards Test (CST) was not used to calculate API scores. Overall, my comparison of the two reports on elementary education suggests a shift from the emphasis on process in *It's Elementary* to an emphasis on products or outcomes in *Elementary Makes the Grade*.

Far from Technical-Rational Policymaking

This brief history of the changes in state testing policy and state standards in California suggests the operation of a political-institutional model of policymaking rather than a technical-rational model of policymaking. March and Olson (1986) argue that political decision-making is shaped by the choices of actors within the system, the conjunction of events that bring possible problems and solutions together, and the institutional structure of the political system that shapes how both processes unfold. In this view, institutions simplify decision-making in a way that violates the fundamental assumptions of rational decision-making and—because they provide order in a complex social world—are the "primary instruments for approximating [comprehensive rationality]" (March and Olson, 1986, 16–17).

In contrast, under a technical-rational model of policymaking, we might predict that the revised curriculum standards would be completed and implemented, and then students' progress would be measured on a test based specifically on the content of the standards. Instead, key stakeholders with competing assumptions about the desired ends of the state testing program—Wilson, Hart, and Honig—were allied long enough to create the initial CLAS program. Once the program was established and the test results were released, there was less room for common ground between the key stakeholders. Ultimately the governor used his political power to revise the program according to his own vision—a testing program that yielded individual scores for students. As a result, an off-the-shelf testing instrument was chosen as the state testing instrument under a compressed timeline and was subsequently institutionalized because it was in place as accountability policies were further elaborated under a subsequent administration (the API school rankings). Thus the outcome of this long saga of California's efforts to assess student learning was the establishment of a testing program that was only loosely coupled to state standards (see also Kirst, 2002).

A description of the policy context helps situate the theories of teaching and learning that were in evidence at Hilltop Charter School and Inspiration School, which I describe in the sections that follow. Here, I illustrate how policies generated at the state level interact with local circumstances to generate strategies of action for teachers and administrators within schools (Swidler, 1986).

Hilltop Charter School: Learning is Growth, Teaching Is Tailoring Activities to Students' Needs

As I detailed in chapter 3, at Hilltop Charter School the developmental model provided the overarching rationale for most aspects of the school's organizational structure, including the classroom cluster arrangement, which allowed for team teaching and mixing students of different language abilities. The teachers were in basic agreement around what teaching developmentally meant, describing it minimally as taking a child "where they are" and thus echoing the Developmental Primary Task Force report referenced in their charter. What was not often articulated as clearly was the assumption that children come into a classroom "where they are" on a continuum of "age-appropriate" skills that they progress through at their own individual paces. Thus, implicit in both the district task force report and many teachers' descriptions of developmental teaching was a more fluid and dynamic understanding of ability—students were viewed not as *unable* but rather as *not ready* to master a particular skill. One teacher alluded to this directly in a meeting when she drew a distinction between "intelligence" and "developmental" (clearly favoring the latter) in a discussion about teaching.

According to this view, it is the teacher's role to focus on a child's growth, to help that student achieve his or her own higher level of understanding of the subject or concept that is being taught. This scene from a kindergarten classroom about a month after school began highlights how this belief system was enacted in a classroom:

> Ms. Clark started the lesson by showing the students two of Jorge's (a student from the previous year) journals; the first was from November and the second was from May. In the first journal Jorge was copying things that were on the walls in the room, which she told the students was "fine" and that they could also do that if they wanted to. Then Ms. Clark showed them the second journal, which had a picture and, on the lines printed directly underneath, a sentence. She commented that by this journal, Jorge was writing on the lines, which was "beautiful." Then she asked the class, "does writing have to be like Ms. Clark's?" and answered her rhetorical question by saying "no, because we are learning." Next Ms. Clark told the students if they made lines and shapes that looked like letters that would be fine and emphasized that this is where they should be [in kindergarten]. She reminded the students that we write from left to right with a preface she used often: "remember when we talked about how...." One student asked a question about writing big or small and she told the students that she didn't care what they did as long as they tried. Ms. Clark added that she really wanted them to have pictures that would "tell me what you are trying to say." Then she told the class her journal was going to be about bugs flying over flowers and asked the class what the picture should have on it [when she reviewed the students' work with the whole class she reminded them how they had talked about using detail in their pictures]. Next she asked them how many words her sentence would have and someone responded five, which she reinforced by repeating that sentences should have five words. Finally, Ms. Clark told the students that she wanted them to try their best.

Here Ms. Clark emphasized progress with these students, who were at the first stages of learning how to write—many were also in the first month of their formal schooling. Ms. Clark encouraged her students by telling them their writing should not look like her writing and that it was acceptable to draw shapes that looked like letters. Yet she also had clear standards for this task (detailed and finished pictures, writing five words) and emphasized skills that were important for these early learners (e.g., writing left to right).

Many teachers contrasted the underlying conception of what teaching and learning looks like in a developmental model to the understanding of student ability and the styles of teaching and learning they viewed as implied in standards, that is, that there are clearly defined sets of abilities that correspond to each grade level. For example, one teacher commented that she saw the current emphasis on standards as:

> ... Generic, one way of teaching, one way of—generic learning styles that they say now [you are teaching first grade] students, that is first grade work. I think that is ridiculous. I don't think you can put a paper on the wall and say that is an example of what a first grade [paper] should look like.

Many teachers at Hilltop Charter School associated this conception of how students learn with a model of curriculum and teaching that was tightly prescribed, to the point of defining the page in the reader or math book they should be teaching at a given point in the school year. They viewed this way of teaching as very limiting because it would allow them to "meet the needs" of only a handful of students in their classrooms. Similarly, another common refrain at the school was that kids do not "come in packages" that teachers can plug into a set curriculum. In contrast, teachers described children—even within a single-grade classroom—as ranging widely not only in their skills but also in the points at which they are able to master particular skills.

At the same time, the teachers at Hilltop Charter School were not against standards per se but tended to view them as broad guidelines, or, as one teacher put it, "expectations," for the content areas that they were supposed to cover with their students. Teachers at Hilltop Charter School saw standards as a tool to help them structure the learning environment, but did not want to use standards as an absolute ruler against which a child's progress should be measured because the latter shifted the evaluative frame away from seeing a child's growth over time:

> Developmental learning means that you try to make lots of connections for kids and you try to tie everything together and you try to pull from their ideas and their interests as well. So everything is not just set in stone and this is what you are going to teach and for how many minutes. Of course you still need standards and you still need a curriculum, but within that you tie things together, you make the learning environment about themes and topics, and you work together towards that. And another thing is accepting

each child where they are at developmentally. Which comes into conflict with having standards at all, for kids. Every kid is never going to be at the same place. So you have a standard but you want every kid to meet that but you know that you have to take the kid where they are at and focus on growth. The teacher can focus on the standard and developing lesson plans that meet the standards, but the focus for the child should be on growth. And if a child has grown tremendously over the course of the year then you have been successful.

Teaching developmentally, then, was trying to reach that difficult balance between not viewing a child who was below grade level as deficient, supporting their growth and progress, and also having a vision about where they can be, or, as one teacher put it, "[f]iguring out where children are and moving forward with high expectations." For example, this teacher echoed the idea that students will progress at their own pace, but also added at that the same time, it is important for students to be continually exposed to challenging material:

> I just read a great article I found written in the sixties. And it used an analogy about growth ... it said that farmers really know what developmental is. They know there is a time to plant and to sow, and plants need certain things in order to sow, but you can't rush it. You can't go outside and say, when are you growing? What is wrong with you? Come on, come on, let's go. And it grows when it grows. And that is, in a sense, what developmental is. Which doesn't mean you don't expose them. I expose my [first grade] kids to literature that is fourth grade. I read it to them.

The implicit distinction made by this teacher maps on to a distinction made in *Elementary Makes the Grade* between content standards and performance standards (Elementary Grades Task Force, 2000). Most teachers at the school advocated content standards, that is, a general outline of what students should learn. However, many—though not all—were wary of performance standards, which they saw as dictating when students should master particular tasks or skills.[5]

However, it should also be noted that the apparent consensus around what "developmental" was tended to break down in teacher's views of the specific teaching practices that fall under the broad rubric of teaching "developmentally." Most teachers agreed about what "developmental" was not: teaching based on worksheets. For example, one teacher commented that "[w]e want to teach in developmental ways, we don't want children doing worksheets, sitting down and reading a book of the same level." Yet, beyond the minimum of utilizing a range of instructional methods, the category of developmental teaching practices was much more fluid and harder to pin down, as reflected in the admission of some teachers in meetings and in interviews that they did not know precisely what "developmental" meant.[6]

When asked in interviews what "developmental" looked like in practice, or as they discussed developmental approaches to teaching and learning during school hours, rather than articulating a common vision of the classroom practices associated with "developmental learning," teachers tended to mention a variety of techniques, none of which perfectly coincided although many overlapped. Teaching developmentally, then, was understood as an approach or an orientation to teaching and learning that accommodated a broad range of teaching practices. The use of centers—small group, "hands-on" activities using a variety of manipulative instructional materials—was most frequently cited. Some teachers elaborated on centers by describing them as a way to organize activities that all students in the class can benefit from, regardless of their levels of proficiency. Other teachers echoed another theme, also touched upon by the first teacher, the importance of multisensory activities to promote children's learning so that if a child was struggling there would be a greater chance of finding the "modality" that worked. Finally, many teachers emphasized the importance of careful observation of students' progress through assessments and ongoing informal observations.

Yet the emphasis on standardized testing in California was not always compatible with this approach. For example, one teacher commented that "[teacher observation of more open-ended student exploration] may work for kindergarteners, but it certainly doesn't work for first graders, especially when they are going to be given a test in second grade that says fill in the bubbles, who was the President during the time of the Civil War? So it doesn't work, which is kind of sad." As teachers described the impact of standardized testing on the school, there were three distinct themes running through their comments. First, teachers noted that the standardized tests did not measure growth. Second, Hilltop teachers were critical of what they saw as a mismatch between the standards and the test. Finally, some teachers claimed that the test tapped into language and other experiential differences between their students and English-dominant and middle-class students.

When asked if the test was compatible with the school's developmental model, one teacher responded:

> No, not what I have seen of the test. Then they need to come up with a different kind of test—a test that is designed to show some sort of growth—because that is what we are interested in....[M]y second language kids coming to me as fourth graders generally are reading a couple of grade levels below. I can give them the SAT 9 in the fourth grade and they are going to

fail. They are going to be in the bottom 20th percentile. But if you design the test to say, OK, here is where they were in October, and now here is where they are in April, that means something to me. Have I taught them anything?

This teacher suggested that her students would not perform well on a test that was scored using national norms based on the performance of native English speakers. In this context, the tests were seen primarily as a political hurdle for the school rather than as a source of useful information for teachers in the day-to-day demands of their jobs.

> I think too much emphasis is placed on the test. I want all of my students to succeed. I would love to give that test and have everybody get the highest score possible. But I also feel like the tests don't match anything. They don't match the standards, they don't match what the teachers do in their rooms. And not the information, but the way it is tested. And the reason that test is like that is because they have to compile tons and tons of data. And some of the questions on the test are stupid, there is no other way to get around it. And I don't feel they test what we should be testing them on. And I know that this is unpopular, for whatever reason, parents didn't like the personal disclosure, but the CLAS test which is . . . a performance-based test where students were actually writing, and they had science problems to solve. Which is the way you teach it and the way you use it in the real world. The reason that I want my students to be successful on standardized tests—I do practice and teach them test-taking techniques and all that—is because unfortunately that is the way to succeed all the way through education. I want them to do well on the SATs, I want them to get into college. I want them to do well on the GREs. And basically to do well on those, it is lifelong learning how to do those tests.

Finally, in what can be read as a "cultural capital" critique of the test, teachers argued that the SAT 9 tapped into language and class-based experiential differences that advantage middle-class English-speaking students and their schools. Hilltop Charter School served a large population of second-language learners, a majority of whom were Spanish speakers. While these students performed well on a norm-referenced test administered in Spanish, on the SAT 9 they did not test as well as their English-speaking peers. Because the results of the SAT 9 testing program were readily available and much more widely reported than the Spanish language tests, it had consequences for how the school was perceived. Teachers were frustrated because the Spanish language tests were a less legitimate measure of their student's progress and also because the SAT 9 results did not seem to reflect the English-language skills they saw their students developing in their classrooms. In this context, fluency in English became a form of cultural capital. This teacher also linked her critique of testing to the patterns of class segregation within the Geary Unified School District.

> We are never going to win the standardized testing battle. And we will certainly, every year, work hard to improve it and get test prep material, and we sent our teachers to conferences and certainly we are concerned about it. But on the other hand, we are not going to give up our entire curriculum to focus on testing.... [T]here is a huge difference between the children we teach and the children in [names an affluent area of the city]. There is nothing that anybody at this school can do to make up for the first five years of a child's life. And the child that has had all of the experience, and has had all of the books read to him before he enters school is always going to be well ahead. Not to mention that a lot of middle class parents give a damn about the test. A lot of our parents don't know about the test, and if they do, they don't care. It is not pushed. In a different neighborhood it is, "how did you do on the test? I am going to make you bacon and ham and eggs so you have energy." It is a whole different competitive thing that goes with a whole different class of people. And I am not saying our children don't learn. Our children learn a ton. I wish [the superintendent] could see the kindergartener that comes into our school that knows nothing. They haven't seen the beach, they haven't been on the freeway, they don't know a letter from a number, they can't hold a pencil. This isn't the occasional kid we get, a good number of our students come to us like this every year. So I am not saying that they are not learning. I am just saying are they ever going to show their learning on a middle class test? No. We are never going to be in the 80th percentile. Unless we worked our tails off and gave up our curriculum and focused on testing strategies for an entire year.

This quote highlights some of the complexities involved in standardized testing. While, on one hand, it would be easy to interpret these comments as an instance of a teacher dismissing the potential of working-class children (e.g., Bowles and Gintis, 1976; Anyon, 1997), they might be more productively read as shaped by the contradictory political space the school occupied. For example, the teacher began by describing about the differences in experiences between middle-class and working-class and poor students, differences that have implications when schools' standardized test results are very publicly reported. These teachers are aware that they are working in what has been labeled as a below-average school by a seemingly objective measure. Yet at the same time they believe in creating learning spaces that do not "teach to the test" (which departed from Bowles and Gintis' claims about predominantly working-class schools). However, the shift in the policy environment brought with it the possibility that their school would not perform as well as other schools that "teach to the test," and increasing pressure to teach to the test at the expense of their education program.

Moreover, by asserting that the students at the school learned a lot, this teacher provided an experientially grounded theory of the role of social class in shaping students' learning, which echoed the findings of Entwhistle, Alexander, and Olson (1997)—the gains of students of low SES students were similar to those of high SES students *while school is in session.*[7] Measured in a zero-sum ranking of absolute scores, the persistent gap between schools—and by extension students—became the predominant focus. In addition, by highlighting the differences in performance across schools and linking them to geographically bound class differences, this teacher invoked one of the central features of the cultural logic of American schooling: the binary of success/failure. As Varenne and McDermott (1998) note:

> Success and failure are products of the same America. Failure allows the definition of success, and together they frame everyone: children, teachers, parents and researchers in the United States (and other parts of the world caught by the school system that evolved in Europe). By the same logic, an understanding of the failure of urban schools requires an understanding of the success of suburban schools. Inner city and suburb do not belong to different worlds. They belong to the same differentiated world. (4–5)

Yet at the same time, while critical of this logic, this teacher is also inexorably caught in it by invoking class-based differences in values, an idea associated with cultural deficit models for understanding student achievement. This suggests that in a political climate where there is a persistent critique of failing schools and teachers, this policy talk can push teachers toward a deficit model of explaining student achievement. If the dominant policy talk focuses on teachers as the problem, it should not surprise us when teachers construct counter-narratives focusing on students' social backgrounds. While teachers at Hilltop Charter School were not unconcerned with student achievement, they saw it as one among a number of goals. Yet they were also aware of the larger political context in which they were operating, which privileged measures they saw as less relevant to their understanding of teaching and learning. Finally, the ambivalence about standardized testing at Hilltop Charter School is also more intelligible if we place the school more squarely within the context of the policy trends described at the outset of this chapter.

In the years before Hilltop Charter School was established, the Geary Unified School District's policies on standardized testing had also shifted. Since the early 1980s, the district had been testing pupils in grades five, seven, nine, and eleven annually using the Comprehensive Tests of Basic Skills (CBTS). In 1990, Geary transitioned to a new norm-referenced test, the ASAT. As this process of selecting the new test started, the professional testing and assessment community also questioned the efficacy of conventional forms of standardized testing (i.e., multiple-choice formats). As a district official noted:

> It also became apparent that with the recent significant changes in the curriculum (e.g., whole language instruction, new curriculum standards by the National Council of Teachers of Mathematics (NCTM), and the new California curriculum frameworks) that a conventional nationally-normed NRT [norm-referenced test] would not meet [the district's] needs. Furthermore, with [the district's] school staffs being encouraged to restructure their instructional programs to better meet the unique needs of their students, it became even more apparent that a flexible testing system was needed, not simply a new NRT.

Here, the district's testing policy is linked to changes in state and national curriculum standards as well as the district's restructuring effort described in chapter 4, which provided fertile soil for the creation of Hilltop Charter School. This district-level discourse about testing mirrored a wider discourse within state agencies (i.e., the California Department of Education and the Elementary Grades Task Force) critiquing the efficacy of standardized tests for measuring student performance. For example, in an overview of California's assessment system in the early 1990s, a former California Department of Education official wrote:

> Critics of testing are becoming more vocal about the exclusive use of simple, multiple-choice tests, which result in curricula narrowing. . . . Such tests can be administered quickly and cheaply, but ignore the breadth and depth of a more rigorous curriculum. California has started to move from an overreliance on "bubble" tests, which ask students to choose the correct response from among alternatives, to "beyond the bubble" tests, on which students respond to performance items that require them to analyze, organize, interpret, explain, evaluate, and communicate. (Alexander, 1992, 138)

These shifts in the policy context played out locally at Hilltop Charter School. For example, an early (pre-charter) request for a waiver of the requirement that the school utilize the district's traditional report card in favor of a site developed "developmental progress report" invoked the recommendations of the Developmental Early Primary Task Force and cited the school's participation in contemporaneous efforts to create alternative report cards, including the California Learning Record. The school's revised charter for its charter renewal in 1998 noted that part of the California Learning Record was incorporated into the school's report card, entitled the "Hilltop Charter School Growth Record." While the Growth Record evolved over the years, in part to make it easier for parents to understand, the reading and writing continua, which were elaborated versions of the scales in the California Learning Record, remained part of the Growth Record. In addition, the Growth Record also reported students' test scores on a range of standards-based assessments.

Similarly, the 1998 charter noted that the staff at Hilltop Charter School had hoped to be waived from standardized achievement testing. Instead the staff wanted to use performance-based assessments to chart their students' progress. However, the school struggled to create an in-house system for data collection and analysis that would allow it to effectively accomplish this goal. Yet the school compared favorably to the district and state averages on the 1994 administration of the CLAS, which suggests that there was some basis in experience for the schools' orientation toward testing and not simply that teachers are unwilling to be measured—the easy interpretation when standardized testing holds sway.

As the discussion of the policy shifts in testing and elementary education at the beginning of this chapter suggests, there is also a more detailed story behind the discussion in the renewal document. The available evidence suggests that the staff's desire to pursue a waiver from standardized testing was a more legitimate course of action during the school's early years, when there was a broader critique of standardized testing and— not inconsequentially—institutional support at the state and district levels for alternative assessments such as the CLAS and the California Learning Record. Hilltop Charter School even participated in the development of the CLR until 1995. By then, the internal political turmoil at the school, described in chapter 4 resulted in the replacement of the school's founding principal with a candidate chosen by the sponsor district in the spring of 1996. Mrs. Carmichael, the school's second principal, saw herself as more supportive of standardized testing than most of her staff. However, the external policy environment had also shifted, making the school's original position on standardized testing less tenable. As the 1998 renewal document noted, "the new age of accountability for schools was becoming firmly established." The state's experiment with performance-based assessment was over and standardized testing was now, in Mrs. Carmichael's words, the "coin of the realm."

Inspiration School: Learning Is What Is Measurable on Standardized Tests, Teaching Is What You Do to Get There

As I suggested in chapter 3, one focus of Inspiration School's charter was the content of academic knowledge. The other dominant theme in the school's charter was an emphasis on assessment. The school's charter stated that student and staff achievement would be continually measured, and the main indicator of student achievement was standardized test scores. Likewise, school performance would be assessed by comparing the school's test scores with similar schools in the district and across the country. This focus on the measurement of student and school performance was empha- sized by representatives of Educational Enterprise Corporation in their descriptions of the school's educational model in public forums such as conferences, editorial columns, and testimony at congressional hearings. For example, one of the company's executives noted at a conference:

> [Our schools are] in areas poorly served by public education. In fact, if you were to have the API in those areas, you would see they were ones. Probably should be zeros if there were such a number. Those schools that we started three or four years ago are doing very well. In fact, they are nines on that scale, and we are proud of that. The situation is fairly simple. All we really did was chose teachers, chose principals, put them in an atmosphere where there were consequences to their actions, and provided them with freedom to use the data that they had, i.e., the data on [each] child, to come up with how they should be judged for the performance of that child, and rewarded them for excellent performance, and if they didn't achieve excellent perfor- mance, put them in a situation where that performance could be proved the next time around.

Not surprisingly, then, the culture of teaching at the school reflected the strong emphasis on test scores as an indicator of the school's success. This was also one of the most consistent themes in school materials from a range of sources as well as interviews with staff members:

> I will go back again and say that the whole staff has a goal in mind, to raise test scores, but also to improve student achievement. At other schools, you might have just one teacher over here that says, I want my kids to be ready for the SAT 9 test, this is going to be my main thing this year. They are going to know what they need to know on this test. I am not going to wait a month before or three weeks before to prep my kids. Everybody on the whole staff, they are not teaching to the test, but they are making sure that their kids are learning well as [they can] and being prepared for that test. And they all have that drive. They all have that desire, for it to happen. And the only way that we are going to be able to prove our point as [a charter school] is to show that we can do it. That we can raise those test scores.

One of the ways this belief system was enacted was through the frequent administration of standardized tests at all grade levels, including kinder- garten and first-grade. In addition to the state-mandated testing program, which took place in the spring, the school also administered a pretest ear- lier in the year. In an interview, one first-grade teacher commented that in her two years at the school, she had administered six standardized tests. Perhaps not surprisingly, then, on the day that the class took a practice test for the SAT 9, one student in this teacher's classroom wrote in her journal earlier in the day: "Today we will take a practice test and if we don't try hard we will get an 'F.'" When she finished writing she turned to me asked whether an "F" meant that you did poorly on a test. Later that day, during the practice test:

> Ms. Bradford reminded the students that they should not write in the book. She described this as a "big rule" and explained that the students could get marked wrong if they write in the book where they are not supposed to. Ms. Bradford explained that the second important rule for the students was that they had to move on. She repeatedly emphasized to the students that should not move on too quickly and fill in the question without reading it because they would get the answer wrong. Ms. Bradford described the "whole test" as trying to "trick you" and then asked the class "which kids can be tricked?" Then she addressed the class, asking "Can you be tricked?" No. "Because you are smart and you are thinking and if you move on, you might be tricked." At this point, a student got nervous and started to cry.

Other markers of student progress were also highly visible at the school. In contrast to Hilltop Charter School's ambivalence about performance standards, at Inspiration School, grade-level progress was often emphasized. During lessons, teachers frequently announced to students that they were doing above grade-level work. Students who were not at grade-level did not participate in afternoon enrichment activities such as dance or martial arts and instead worked with their teachers on reading and math. One day during recess, I observed a student complaining to a teacher because other students were describing her with the apparently pejorative label of "below grade level."

However, there was little evidence of a commonly held philosophy of teaching within the school. Instead, many teachers emphasized the importance of having the freedom to teach how they wanted to in their classrooms. As I noted in chapter 3, the school was in the early stages of implementing the Grand Heritage curricular model. The teachers were highly supportive of this curriculum because they saw it as challenging and academically rigorous. In addition, the language arts program adopted by the school was also structured around a "back to basics" model (i.e., a series of basal readers and sets of accompanying workbooks), which was explicitly marketed by the publishing company as a product that would raise students' test scores. Thus the materials that were readily available to teachers tended to promote teaching in the model of whole-class, teacher-directed activities and "seatwork."

Instead of a set of pedagogical practices, the shared belief system at the school crystallized around the notion that the teachers fundamentally drove the school's success, which can be attributed in part to the hierarchical organizational structure. Inspiration School was organized much like a traditional school with the exception that most decisions about the school's program were made by Educational Enterprise Corporation rather than the school district. Teachers described having little influence over school policy and also that they were not getting the basic resources they saw as necessary to support student achievement. For example, a number of teachers reported that they did not have books for their classrooms at the beginning of the school year.

At the same time, as suggested by the Educational Enterprise Corporation executive's reference to performance, the school's administration placed a great deal of importance on test scores. Some teachers commented that without strong test scores their teaching contracts would not be renewed the following year. This combination of "one-way accountability"[8] in the context of a highly centralized organizational structure produced a very strong teacher culture where the teachers overwhelmingly emphasized how the students' and school's success (as measured by test scores) was largely—if not entirely—attributable to their own hard work and "dedication" as a group (Gallagher, 2000, p. 501; see also Elmore, 2004). Note too that even though this teacher is critical of the emphasis on test scores, she still described it as a "pressure" twice, which suggests that it was not easily ignored.

> Our school is very academically focused. But I think that is very much the teachers who are here. I think the school pressures, good test scores, good test scores. I think the school puts that pressure on. But we don't teach the kids to get good test scores. I worked every day to get them to achieve. I am not here to babysit them or let them play around. That is what a good teacher does. Every day they are trying to teach their students. Is there anything the school does to help me? No. No, they don't have anything in place to help me do what I am trying to do. It is all very much in my heart to do it. And it is in the hearts of the other teachers I work with. Because it is for the kids. If they are not successful in school, then they have less of a chance in life than they would have had. We do it out of the goodness of our hearts because we care about the kids because we want them to succeed in life. But the pressure to get good test scores is not relevant to me, they don't offer me much support or anything to get it done.

Likewise, this teacher placed particular emphasis on the cohesion of the teachers at Inspiration School:

> I think that among the teachers, yes, we all have a vision. We want to take these kids places where kids have never been able to go in the specific grades

they are in. I have kids in this room—all of my kids in my [first grade] classroom can read. And I don't know if most first grade classrooms can say that. I think that all the first graders can read. Our test scores last year were outstanding so I knew we were doing good things as far as that is concerned.... Our dream is to take these kids to be better than whatever is going on out there. That is our dream as teachers. But I am not going to say any more.

This consistency was striking, particularly since teachers were relatively atomized during the instructional day. While teachers also identified other practices as more helpful gauges of individual student progress on a day-to-day basis, they focused a lot of time and attention on raising test scores. Many also described the school's high test scores as a measure of the school's success. For example, one teacher evaluated the district's curriculum in highly negative terms because in her opinion it could not help her adequately prepare her kindergarten students for the SAT 9.

When teachers and other staff members were critical of standardized testing, few consistent themes emerged from their comments. For example, some respondents described how students might be having a "bad day" on the day the test is administered. However, what was striking was the relative absence of the cultural capital critique of testing, which could be partially attributable to the relative advantage of the school's population. Unlike most other schools in the Geary Unified School District, Inspiration School did not serve English-language learners.[9]

Discussion

The comparison between the two schools described here highlights some of the complex issues involved with standardized testing. Connecting the two schools to larger trends in education policy also helps us shift the evaluative frame away from the more conventional terms of the debate, that is, whether or not the schools are "good" or "bad" schools, and think more broadly about how these schools fit in the larger policy context, because it is perhaps in this contrast that we see most clearly how charter schooling intersects with other reforms. It is also important to note that all of the teachers and school staff that I encountered at both schools obviously cared a great deal about their students, and this care was evident in ways that were too numerous to describe. Perhaps the best indicator of the teachers' care at both schools was that many students at both schools were not only friendly with me, an outside observer they saw as a "teacher," but eager to share details of their lives and demonstrate how much they were learning.

However, in the current policy climate with its increasing emphasis on ranking and labeling schools based on test scores, Inspiration School will be a "good"—or at least better—school. Indeed, in its focus on outcomes or, more to the point, one particular outcome, its aim was to be "good" in these terms. Thus we see a strong match between the goals of the school and the broader policy context, which provided it with increased legitimacy as an organization. Yet at the same time, trying to adjudicate which school is "better" might also be unproductive. Both schools were providing good, safe educational experiences for their students and as such both schools were meeting one of the central goals of charter school legislation—to provide choices within the education system. By this criterion, then, Hilltop Charter School and Inspiration School were successful.

What is the outlook for these schools in the face of this contradiction in public policy? If sociological studies of organizations are to be any guide, schools such as Hilltop Charter School have experienced increased pressure to raise test scores since NCLB. While one positive outcome of this process at Hilltop Charter School was a more critical examination of school practices, it struggled to fully enact a "developmental" education program and also raise test scores. We might also consider how these pressures are in all likelihood greater for charter schools serving low-income students, given the strong association between school demographic characteristics and school rankings (Powers, 2004a, 2004b; see also Elmore, 2004). Finally, the comparison also illustrates some of the tensions within the charter school movement and education policy more generally. If the goal of charter school reform is to create schools that are "different," will accountability polices allow them to maintain their distinctiveness? Or, does the system contain a tendency toward centralization? We might also think about how this type of de facto centralization might disproportionately affect low-income charter schools.

Unpacking the distinct theories of teaching and learning at each school and placing them within the context of the shifts in state policy on standardized testing helps bring into sharper focus the effect of the policy context in "imprinting" charter schools' teaching cultures. At the same time, as my analysis also demonstrates, the policy environment does not remain stable, which has implications for whether or not a school can continue to enact the model for teaching and learning outlined in its charter. To be more specific: what are the consequences for schools imprinted by a policy environment that enables a certain type of organizational form when the policy environment subsequently undergoes a radical shift?

On the one hand, charter school legislation is intended to foster variation among schools and local control. On the other hand, state and national testing policies have generated increasingly sophisticated methods of ranking schools. In this case, the policy context places limits on the extent to which charter schools can take advantage of the freedom afforded by decentralization depending on the fit between the school's culture and the policy environment, a process that may also be mediated by student background characteristics. Finally, to return to an issue I discussed at the beginning of this chapter, the account of the changes in the state testing program and curricula highlights the discontinuous and highly politicized nature of education policymaking—a stark contrast to the technical-rational view of education policy and policymaking embedded in much of the policy talk related to education reform.

CHAPTER SIX

THE RELATIONSHIP BETWEEN
POLICY TALK AND IMPLEMENTATION

In this chapter I look at charter school implementation nationally using the 1999–2000 Schools and Staffing Survey (SASS). I focus on a key component of the policy talk related to charter school reform, accountability. As the analysis of the statements of legislative intent in chapter 1 illustrated, while many policymakers saw charter schools as a method of increasing accountability in public education, they rarely specified (1) who schools should be accountable to and (2) how schools should be held accountable (see also Bulkley, 2001; Fusarelli, 2001; Wells et al., 2002). I begin by first considering how researchers have understood charter school accountability, and how these conceptualizations of charter school accountability overlap with a framework for analyzing performance accountability.

Analyzing Charter School Accountability

In their national study of charter school accountability, Hill, Lake, and Cielo (2002) identified three dimensions of charter school accountability. The first is internal accountability, or accountability to the immediate stakeholders within the school, which they defined as the "set of processes where teachers apply shared expectations to their own work and that of colleagues" (Hill et al., 2002, 25). The remaining two dimensions are both forms of external accountability or accountability to stakeholders outside of the school: (1) accountability to authorizing agencies and (2) accountability to other partners that are independent of the public school system. Inspiration School's relationship with Educational Enterprise Corporation is an example of this second form of external accountability.

In contrast, Garn and Cobb (2001) distinguished between (1) bureaucratic accountability; (2) performance accountability; and (3) market accountability. In a system of bureaucratic accountability, a school is judged successful (or not) based on how well it follows rules and procedures. Under a system of performance accountability, a school's performance is assessed in relation to its performance on a set of measurable outcomes. Finally, in a market accountability system, schools are accountable to the immediate constituents of schools: parents and students. These direct consumers of education have the option of changing schools if they are dissatisfied with their educational experiences.[1] While the Hill et al. (2002) framework focused on the sets of actors, or who schools are accountable to, the Garn and Cobb (2001) framework was primarily concerned with the methods of accountability, or how schools are held accountable.

An earlier framework that was developed in the context of a study of school restructuring (Newmann, King and Rigdon, 1997) engaged issues raised by both Hill et al. (2002) and Garn and Cobb (2001). Here, the focus was on one dimension of the Garn and Cobb framework, performance accountability. Like Hill et al. (2002), Newmann et al. (1997) were also interested in who sets performance standards for schools, and also distinguished between external and internal accountability. Schools are externally accountable when standards for teaching and learning are imposed on schools by outside entities (e.g., the school district, state, or federal government). Schools are internally accountable when standards for teaching and learning are generated within schools. Yet Newmann et al. (1997) also argued that focusing solely on standards without considering the resources schools need to meet standards is insufficient. Thus while internal and external accountability describe how a school's goals for teaching and learning are determined, Newmann et al. (1997) proposed an additional concept, organizational capacity, to assess the degree to which the "human, technical, and social resources of an organization are organized into an effective *collective* enterprise" focused on student learning (47).

Organizational capacity encompasses three dimensions: (1) knowledge and skills; (2) power and authority; and (3) shared commitment and collaborative activity. In general, internal accountability is associated with organizational capacity. That is, depending on the circumstances, internal accountability can either generate organizational capacity or it can be an outcome of organizational capacity. However, the relationship between external accountability and organizational capacity is less clear-cut. The presence of external accountability may not necessarily foster organizational capacity. For example, as we saw in chapter 5, Hilltop Charter School was struggling with a new form of external accountability that was not compatible with the school's internal understanding of what teaching and learning should look like.

As the discussion above suggests, the Newmann et al. (1997) framework is particularly useful for looking at the relationship between policy talk and implementation because it engages a central theme in charter school policy talk, accountability (see also Finn, Manno, and Vanourek, 2000).

In this chapter I widen the frame of the analysis to include both charter schools and conventional public schools using data from the SASS to compare the relationship between policy talk and implementation in charter school reform. If there is a strong fit between charter school policy talk and implementation, then charter schools should look substantially different from conventional public schools on indicators of performance accountability and organizational capacity.

Data and Variables

While I discussed the SASS in the Introduction, a few features of the data are worth repeating here. Designed to facilitate cross-sector comparisons, the 1999–2000 Schools and Staffing Survey combined a nationally representative sample of conventional public schools with almost the full population of charter schools that were operating in 1998–1999 (the year prior to the survey). In the analysis presented here, I draw primarily from the principals' and the teachers' surveys (NCES, 2000). The SASS is ideal for assessing the relationship between policy talk and implementation in charter school reform because it was collected eight years after the first charter school law was passed and seven years after the first charter school opened its doors in Minnesota in 1992. By this time, we can expect that charter schools have developed into a relatively mature education reform, particularly in states such as California and Arizona, which were among the earliest states to pass charter school legislation and also have large numbers of charter schools. In addition, the 1999–2000 SASS data was collected before NCLB was passed in 2002, at a point when state accountability systems were at a relatively early stage in their development and implementation. NCLB changed the accountability requirements for all public schools. It is likely that after 2002, charter schools and conventional public schools were more similar in terms of accountability. As a result, this data allows us to assess the relationship between policy talk and implementation without the confounding effects of a change in federal policy that affected all public schools. In the sections that follow, I describe the variables from the SASS in more detail.

Accountability

A number of questions in the SASS provided indicators of the locus of accountability in charter schools and conventional public schools. Principals were asked whether or not the school had district or state performance goals and whether or not they met those goals (yes/no). Principals who reported that their schools did not meet district or state performance goals were asked if their schools were subject to a list of consequences for not meeting those goals (yes/no). The presence of accountability to district or state performance goals will indicate external accountability; the consequences for schools will provide indicators of the degree of external accountability.

A second set of indicators of internal versus external accountability are survey items that asked principals to rate their own influence on the performance standards for the students in their schools on a 5-point Likert scale, where 1 indicated "No influence" and 5 indicated "A great deal of influence" (NCES, 2000, Form 2D, 7). The principals were also asked to use the same scale to rate the influence of other parties: state-level officials, their local school board, school district staff, the school site council, teachers, and the parent association. If principals in charter schools reported that parties within the school had more influence on performance standards than principals and teachers in conventional public schools, we might conclude that charter schools have greater internal accountability. If principals in conventional public schools indicated that parties outside the school had a great deal of influence on the standards for their students compared to principals and teachers in charter schools, it would suggest that conventional public schools were subject to greater external accountability than charter schools.

Like the principals, teachers were asked to rate their own influence on setting their schools' performance standards. In addition, teachers rated the extent to which district and state standards and assessments shaped their teaching practices on a 5-point Likert scale, where 1 indicated "Not at all" and 5 indicated "To a great extent" (NCES, 2000, Form 4A, 34). Another series of questions asked teachers whether or not they received their students' scores on state and local achievement tests (yes/no) and if so, the extent that they used the test results to alter their teaching practices, using the same Likert scale described above. A last set of questions asked principals whether or not their schools had formal school improvement plans, and if so, how they assessed their schools' progress on the plan.[2]

Organizational Capacity

As noted above, there are three dimensions of organizational capacity: (1) knowledge and skills; (2) power and authority; and (3) shared commitment and collaboration. For indicators of knowledge and skills, the first dimension of organizational capacity, I used survey items that asked teachers whether or not they participated in different types of professional development related to teaching and learning during the twelve months prior to the survey (yes/no). An additional set of questions asked teachers more detailed questions about the topics of the professional development activities they participated in, and also the amount of time they spent in activities related to each area. Teachers were asked to chose the category on an ordinal scale that best fit the number of hours they spent in professional development activities in that area. As indicators of power and authority, the second dimension of organizational capacity, I used questions that asked principals and teachers to assess the degree of influence they had over different areas of decision-making at their schools: establishing curriculum, determining the content of in-services, hiring and evaluating teachers, and determining the budget and disciplinary policies.

I used two sets of questions to assess shared commitment and collaboration, the final dimension of organizational capacity. The first set was drawn from the teachers' surveys. I selected questions assessing the degree to which teachers perceived that they and their colleagues (including administrators) had a common vision of the school's mission, supported each other, and worked cooperatively. For example, compared to teachers in conventional public schools, were teachers in charter schools more likely to report that they and their colleagues had similar beliefs about what the central mission of their schools should be? Are teachers in charter schools more likely to report that their principal knew what kind of school she/he wanted and communicated it to the staff than did teachers in conventional public schools? It should be noted that the scale for this latter set of questions is the opposite of the scale used in the other analyses in this chapter. In this case, a response of 1 indicated "Strongly agree" whereas 4 indicated "Strongly disagree" (NCES, 2000, Form 2A, 40). As with the analysis of school climate in chapter 1, I ordered the items in the table based on the charter school teachers' average responses from lowest to highest so that the items at the top of the table are the items that charter school teachers most strongly agreed with. The second set of questions used to assess shared commitment and collaboration were drawn from the principals' survey. Principals were asked to report how many times in the month prior to the survey that they (1) "facilitate[d] the achievement of the school's mission through such activities as consensus building, planning, obtaining resources, monitoring progress, etc."; (2) "facilitate[d] student learning (e.g., eliminate[d] barriers to student learning, and establish[ed] high expectations for students)"; and (3) [built] professional community among the staff (NCES, 2000, Form 2D, 16).

Results

In the sections that follow, I present descriptive analyses of the variables described above.[3] Answers to yes/no questions were tabulated as percentages.

Reponses measured on a 4-point or 5-point Likert scale were reported as means. When relevant, differences in means are presented in the third column of each table; this figure is the difference between the charter school mean and the conventional public school mean. A plus (+) indicates that the charter school mean was higher than the conventional public school mean on the variable of interest. Conversely, a minus (–) indicates that the charter school mean was lower than the conventional public school mean. In addition, t-tests were used to assess the significance of the differences in means across the two school types, which is denoted by a series of asterisks (*). For example, in table 6.3, the difference of –0.36 in the last column of the first row indicates that as a group, charter school principals tended to report that state officials had less influence on how performance standards were determined for students at their schools. The asterisks indicate that the differences in means across the two sectors was statistically significant at $p \leq 0.001$.

Accountability

As table 6.1 illustrates, compared to principals of conventional public schools, slightly higher percentages of charter school principals reported that their schools either did not have performance goals set by their state or district, or if they did have performance goals, their schools were not required to meet them. Likewise, a slightly lower percentage of charter school principals reported being required to meet district and state performance goals. The percentage of schools of each type that met their performance goals (whether required or not) was approximately even.

Table 6.2 shows the consequences reported by the principals for the 29 percent of schools that did not meet their performance goals. These

Table 6.1 Did School Have and Meet District or State Performance Goals?

	Conventional Public Schools in Charter States N = 53,712 (%)	Charter Schools N = 988 (%)
School had no performance goals	9.3	11.9
School had performance goals but was not required to meet them	7.5	9.1
School had performance goals and was required to meet them	83.2	79.0
Of the schools that had performance goals		
Did not meet performance goals	28.9	28.8
Met performance goals	61.8	59.3

Table 6.2   Consequences for Schools That Did Not Meet Performance Goals

	Conventional Public Schools in Charter States N = 15,524 (%)	Charter Schools N = 285 (%)
Required to write a school or program improvement plan	74.4	58.6
Put on an evaluation cycle with required targeted improvement dates	46.7	34.1
Provided with technical assistance by outside experts	37.2	36.5
Provided with additional resources	46.4	45.6
Required to replace the principal	3.5	5.0
Subject to reconstitution or takeover regulations	0.5	0.4
Penalized by a reduction in state funding	2.7	4.5
Percentage subject to none of these sanctions	25.0	27.3
Percentage subject to one of these sanctions	31.4	35.9
Percentage subject to two of these sanctions	24.7	21.2
Percentage subject to three or more of these sanctions	19.0	15.5

results suggest that, contrary to charter school policy talk, within the group of schools that did not meet their performance goals, charter schools were less externally accountable than conventional public schools for not meeting their performance goals. For example, fewer charter schools than conventional public schools were required to write a school or program improvement plan or were put on an evaluation cycle. Compared to conventional public schools, slightly higher percentages of charter schools reported being required to replace their principals or experiencing a reduction in state funds as a result of not meeting performance goals. However, fewer than 5 percent of either type of school reported being subject to any of these consequences. At the bottom of the table I provide a breakdown of the total number of sanctions each group of schools were subjected to. Compared to conventional public school principals, a slightly smaller percentage of charter school principals reported that their schools did not experience any of these sanctions after not meeting their performance goals. Charter school principals were also more likely to report that their schools were subject to fewer combinations of sanctions.

While the findings in table 6.2 are based on the reports of 29 percent of the principals in each group, a similar conclusion can be drawn from the comparison of the full sample of principals' reports of the relative influence that different groups had on setting performance standards for the students at their schools, which are shown in table 6.3. Compared to

Table 6.3 Influence in Setting Performance Standards

Influence on Setting Performance Standards 1 = No Influence; 5 = A Great Deal of Influence	Conventional Public School Principals Weighted N = 53712 Mean (S.D.)	Charter School Principals Weighted N = 988 Mean (S.D.)	Difference
State dept. of ed. or other state bodies	4.32 (0.92)	3.96 (1.11)	−0.36***
Local school board	4.01 (1.02)	3.27 (1.34)	−0.74***
District staff	4.00 (0.92)	3.28 (1.44)	−0.72***
Principal	4.06 (0.90)	4.36 (0.83)	+0.30***
Teachers	4.02 (0.97)	4.31 (0.86)	+0.29***
School Site Council	2.00 (1.34)	2.01 (1.40)	+0.01
Parent association	2.71 (1.08)	3.00 (1.24)	+0.29***

principals of conventional public schools, charter school principals tended to report that parties outside the school (e.g., district staff or school board) had less influence on the school's performance standards. As table 6.3 also illustrates, principals in charter schools were more likely to report that participants at the school site (principal, teachers, the parent association) had more influence on setting the performance standards used to evaluate their students than their counterparts in conventional public schools. The t-tests indicate that, with the exception of the influence of the school site council, all of the differences in means across the two types of schools were statistically significant.[4] Like the findings reported in table 6.2, these findings also suggest that charter schools were less subject to external accountability than conventional public schools. The greater influence (on average) of the principal, teachers, and parent associations on setting performance standards in charter schools suggests that charter schools tend to have more internal accountability than conventional public schools.

The principals' reports are consistent with teachers' responses to survey items related to standards and assessment (shown in table 6.4), which also suggests that charter schools were less subject to external accountability than conventional public schools but were more internally accountable. As a group, teachers in charter schools were more likely to report that they had a great deal of influence over the performance standards for the students at their school. Similarly, charter school teachers were less likely to report that districts and state standards guided their instructional practice than teachers in conventional public schools. The last section of the table compares teachers' responses on a set of questions that asked if they received their students' standardized test scores, and how they used them. Compared to teachers in conventional public schools, a slightly higher

Table 6.4   Teachers' Influence on Standards and Use of Test Scores

	Conventional Public School Teachers Weighted N = 2014596 Mean (S.D.)	Charter School Teachers Weighted N = 17477 Mean (S.D.)	Difference in Mean
1 = No Influence; 5 = A Great Deal of Influence			
Teachers' Influence on Setting Performance Standards	2.99 (1.25)	3.47 (1.29)	+0.48***
1 = Not at All; 5 = To a Great Extent			
Teachers Use State or District Standards to Guide Instructional Practice	4.10 (1.03)	3.86 (1.14)	−0.24***
1 = Strongly Agree; 4 = Disagree			
Worried about job security because of student performance on state or local tests	3.04 (0.97)	3.05 (0.98)	+0.01
Received students' scores on standardized tests (%)	61.5	66.8	
How teachers used the scores			
1 = Not at All; 5 = To a Great Extent			
To group students into instructional groups by ability	2.61 (1.36)	2.44 (1.36)	−0.17***
To assess areas where you need to strengthen your content knowledge or teaching practice	3.63 (1.20)	3.51 (1.24)	−0.12***
To adjust your curriculum in areas where students encountered problems	3.78 (1.56)	3.61 (1.20)	−0.17***

percentage of charter school teachers reported receiving their students test scores. However, as a group, teachers in charter schools were less likely to report that they used the test results to change how or what they taught in their classrooms. The pattern in the teachers' responses across the three questions could be a function of when teachers received their students' test scores. More specifically, both groups of teachers reported using test scores to group students to a lesser extent than they used test scores to reflect on their own content knowledge and adjust their teaching practices. If students were tested in the spring and teachers received the scores in the summer after the academic year had ended, then the scores will be of little use for grouping students. However, teachers could use test scores they receive during the summer months to plan their curricula or professional development activities for the following academic year.

Finally, these results also dovetail with principals' responses to a series of questions asking if their school had a formal school improvement plan and, if so, how they gauged their school's progress on the plan (see table 6.5).

Table 6.5 Did School Have a Formal School Improvement Plan?

	Conventional Public Schools N = 53,712 (%)	Charter Schools N = 988 (%)
No	11.3	29.2
Yes	88.7	70.8
Instruments Used to Assess School's Progress on School Improvement Plan		
State or national tests	96.0	95.9
Parent or student surveys	83.8	92.6
Portfolio products	62.2	77.0

Fewer charter schools than conventional public schools had formal school improvement plans (71 percent compared to 89 percent, respectively). Of these schools, similar percentages of charter schools and conventional public schools used state tests to assess their progress on their school improvement plans. Within this group of schools, charter schools were also more likely to use parent or student surveys to determine their progress, which suggests that charter schools were slightly more attuned to issues of market accountability. Yet at the same time, the responses of conventional public school principals also highlights how these school leaders paid attention to their "markets." Eighty-four percent of the conventional public school principals whose schools had formal school improvement plans reported using parent and student surveys to measure their progress on their plans. This latter finding suggests that the charter school policy talk that claims conventional public schools are buffered from market accountability is an oversimplification and that conventional public schools are not inattentive to market dynamics.

Organizational Capacity

Knowledge and Skills

Teachers in conventional public schools and charter schools reported participating in roughly the same types professional development activities in the year prior to the survey (see table 6.6). Though not shown, conventional public school teachers and charter school teachers also reported participating in the same number of professional development activities in the year prior to the survey (the average was approximately four for both types of teachers). Across most of the categories the percentages in the two groups of teachers are strikingly similar. The largest difference in teachers' participation in professional development across the two sectors

Table 6.6 Percentage of Teachers Reporting Participating in Professional Development Activity by Type

	Conventional Public School Teachers Weighted N = 2014596 (%)	Charter School Teachers Weighted N = 17477 (%)
University courses related to certification in main teaching field	31.5	33.8
Other university courses in main teaching field	23.8	26.6
Observational visits to other schools	34.5	40.9
Individual or collaborative research	47.1	51.6
Regular collaboration with other teachers around instruction	75.1	73.9
Mentoring and/or peer coaching	42.9	47.8
Participating in teacher network	24.9	26.3
Attending workshops/trainings	94.4	90.1
Presenting workshops	22.3	25.4

is that a higher percentage of charter school teachers reported participating in observational visits than conventional public school teachers (41 percent compared to 35 percent). Overall, charter school teachers appear to participate in most types of staff development at slightly higher rates than conventional public school teachers. The most common form of professional development for both groups of teachers was attending workshops, followed by regular collaboration with other teachers around instruction, with three quarters or more of all teachers, regardless of school type, reporting that they engaged in these activities.

While the types of professional development activities teachers participate in provide a very general overview of the professional development activities of the two groups of teachers, a better indicator of the knowledge dimension of organizational capacity as conceptualized by Newmann et al. (1997) is the extent to which teachers participated in professional development activities related to teaching and learning. Table 6.7 reports the percentages of teachers who engaged in this subcategory of professional development activities by topic and school type; the numbers directly below indicate the amount of time those teachers reported spending in professional development on a particular topic. For example, 60 percent of conventional public school teachers reported participating in professional development activities related to in-depth study of content in their main teaching field. Of these, 19 percent reported spending eight hours or less in professional development activities related to in-depth study of content, whereas 32 percent spent thirty-three or more hours. In each category, slightly fewer charter school teachers reported participating in professional

Table 6.7 Percentage of Teachers Reporting Participating in Professional Development Related to Teaching and Learning by Type and Hours

	Conventional Public School Teachers Weighted N = 2014596 (%)	Charter School Teachers Weighted N = 17477 (%)
In-depth study of content in teachers' main teaching field	59.7	54.4
Hours spent by participants		
8 hours or less	19.0	17.7
9–16 hours	26.4	22.2
17–32 hours	23.1	22.8
33 hours or more	31.6	37.3
Content and performance standards in main teaching assignment	72.4	63.4
Hours spent by participants		
8 hours or less	33.5	31.2
9–16 hours	32.0	28.6
17–32 hours	18.7	18.8
33 hours or more	15.7	21.3
Methods of teaching	73.6	71.4
Hours spent by participants		
8 hours or less	40.6	38.1
9–16 hours	28.7	26.1
17–32 hours	16.0	19.3
33 hours or more	14.7	16.4
Student assessment	62.5	59.8
Hours spent by participants		
8 hours or less	60.8	55.2
9–16 hours	23.0	24.4
17–32 hours	9.3	12.0
33 hours or more	6.8	8.4

development activities focused on teaching and learning. However, the charter school teachers that did participate in these professional development activities tended to participate in more hours of professional development than conventional public school teachers.

Notably, the largest difference in participation across the two groups was their participation in professional development activities related to content and performance standards, which is consistent with the findings on accountability I presented above. Sixty-three percent of charter school teachers participated in professional development activities related to content and performance standards, compared to 72 percent of conventional public school teachers. As a group, charter school teachers tended to be less oriented toward content and performance standards in both their daily

Table 6.8 Principals' Reports of Frequency of Activities Related to Knowledge and Skills During the Month Prior to Survey

	Conventional Public School Principals Weighted N = 53712 (%)	Charter School Principals Weighted N = 988 (%)
Guide the development and evaluation of curriculum and instruction		
Never	2.7	2.7
Once or twice a month	30.0	31.0
Once or twice a week	39.7	36.3
Every day	27.5	29.9
Provide and engage in professional development activities		
Never	2.1	2.0
Once or twice a month	58.8	53.2
Once or twice a week	30.7	35.4
Every day	8.5	9.3

teaching activities and in their professional development activities than conventional public school teachers.

The SASS also asked principals how often they engaged in different types of activities in the month prior to answering the survey. Table 6.8 reports the results of the questions related to knowledge and skills. Overall, charter school principals participated in activities related to the knowledge and skill dimension of organizational capacity at the same or slightly higher rates than conventional public school teachers. In general, principals of both conventional public schools and charter schools spent similar amounts of time guiding the development of curriculum and instruction. Compared to conventional public school principals, charter school principals were slightly more likely to report spending more of their time providing and engaging in professional development activities.

Power and Authority
Tables 6.9 and 6.10 report principals' and teachers' perceptions of their influence over different areas of school policy by school type. In general, both principals of charter schools and conventional public schools reported having a considerable amount of influence over school life. The means for all questions across the two groups was 4 or greater on a 5-point scale, where 5 indicated a great deal of influence. Yet while all principals tended to perceive themselves as having a great deal of influence on school policy, there were also some notable differences across the two groups. In general, principals in charter schools tended to rate their influence across all of these areas more highly than conventional public school principals.

Table 6.9 Principals' Reports of Their Influence on School Policy

Principals' Reports of Influence on 1 = No Influence; 5 = A Great Deal of Influence	Conventional Public School Principals Weighted N = 53712 Mean (S.D.)	Charter School Principals Weighted N = 988 Mean (S.D.)	Difference
Curriculum	3.99 (0.88)	4.33 (0.86)	+0.34***
Professional development	4.20 (0.82)	4.47 (0.76)	+0.27***
Evaluating teachers	4.74 (0.48)	4.75 (0.62)	+0.01
Hiring new teachers	4.66 (0.72)	4.75 (0.60)	+0.09***
Setting discipline policy	4.63 (0.62)	4.69 (0.62)	+0.06
Deciding how the school budget should be spent	4.26 (0.90)	4.39 (0.90)	+0.13***
Percentage of schools with own professional development budgets controlled by the principal (%)	74.0	84.5	

Table 6.10 Teachers' Reports of Their Influence on School Policy

Teachers' Reports of Influence on 1 = No Influence; 5 = A Great Deal of Influence	Conventional Public School Teachers Weighted N = 2014596 Mean (S.D.)	Charter School Teachers Weighted N = 17477 Mean (S.D.)	Difference
Curriculum	3.16 (1.23)	3.70 (1.30)	+0.54***
Content of professional development	2.85 (1.20)	3.10 (1.31)	+0.25***
Evaluating teachers	1.79 (1.04)	2.30 (1.28)	+0.51***
Hiring new teachers	2.02 (1.19)	2.53 (1.41)	+0.51***
Setting discipline policy	2.77 (1.23)	3.23 (1.33)	+0.46***
Deciding how the school budget should be spent	2.14 (1.16)	2.24 (1.30)	+0.10***

The differences in ratings were statistically significant in the areas of curriculum, professional development, hiring new teachers, and deciding how to spend the school budget.

Similarly, while teachers working in both charter schools and conventional public schools tended to view themselves as having comparatively little influence over school policy, as a group teachers in charter schools reported greater levels of influence than teachers in conventional public schools across all areas. Teachers in charter schools were also more likely

Table 6.11   Teachers' Perceptions of Control Over Their Classrooms

Teachers' Perception of Control Over 1 = No Control; 5 = A Great Deal of Control	Conventional Public School Teachers Weighted N = 2014596 Mean (S.D.)	Charter School Teachers Weighted N = 17477 Mean (S.D.)	Difference
Selecting Instructional Materials	3.42 (1.21)	3.66 (1.29)	+0.24***
Selecting Content, Topics and Skills	3.50 (1.21)	3.78 (1.18)	+0.28***
Selecting Teaching Techniques	4.35 (0.85)	4.37 (0.92)	+0.02
Evaluating Students	4.43 (0.78)	4.43 (0.83)	0.00
Disciplining Students	3.97 (0.96)	4.03 (0.98)	+0.06***
Homework	4.42 (0.87)	4.36 (0.96)	−0.06

to report having more control over aspects of their classrooms than teachers in conventional public schools (table 6.11). The biggest differences between the two groups were in teachers' abilities to select instructional materials and the content, topics, and skills they covered in their classrooms. Overall, the general pattern that emerges from the two tables is that charter school principals and teachers were more likely to perceive that they had a great deal of influence over school policy compared to conventional public school teachers.

Finally, one set of questions that bridges two of the three dimensions of organizational capacity, (1) knowledge and skills; and (2) power and authority is principals' reports of the factors that influenced teachers' professional development activities at their schools, which are shown in table 6.12. Overall, principals in conventional public schools tended to report that state or district initiatives and state or local standards were important in determining the in-service professional development activities for teachers. Conventional public school principals were also more likely to report that professional development activities were intended to support either their districts' improvement goals or the implementation of state and local standards (see the bottom half of table 6.12). However, even though on average, charter school principals rated these factors as having less influence over professional development, the standard deviations for the charter school principals' responses on these questions tended to be higher than those of conventional public school principals, which suggests that there was much greater variation within the responses of charter school principals than conventional public school principals. Conversely, charter school principals were more likely to report that teacher preferences were an important factor shaping teachers' professional development activities compared to conventional public school principals. Notably, compared to

Table 6.12 Principals' Reports of the Factors That Shape Teachers' Professional Development Activities

Importance in Determining In-Service Professional Development Activities 1 = Not important at all; 5 = Very important	Conventional Public School Principals Weighted N = 53712 Mean (S.D.)	Charter School Principals Weighted N = 988 Mean (S.D.)	Difference in Mean
State level initiatives	3.51 (1.07)	3.07 (1.23)	−0.44***
District level initiatives or district improvement plan	4.31 (0.78)	3.37 (1.41)	−0.94***
School improvement plan	4.48 (0.74)	4.17 (1.05)	−0.31***
Implementation of state or local academic standards	4.39 (0.76)	4.14 (1.03)	−0.25***
Implementation of state or local skills standards	4.21 (0.88)	3.97 (1.11)	−0.24***
Teacher preferences	3.88 (0.89)	4.11 (0.90)	+0.23***
How often is professional development for teachers 1 = Never; 5 = Always			
Designed or chosen to support the school's improvement goals	4.21 (0.69)	4.23 (0.71)	+0.02
Designed or chosen to support the district's improvement goals	4.14 (0.69)	3.51 (1.25)	−0.63***
Designed or chosen to support the implementation of state and local standards	4.03 (0.73)	3.76 (0.92)	−0.27***
Accompanied by the resources teachers need (e.g., time and materials) to make changes in the classroom	3.54 (0.86)	3.83 (0.84)	+0.29***

conventional public school principals, charter school principals' responses suggested that their school improvement plans were less important in shaping professional development activities, which is consistent with the findings related to accountability presented above.

Shared Commitment and Collaborative Activity

Based on findings from prior research on charter schools, we might expect that participants in charter schools have a stronger sense of shared commitment and collaboration compared to their counterparts in conventional public schools (Hill et al., 2002). On average, conventional public school teachers were more satisfied at their schools than charter school teachers and were slightly more likely to agree that their principals communicated their expectations to their staffs. However, on most of the other measures related to shared beliefs (see table 6.13), the charter school teachers' means were lower than the means of the conventional public school teachers. Recall that on this set of questions an answer of 1 indicated "Strongly Agree." A mean that is close to 1 indicates that the teachers responded

Table 6.13 Teachers' Perceptions Related to Shared Commitment and Collaboration

Teachers Agree/Disagree with 1 = Strongly Agree; 4 = Disagree	Conventional Public School Teachers Weighted N = 2014596 Mean (S.D.)	Charter School Teachers Weighted N = 17477 Mean (S.D.)	Difference
I am generally satisfied being a teacher at this school	1.59 (0.75)	1.67 (0.80)	+0.08***
Principal communicates the type of school he/she wants to the staff	1.74 (0.86)	1.69 (0.88)	−0.05**
Principal communicates expectations to staff	1.67 (0.80)	1.71 (0.85)	+0.04***
Colleagues share my beliefs and values about the school's mission	1.87 (0.75)	1.74 (0.75)	−0.13***
There is a great deal of cooperative effort among the staff	1.94 (0.84)	1.75 (0.82)	−0.19***
Principal enforces school rules for student conduct and backs me up	1.76 (0.88)	1.75 (0.91)	−0.01
Administration's behavior toward staff is supportive	1.88 (0.93)	1.78 (0.93)	−0.10***
I make a conscious effort to coordinate content with other teachers	1.81 (0.78)	1.81 (0.79)	−0.00
The staff is recognized for a job done well	2.16 (0.93)	2.03 (0.93)	−0.13***
Principal talks with me about instructional practice	2.68 (0.95)	2.56 (0.99)	−0.12***
I am worried about my job security	3.04 (0.97)	3.05 (0.98)	+0.01
It is a waste of time to do my best	3.39 (0.90)	3.49 (0.85)	±0.10***

affirmatively to that survey item, while a mean that is close to 4 indicates that the teachers responded negatively to that survey item. Compared to conventional public school teachers, charter school teachers were more likely to agree that their principals communicated the type of schools they wanted. Charter school teachers were also more likely to agree that their colleagues shared their beliefs than conventional public school teachers and that there was a high level of cooperation among the staff. Finally, compared to conventional public school teachers, charter school teachers were more likely to disagree that it was a waste of their time to do their best. These differences in shared commitment and collaboration should be attributable to the smaller size of charter schools compared to conventional public schools (see table 1.6 in chapter 1).

Table 6.14 reports principals' responses to questions related to shared commitment and collaboration. While charter school principals reported engaging in activities related to facilitating the school's mission at a slightly higher rate than conventional public school principals, there was little difference across the two groups in the extent to which they facilitated student learning. Both types of principals spent approximately the same amount of time building professional communities at their schools.

Table 6.14 Principals' Reports of Frequency of Activities Related To Shared Commitment and Collaboration in the Month Prior to Survey

	Conventional Public School Principals Weighted N = 53712 (%)	Charter School Principals Weighted N = 988 (%)
Facilitate the school's mission		
Never	1.7	1.6
Once or twice a month	24.6	19.8
Once or twice a week	31.7	32.6
Every day	42.0	46.0
Facilitate student learning (e.g., eliminate barriers and set high expectations)		
Never	1.0	1.1
Once or twice a month	15.1	14.4
Once or twice a week	29.5	30.4
Every day	54.7	54.1
Build professional community among faculty and other staff		
Never	1.7	2.2
Once or twice a month	28.8	26.8
Once or twice a week	28.8	30.7
Every day	40.7	40.3

Discussion

Overall, these analyses provide a complex picture of the differences between conventional public schools and charter schools on accountability and organizational capacity. Charter schools appear to be less subject to external accountability than conventional public schools—a surprising finding. As I documented in the Introduction and chapter 1, charter school policy talk claims that charter schools will be more accountable than conventional public schools. However, the results presented here suggest that, in practice, charter schools have fallen short of this goal. Yet there is also evidence to suggest that charter schools are more internally accountable, which is consistent with charter school policy talk. Charter schools also appear to be somewhat higher on two of the three dimensions of organizational capacity (power and authority, and shared commitment and collaboration) than conventional public schools. But charter schools and conventional public schools are similar on the knowledge dimension of organizational capacity, which suggests that charter schools are largely an organizational innovation. That is, charter schools provide the teachers working in them with more autonomy and either foster or attract teachers with higher levels of commitment to their missions but do not tend to be more focused on teaching and learning than conventional public schools.

The differences between conventional schools and charter schools are systematic and patterned. That is, on all of the questions related to accountability, both charter school principals and teachers responded similarly and consistently. For example, both charter school principals and teachers tended to report that they had more influence on setting standards for their schools than their counterparts in conventional public schools. Overall, a comparison of the responses across the two sectors on all of the questions related to accountability suggest that charter schools experienced less external accountability than conventional public schools but that charter schools also had more internal accountability. Likewise, charter school teachers' and principals' responses suggest that, on average, they had higher levels of power and authority than conventional public school teachers and that shared commitment and collaboration tended to be higher at charter schools.

Yet there is also a good deal of similarity in participants' responses across the two sectors.[5] That is, while charter school principals' and teachers' responses were consistent within and across the three domains (accountability, power, and authority, and shared commitment and collaboration), their responses were also not radically different from those of conventional public school teachers. For example, in table 6.13, which reported the teachers' responses on items related to shared beliefs and commitment, the question that charter school teachers and conventional public school teachers most strongly agreed with (job satisfaction) and the question that the two groups most disagreed with (waste of time to do my best) were the same. Moreover, the overall averages across the two groups on most questions were fairly similar. Likewise, principals' responses about how they spent their time and the amount of influence they had over many areas of school life were remarkably alike.

These findings echo the perspectives of the charter school teachers at Hilltop Charter School, Hearts and Hands Community School, and Inspiration School described in chapter 4. While teachers at all three schools saw charter schools as different from conventional public schools, when queried deeper they tended to suggest that the differences between the two types of schools were more relative rather than absolute. Rather than reinvent public education then, if we consider that charter schools comprised only 2 percent of all public schools in 2005–2006, charter schools instead seem to be creating incremental changes in a very small corner of the public school sector.

Conclusion: Charter School Reform—Sweeping Claims and Modest Progress

As I suggested in the Introduction, charter school policy talk imagines a reform that will transform public education. The evidence presented here suggests that rather than radically changing public education, charter schools have had much more modest and local successes. Indeed, this is not surprising given the nature of charter school reform. Charter school reform is a form of decentralization within what is already a highly decentralized system of public education. At its core, charter school reform is largely a school-by-school reform that is shaped by features of the state and district contexts. The creation and evolution of individual charter schools is dependent on the opportunities and constraints available to teachers, parents, and community members in local settings.

The goal of this book was to provide a comprehensive picture of charter school reform by examining each stage of the policy-making cycle proposed by Tyack and Cuban (1995). I began by discussing charter school policy talk. Policy-makers propose ambitious reforms for schools, but as the analyses presented here suggest, the trajectory from goals to practice is complicated. While there are some variations across state contexts, charter school policy talk shares some common themes. Not surprisingly, one of the most common goals for charter schools was to improve student learning—a goal we might expect for any education reform. Likewise, expanding school choice is a fairly self-evident goal for a school choice policy. There was less agreement in the more specific goals for charter school reform. For example, many state policymakers saw charter schools as a way to increase accountability in public education, but there was little consensus on how schools should be held accountable.

Similarly, the processes whereby charter school policy talk is translated into policy action are shaped by individual states' political contexts. In California, the policy precursor to charter school reform was the restructuring movement, the "second wave" response to the dramatic calls for education reform in the mid-1980s. Another important influence on charter school policy action in California was the threat that voters would approve a large-scale school voucher program by ballot initiative. In Arizona, charter school reform was more squarely an effort to create market competition in education. This goal is succinctly summarized in the current mission statement of the Arizona State Board for Charter Schools: "To foster accountability in charter schools which will improve student achievement through market choice" (Arizona State Board for Charter Schools web site). Finally, compared to California and Arizona, charter school reform in Missouri was more of an afterthought. Although state lawmakers had proposed charter school legislation in the years before Missouri's charter school legislation was passed, it never gained traction. Charter school reform was included as one set of provisions in a broader bill passed in 1998 aimed at ending court-ordered desegregation in Kansas City and St. Louis in 1998. A decade later, these districts remain the only districts in Missouri in which charter schools can be opened.

At the heart of the book is an examination of charter school implementation in three schools. On the ground, as it is realized in individual schools, charter school reform provides an opportunity to analyze the complex links between state policies, local school cultures, and the agency of educators. The concepts of organizational structure and school culture provided an initial conceptual window through which we can view school life. Yet it was also important to expand the analysis beyond the boundaries of the school to understand the different contextual factors that shaped the schools as the people working within them attempted to enact the broad principles outlined in their school charters. My goal was to document and analyze the dynamism in schools and dynamism in policy contexts and how they influence each other.

I began by analyzing the relationship between organizational structure and school culture at the three school sites. While each school's charter provided a blueprint for the educational and organizational principles that were intended to animate school life, these had to be taken up by actors in each school and actively maintained. For example, at Hilltop Charter School, developing and sustaining a school culture based on a developmental education program and shared decision-making was dependent on maintaining an experienced teaching staff at the site and socializing teachers into the school's model of governance. When long-term staff members left the school, they were often replaced by new teachers who found it challenging to implement this relatively undefined educational model. Moreover, the institutional support for developmental education at the district and state level declined. Likewise, shared decision-making can be time-consuming and challenges taken-for-granted cultural beliefs about hierarchical authority within schools. Yet despite these constraints, these concepts were woven into the normative life of Hilltop Charter School, due in no small part to the activism of both original and newer staff members who expended enormous amounts of energy keeping these ideals alive.

Taken together, the three case study chapters suggest that understanding the distinctive organizational structures and school cultures enacted at each school required tracing the components of each to features of the policy environment at the time of the school's founding. Compared to conventional public schools, charter schools may be more susceptible to "imprinting" where they acquire features at their founding that are rooted in the extant policy context. This process of imprinting is in part a consequence of the nature of charter school reform. Charter schools are a conceptually empty reform waiting to be filled with cultural content. While the organizational form of a charter school is enabled by state-level policy action (a charter school law), local actors have to take the opportunity to envision a charter school (write the charter), get their charter approved by a sponsor (e.g., a school district), and then enact the vision outlined in that charter. The policy context is an important source of cultural resources as this process unfolds. During different "waves" of education reform, different organizational models were legitimized that were woven into the fabric of these schools. More specifically, we see the emphasis on teacher empowerment in the second wave of restructuring reform in Hilltop Charter School, and the reframing of decentralization around the market model characteristic of the third wave of restructuring reform in Inspiration School.

The degree of fit between the policy context and the type of education program enacted at a school influences the school's stability and legitimacy over time. Schools based on what were at the time of their founding more "mainstream" educational models, here Hilltop Charter School and Inspiration School, were less vulnerable to external challenges—unlike Hearts and Hands Community School. Yet the policy context is also in flux, which can affect whether or not the schools can maintain the educational model outlined in their charters in the face of shifts in the policy context. Examples of this dynamism include the increased tension between the "Waldorf-inspired" and "district" educational models at Hearts and Hands Community School as the Geary Unified School District's reform gained momentum, and the impact of the increased emphasis on standardized testing on Hilltop Charter School. I expand on this latter point in more detail below.

The comparison of the three school's trajectories also suggests another significant contextual factor that provides an important source of legitimacy—the ties schools have to external organizations. Hilltop Charter School's founding was supported by important external organizations, in this case the school employees unions, which was significant because the unions were early opponents of charter school reform. The employees unions, and in particular the teachers union, was able to shape the form of "shared decision-making" that emerged at the school. In addition, the school was also participating in high-profile national and state reform efforts, which not only provided funds for professional development activities and other school programs, but also gave the school a reputation for being "cutting edge."

In contrast, while Hearts and Hands Community School had the active support of a member of the Board of Education, and ultimately a majority of the school board voted to approve the charter, district employees recommended turning the proposal down. The school employees union initially challenged the charter because their concerns were not addressed during the public hearing before it was approved. However, by the time Inspiration School's charter was being approved, the unions had unsuccessfully challenged Hearts and Hands Community School in the courts. Moreover, the national headquarters of the teachers union was supporting efforts by its local branches to open union-sponsored charter schools, including a school in the Geary Unified School District. Inspiration School also benefited from the symbolic support and ongoing ties to prominent local business and community leaders.

The analysis in chapter 5 highlights how the respective theories of teaching and learning at Hilltop Charter School and Inspiration school can be traced to features of the policy environment at the time of each school's founding. While the policy environment provided cultural and organizational resources that facilitated the founding of each school, over time state policies related to accountability and standardized testing changed considerably. These had the greatest impact on Hilltop Charter School, the more established of the two schools. As the comparison between Hilltop Charter School and Inspiration School suggested, there was relative stability in the cultural "tool kits" enacted at these schools (Swidler, 1986). Each of these tool kits reflected different conceptions of teaching and learning that were rooted in the dominant policy trends at the time of each school's founding. When Hilltop Charter School was no longer isomorphic with the policy context, it became increasingly difficult for the school to maintain its early vision.

Given this dynamism, it is not surprising that a pendulum has been a popular metaphor to describe education reform. In the state policy context, California's charter school legislation has evolved over time, the curriculum standards were revised, and state programs and policies around testing and accountability were transformed. In the district policy context, a change in administration resulted in shift in the foci of district policies.

Whereas the reforms under Superintendent Carl Nelson and his successor Ellen Temple were largely concentrated on issues of school organization (i.e., implementing restructuring and shared decision-making), the reforms implemented by John Tower's administration were focused more squarely on instruction and specific technologies of teaching. While charter schools are organized to implement the education programs described in their charters, as schools also authorized locally by the Geary Unified School District, these schools were not immune from pressure to implement the district's reforms to some degree or other. Likewise, the school district was not unambiguously friend or foe. At times it granted charter schools relatively more autonomy and at other times restricted it—whether perception or practice, district control nonetheless shaped school life.

Despite the differences across the schools, there was also evidence of a more institutionalized way of speaking about charter school reform that mapped onto charter school policy talk. For example, participants from all three schools tended to describe conventional public schools as highly bureaucratic and saw working in a charter school as offering them freedom in various ways. However, the three schools' experiences raise questions about the extent to which charter schools are able to transcend bureaucracy in practice. The high level of corporate centralization at Inspiration School was not consistent with charter school policy talk that argues for deregulation. Much like a school district, Educational Enterprise Corporation had a great deal of control over school policies. Yet as its sponsor the Geary Unified School District also had authority over Inspiration School. The two schools that were more decentralized, Hilltop Charter School and Hearts and Hands Community School, struggled to find a good balance of power among the stakeholders within the site. While granting more control of decision-making to school sites can indeed foster democratic participation within schools, it can also raise thorny procedural questions as schools attempt to reach what can be an elusive balance between broad participation and timely action.

Likewise, while participants in charter school reform placed a high premium on being "different," that difference often consisted of incorporating existing educational or organizational models into a school's organizational design. "Difference" was more relational rather than absolute; participants understood charter school difference by way of contrast—primarily with other schools in the district. In the portraits of these schools we see schools that largely have not altered—either by default or by design—familiar and resilient cultural models of schooling (Weick, 1976; Tyack and Cuban, 1995). As the trajectory of Hilltop Charter School suggests, even more ambitious efforts at education reform can be diluted as a result of internal instability, staff turnover, and pressures related to accountability and standardized testing.

While participants in charter school reform tended to perceive their schools as different, if we compare charter schools and conventional public schools in charter states, we find that the differences between them were less stark than charter school policy talk would suggest. While many policymakers have argued that charter schools will be a vehicle for increasing accountability in public education, in general charter schools tended to be less externally accountable than conventional public schools. Moreover, these findings were consistent across a range of measures of accountability. However, there is some evidence to suggest that charter schools had greater internal accountability, that is, a collective sense of their schools' own standards for teaching and learning. In general, charter schools also tended to have greater power and authority and shared commitment than conventional public schools which may be because charter schools tend to be smaller.

Three main policy implications can be drawn from the analyses presented here. First, the apparent coherence of policy talk masks a considerable amount of diversity in implementation. Second, education reform is best understood as a process rather than a single event. Finally, a single policy is rarely implemented on its own. Policy analysts should strive to understand how multiple policies work in tandem. I explain each of these points in greater detail below.

Much like restructuring reform, charter school reform is not a monolithic policy but a set of policies that vary from state to state. This is not a particularly surprising observation, given that charter school reform is aimed at decentralizing public schools. However, it could be argued that this lack of coherence is a more general characteristic of education policy in the United States. For example, although NCLB greatly expanded the federal government's role in education, its accountability provisions did not impose a uniform set of accountability provisions on all states, rather they required states to create systems of accountability and submit them to the federal government for approval (Sunderman, Kim, and Orfield, 2005). Many states kept their existing accountability systems in place and layered the NCLB requirements on top of their own accountability requirements.

Education reform is not an event but a process. For example, at Hilltop Charter School, converting to charter school status was one component of a larger constellation of reforms that the school participated in when it was founded. Hilltop Charter School's history also highlights how education reform must be maintained over time. Part of this school's story is the staff's effort to maintain deeply held tenets of school life in the face of policy shifts in elementary education and standardized testing, cultural norms about school leadership, staff turnover, and, intersecting with all of these, internal struggles within the school. In particular, we can see the strong value on "shared decision-making" at Hilltop Charter School as an aspect of context that has been reworked over time. While the vision outlined in Hilltop's original charter remains largely intact, over time all of these factors have tended to push the school back toward a more conventional model of schooling. Likewise, at Inspiration School, simply being a charter school was not a magic bullet that allowed the staff to come together around a shared mission or vision. Moreover, the mission of Educational Enterprise Corporation, to reorganize public schools around a competitive business model, had little traction among the teaching staff.

Schools are subject to a wide array of policy pressures from the federal government, state, and their school districts. How these policy pressures unfold at individual charter schools has a lot to do with how they conflict or complement the school cultures that develop within them. For example, at Hilltop Charter School, the instructional practices associated with the Geary Unified School District's systemic reform were compatible with the school's instructional model, but the top-down implementation of the Balanced Literacy approach was not a good fit with shared decision-making, a key tenet of its school culture. At Hearts and Hands Community School, the district's reform was in tension with the school's Waldorf inspired instructional model and exacerbated a long-simmering conflict at the school. Thus, rather than analyze how a single education policy is implemented, policy analyses should instead consider how multiple policies articulate together to shape practices within schools. The contexts that these schools are embedded in are considerably more complex than the relatively unproblematic vision of deregulation that is often a feature of charter school policy talk.

While charter schools are a relatively small part of the public school sector, they have generated enormous interest among policymakers and researchers alike. Yet the overall impact of charter schools on public education is harder to gauge. As with conventional public schools, there are highly successful charter schools and there are struggling charter schools. What these analyses suggest is that charter schools are best understood in their local contexts—in states, in districts, and perhaps even in neighborhoods. This is not to assert that looking broadly at charter schools as a group is not useful—indeed I provide that type of analysis many times in this book. Rather, the macro-level view of national and state-level analyses of charter school reform is complemented and enriched by finer-grained analyses of implementation within schools and districts that attempts to understand how these schools fit into and are shaped by the multiple and intersecting policy contexts in which they operate.

Notes

Introduction: Charter Schools in the Reform Imagination

1. The eligibility requirements for these programs vary considerably. Most publicly funded voucher programs are restricted to low-income students, students with disabilities, or students who attended schools identified as failing.
2. *A Nation at Risk* was the most influential of a series of reports on the state of American education that was released during that time period. The Twentieth Century Fund, the Education Commission of the States, and prominent education researchers such as John Goodlad and Theodore Sizer also weighed in with their own analyses. Berliner and Biddle (1995), and more recently Glass (2008), have argued that the crisis in American education was, in Glass's words, a "political invention" (54).
3. The other two reforms that Coleman and his colleagues (1997) saw as having the potential to create output-driven schools were: (1) national standards; and (2) the use of private contractors to manage public schools.
4. The school charters ranged from elaborate statements of educational philosophies to thin documents. With many of the latter, it was difficult to discern how the proposed school would differ from any other public school. For example, a few of the earliest approved charters were conversion schools with charters that amounted to little more than brief statements that the schools wanted more flexibility to make curricular and funding decisions. According to one charter school advocate, a revision to California's charter school legislation that took effect in 1999 required charter school organizers to provide "reasonably comprehensive" descriptions of their schools' instructional program and operations because so many early charters were relatively undeveloped (Premack, 1998, 41).
5. In order to mask the identity of the school, I do not identify the specific racial group that was the majority of the school's population. The label "disadvantaged," while imprecise, denotes that this particular minority group has a long history of being underserved by public education.
6. There are two other rough indicators of Inspiration School's relative advantage. First, the school did not offer transportation to its students, so parents had to drive their children to the school. Second, according to the information collected by the school as part of the state assessment program, parental education was relatively high. In 1999, 97 percent of the parents of students tested in grades two and higher responded, and of these only 2 percent had less than a

high school diploma. The corresponding figures for Hilltop Charter School and Hearts and Hands Community School are 29 percent (88 percent response rate) and 18 percent (97 percent response rate).

1 Mapping the Terrain of Charter School Reform

1. Author's calculations using Common Core of Data (CCD).
2. In 1999–2000, 74 percent of charter schools were start-up charter schools. In 2003–2004, 80 percent of charter schools were start-up charter schools (Author's calculations using the SASS).
3. The most well-known EMO associated with charter school reform is the Edison Project. Other EMOs involved in operating charter schools include White Hat Management, Mosaica Schools, and the Leona Group.
4. Statements of legislative intent change over time. The analysis presented here is based on the statements of legislative intent in each state's charter school legislation as of September 2006.
5. After the Detroit City School District, the next largest school district in Michigan is Utica Community Schools, a suburban district within metropolitan Detroit, which had just under 30,000 students enrolled in 2005–2006.
6. A charter school can also be renewed if its sponsor can document that its students would perform at least as well as they would in the public schools they would attend if they did not attend the charter school. The evidence used by the sponsor to make the case that the charter school be renewed must include student achievement data from the state-mandated assessments.
7. The characteristics used to construct the SSI include: pupil mobility, racial demographics, socioeconomic status (measured by percentage of students eligible for reduced or free lunch), teachers' credentials (percentage fully credentialed or emergency credentialed), the percentage of English learners at the school, the average class size by grade level, and the type of school calendar (traditional versus year-round multitrack), grade span, and the percentages of: students in the Gifted and Talented Program, students with disabilities, reclassified fluent-English proficient students, special education students, and students in full-day reduced-size classes.
8. While the SASS data are six years older than the CCD demographic data presented above, the demographic breakdowns for the weighted samples of conventional public schools and charter schools in the analyses that follow are roughly similar to the figures presented in tables 1.3 through 1.5, which suggests that the data are roughly comparable. Standard errors for all calculations using the weighted samples from the SASS are available from the author on request.
9. The locale variable in the CCD follows the Census classification of communities. The CCD locale variable was an eight-category variable, which I recoded as follows. Central city denoted schools located in the central city of a Consolidated Metropolitan Statistical Area (CMSA). Urban fringe indicated that the school was located in an urban area within a CMSA with a central city but outside the central city. Town contains all schools located in nonmetropolitan urban areas with populations greater than 2,500 people. Finally, Rural indicates that the school was located in a rural area (NCES, 2008).

10. Similarly, 35,076 (64.6 percent) of the conventional public schools in table 1.6 served at least one grade between kindergarten and fifth grade. Of these, only 3.3 percent served at least one grade between grades nine and twelve. In contrast, 643 (63.7 percent) of the charter schools served at least one of the grades between kindergarten and fifth grade; 19.3 percent of these schools served at least one grade between grades nine and twelve.

2   State Level Policy Action

1. This narrative, while convenient, oversimplifies a complex story. *A Nation at Risk* both reflected and provided impetus for education reforms that were underway at the state and local levels (see Toch, 1991) and was also the most prominent of a series of reports on the state of American education that was released during that period. The general consensus that emerged from these reports was that the American educational system was in deep crisis.
2. Most analysts agree on this rough timeline of reform efforts as well as the use of the metaphor of successive "waves" of reform efforts. Similarly, most also make a conceptual distinction between the two types of restructuring described here (see, for example, Raywid, 1992), Whether or not commentators describe them as separate waves of reform seems to depend largely on when they are writing. For example, in an early assessment of restructuring, Murphy (1992) describes market-driven choice as a "less central but persistent theme" within the restructuring movement that at the time he was writing was gaining increasing attention, whereas teacher empowerment tended to dominate earlier efforts at restructuring (6, 9). In many ways, the two forms of restructuring have come together under the banner of the charter school movement.
3. NCLB required states to develop accountability systems to assess if schools and districts are making adequate yearly progress (AYP) toward academic achievement; schools that do not make AYP for two years in a row can be targeted for school improvement. Ultimately, if a school fails to make AYP for more than three subsequent years, it can be restructured by its local school district. The local school district could: (1) reconstitute the school as a charter school; (2) replace all or most of the school's staff; (3) contract with a private management firm to manage the school; (4) have the state take over school operations (NCLB, 2002).
4. The California Business Roundtable's efforts were paralleled by similar activities by national business organizations such as the Business Roundtable, the National Alliance of Business, and the Center for Economic Development.
5. Paul Berman, the head of the research team that produced the report, described the impact of the Roundtable on education reform:

> As the new kid on the block, the Roundtable had entered California's contentious political battleground with a nonpartisan approach that enabled it to play a broker's role. The timing was right for change and the political actors were in place. But a powerful yet responsible weight was needed to tip the balance. By committing prestige and resources and developing a clear agenda that was above the partisan skirmishing, the Roundtable may have provided the missing element that had been so conspicuously

absent in past stalemated efforts to achieve education reform in California. (Berman and Clugston, 1988, 130)

6. The latter were drawn from an initial pool of 822 proposals that were narrowed down to 200 finalists. Hilltop Charter School was a grantee in a highly competitive funding process (Chang, Salazar, Dowell, Leong, Perez, McClain, Olsen, and Raffel, 1994).

7. Charter schools are required to meet state standards and administer state assessments. As I detail in chapter 5, both state standards and the state testing program have undergone considerable revision since California's charter school legislation was passed in 1992.

8. There was also considerable, although not uniform, opposition to the initiative within the charter school community. The state charter school organization, the California Network of Educational Charters (CANEC), refused to take a position on the initiative until it was officially qualified for the November 1998 ballot. Ultimately, CANEC also played an important role in shaping the final bill that was passed by the legislature.

9. While KCMSD was the original plaintiff that filed the lawsuit, the presiding judge named the district as a defendant, and a private civil rights lawyer was engaged on behalf of the plaintiff schoolchildren (Morantz, 1996). KCMSD worked with the plaintiffs as "friendly adversaries" to develop their legal strategies and arguments throughout the trial and appeals process (*Jenkins v. State of Missouri*, 593 F. Supp. 1485).

10. In *Milliken*, the Supreme Court struck down an interdistrict desegregation plan in Detroit because the plaintiffs did not prove that the policies and actions of the suburban districts contributed to segregation in the Detroit School District (*Milliken v. Bradley*, 48 U.S. 717).

3 School Level Implementation: Charter School Reform "On the Ground"

1. Selznick's structural-functionalist theory of organizations stresses rational action. Neo-institutional theorists have since questioned the view that organizational behavior is rational (see, for example, Meyer, 1977).

2. I use the terms Principal and Director at different times to describe the school leader because during my tenure at Hilltop Charter School, Mrs. Carmichael, the principal, resigned. When her successor Mr. Arden was hired, the title of the position was changed from Principal to Director.

3. A sheltered classroom is a classroom that is comprised of English language learners (ELLs) who receive instruction exclusively in English; teachers use instructional strategies such as visual cues, linguistic modifications such as repetition, and cooperative learning techniques to help teach ELLs subject-specific concepts (Freeman and Freeman, 1988).

4. The weighted N for each group was 24,791 conventional public schools and 420 charter schools.

5. There was some variation in this structure over the years. For example, one year the committee structure was eliminated to allow teachers to focus their work within their grade clusters, only to be reinstituted the following year

because the staff needed the committees to facilitate work across grade clusters on school-wide issues.

6. The school's first charter was approved by the district in the summer of 1993 and renewed in the fall of 1998. In discussing the school's developmental model, I have drawn from the sections of the renewed charter that was largely consistent with the original charter. The sections of the charter dealing with school governance had been revised substantially. I discuss some of these changes in more detail in chapter 4.

7. Other aspects of the school's original structure had also changed, but less radically. For example, classrooms were originally organized as three-year multiage classrooms. One teacher characterized the decision to covert to two-year multigrade classrooms as positive because teaching classes with a three-year grade span was too much of a stretch for teachers. Similarly, teachers met with their families every day.

8. Author's calculations using the 1999–2000 SASS.

9. Based on my informal observations, less formal teaming seemed to occur more regularly between teachers with English and sheltered classrooms, which is likely attributable to the high levels of primary language support that bilingual students needed, which the non-bilingual teachers were generally unable to provide (although many knew and used rudimentary Spanish).

10. While the "grey binder" was not new to the school, it was updated in the fall of 1999. One of the SSC co-chairs, a teacher who was later promoted to Assistant Director, systematized and revised all of the school procedures and ensured that all staff members had copies.

11. Private Waldorf schools not bound by laws regarding the separation of church and state would focus on the Book of Genesis and have an explicit religious component (Edmunds, 1975).

12. By the end of the school year, the kindergarten students were making smaller versions of main lesson books on the alphabet.

13. See also the description of the Waldorf Curriculum on the Association of Waldorf Schools in North American web site at www.awsna.org.

14. Participation in the program varied widely across state contexts. At the time of the fieldwork, twenty-six states had between one and ten public and private schools implementing the curriculum. Another nine states had between ten and twenty schools, three states had between twenty and forty schools, and eight states had more than forty schools in the process of implementation. According to the organization's materials, schools were considered participants in this curriculum model if they "indicate a commitment" to start implementing the model. Schools could be certified in the Grand Heritage model if they taught at least 80 percent of the program's curriculum sequences and completed a certification process. A much smaller number of schools were certified.

15. As Larry Cuban (2000) pointed out, these are highly charged political terms that often obscure the considerable variation within the respective camps, yet are also resilient features of the policy talk around education reform.

16. Though beyond the scope of the discussion here, it is worth noting that, like Cuban, Delpit is also critical of the sharp dichotomy between "traditional" and "progressive" education (which she indexes in her discussion of the debate between skills and process).

17. After California's school legislation was passed, a community group made an unsuccessful attempt to convert three low-performing and predominantly minority schools into charter schools to be run by a for-profit educational management organization. This effort was unsuccessful because the group did not have sufficient support among the schools' teaching staff. Charter school law required charter school conversions to be approved by 50 percent of the schools' faculty.

18. In early 2000, Educational Enterprise Corporation targeted six county school boards in Florida in an effort to open additional charter schools, although none of those efforts were successful.

19. The Little Hoover Commission is an independent state oversight agency charged with examining the operation of state government with the goal of improving its efficiency, economy, and service.

20. In 2002, Inspiration School discontinued its relationship with Educational Enterprise Corporation. The report to the Geary Unified School District's governing board that was prepared by the district's administrative staff noted that Inspiration School was in violation of its charter because there was little evidence that regular governance meetings were held in accordance with California's public meetings law. The Geary Unified School District also conducted an outside audit and found serious lapses in the financial management provided by Educational Enterprise Corporation to Inspiration School and the three other schools in the district that it managed. Inspiration School submitted a revised charter that the Geary Unified School District approved conditionally; the school had to meet a set of requirements related to fiscal and managerial accountability.

21. One school (not Inspiration School) received a grant of approximately $350,000 during the same year.

22. This figure was drawn from Inspiration School's state-mandated school accountability report card.

23. Tuckman's ([1968]2001) model of group development has since been adapted to explain the stages of organizational development.

4 How Policy Contexts Shape Implementation

1. This contract language was the outcome of a teachers' strike in 1996. Teachers had been working under an expired contract for over six months and had not received cost-of-living raises for six years. Teachers also sought more authority for governance teams at the school site.

2. The New American Schools Development Corporation (NASDC) was a high profile national effort at restructuring formed as part of President George H. W. Bush's America 2000 education plan. America 2000 provided seed money for NASDC, a privately funded nonprofit that funded the creation of designs for "break the mold" schools (Richter, 1991). By July of 1992, eleven design teams were chosen to participate in the initiative. The Geary Unified School District was a district participant on one of the teams: The National Alliance for Restructuring Education. Five Geary schools, including Hilltop Charter School, were chosen to participate in the program.

3. Interestingly, Jensen's earliest vision for the school included a number of creative policies and practices: class sizes as small as ten students; a school

day that started in the early afternoon and ended in the evening to facilitate parental involvement; utilizing students as maintenance workers; teaching parents and children together; and providing health, nutrition, and psychological counseling services to students. That the ultimate form of the school largely conformed to the conventional model of schooling suggests the power of what Tyack and Cuban (1995) have described as the "grammar of schooling" (9).

4. The composition of this group reflected local school politics when Hilltop Charter School was founded. In 1992, prominent local business leaders began to promote education reform. One strategy included supporting the development of charter schools by providing technical assistance. By 1996, this group was a key player in local school politics, endorsing a slate of candidates for the school board and actively promoting its own reform agenda.

5. Shared decision-making was the language used by the union to describe site-based management. According to district documents, as shared decision-making evolved as a formal policy within the district, the employees' unions had a strong influence in shaping the district guidelines on this policy.

6. In subsequent revisions of the charter, this strong statement was toned down.

7. Two other charter schools were in the middle of crises during this period. Hearts and Hands Community School's internal struggle is detailed in this chapter. Another conventional public school that converted to charter school status was also embroiled in internal disputes; the Geary Unified School District revoked its charter in the fall of 1996.

8. Staff members credited Mrs. Carmichael with making important and much needed changes at the school. They most frequently highlighted her efforts to reorganize the school's budget and financial systems.

9. While the school had other sources of funding that allowed it to participate in other reform efforts, the school's charter identified these two reforms, and in particular the 1274 grant, as the most significant.

10. This school remained an important model for Hearts and Hands Community School. Teachers visited the Milwaukee school annually. One teacher who was a grassroots leader described the Milwaukee public Waldorf school as the school that Hearts and Hands Community School needed to be.

11. The other two charter schools that were formed in 1994 were conversion charter schools. Until Inspiration School was approved in 1997, most of the charter schools that were approved by the Geary Unified School District were conversion schools. An additional "start-up" charter school opened in September of 1996. However, the Geary Unified School District revoked its charter within a week because of safety code violations at the school's rented site; this school became a satellite school of a charter school in a neighboring district until Geary approved its own charter.

12. For a good overview of some of the philosophical underpinnings of the Waldorf movement and the controversies surrounding public Waldorf schools, see Ruenzel (2001).

13. In the years that followed, the teacher's union opened its own charter school in the district. This school (which is now defunct) also served as an overflow school housed in a district building. Interestingly, these were issues of contention in the union's lawsuit against Hearts and Hands Community

School—the union argued that since the school was housed in a district-owned building rent-free, the district was in effect subsidizing the school.

14. As I noted in chapter 2, in the years immediately following these lawsuits, charter school law has undergone significant changes, which made some of these issues moot. Specifically, charter school teachers in California are required to be credentialed and charter schools had to declare whether or not they were independent from their district for the purposes of collective bargaining.

15. While Hilltop Charter School's teachers retained all the rights granted to district employees under the union's collective bargaining agreement, the school did not have to hire teachers using the union's post and bid procedure, which was based on seniority.

16. While the case was dismissed, PLANS appealed the verdict in a higher court (Ruenzel, 2001).

17. In other instances, the curriculum is described as a blend between California State curriculum frameworks and a Waldorf educational model. At Hilltop Charter School, district and state standards also seemed to be used interchangeably, in part because the Geary Unified School District had a separate set of standards it adopted in 1998. In January 2001, the district reverted to the California state frameworks.

18. While the district's reform emphasized teaching children to read quickly and early, the school's charter advocated a slower approach: "Each grade has its own course of study that is responsive to the child's stage of physical, emotional, and cognitive development. Because of this, some areas of academic subjects traditionally taught in kindergarten and first grade are introduced more gently and gradually. Specifically, letter and sound recognition is introduced in first grade, while reading is introduced in the first grade and continued in the second grade" (Hearts and Hands Community School, 1993, 8).

19. As a condition for their charter renewals in 1998, both Hilltop Charter School and Hearts and Hands Community School were required to follow the district's accountability plan, which required them to administer all the assessments mandated by the district.

20. There was also some disagreement among the parties about what constituted a clearly defined program and what audience the program document should address. The charter and a teacher's guide contained a skeletal outline of the school's education program in the charter. One teacher argued that these documents would allow teachers to get started and conduct their own research on how to implement the model. Another teacher characterized this assumption as problematic and questioned how people could be effective mentors if they looked down upon people with less Waldorf training. The Curriculum Committee produced a draft of a document intended mainly for teachers that linked the school's education program to state and local standards and highlighted the relationship between the Waldorf-inspired components of the program and the work of child-development theorists such as Piaget. However, some staff members wanted a document that explained the education program more clearly to parents.

21. For example, a school document produced the previous summer listed a series of "collective concerns" that were the outcome of a staff meeting meant to facilitate positive organizational growth and change. One of these concerns was that the "Waldorf component was not clear, not required (how it ties in), not enforced."

22. Information obtained from the Corporations Directory at the Office of the Secretary of State.

23. One of the other schools managed by Educational Enterprise Corporation was a former private school run by a faith-based organization that was reorganized as a charter school. Originally formed under the auspices of Inspiration School's charter, its own charter was approved in 1999. In 1995, a representative of the school testified at a Congressional hearing on education reform in support of school vouchers as a vehicle for a comprehensive reform effort that encompassed the home, religious institution, and educational institutions. He also noted that "the education monopoly, like all monopolies, tends to take its clients for granted and loses sight of its responsibility to those which it serves. Healthy competition is good for any business." Thus while his testimony focused largely on the ways that public schools have underserved minority youth, he also invoked the policy talk of market-driven choice.

24. It could be argued that this is a form of segregation by choice that is analogous to the move into private schools by white parents in the South as a response to desegregation. However, the contexts in which these two sets of choices were made are radically different. Whereas white parents pulled their children out of public schools to resist the change in power dynamics that desegregated schools represented, in contrast, many of the local actors involved with this charter school saw it as a response to how minority students have been underserved by public schools. The only way that we can equate these choices is if we strip them from the wider political and historical contexts that give them meaning (Gotanda, 1991). Moreover, highly segregated urban public schools are themselves the outcome of public policy choices. As Lipsitz (1998) demonstrates, long-standing patterns of residential segregation and "white flight" from public schools in central cities were facilitated by both governmental policies and informal practices (see also Katznelson, 2005; and Kimble, 2007). Moreover, in some instances, white parents have been able to use charter school reform to create schools that have become, in essence, exclusive enclaves for white middle class families (Stambach and Becker, 2006).

25. For a more recent example of this argument, see Stossell (2006).

26. These competing pressures were highly visible at a meeting of a local business group that sponsored an organization that offered technical and legal support for charter schools. Once a year, members of the charter school group were invited to the meeting of the business group. One of these meetings occurred a week before the school board passed the *Plan for Student Success*. The superintendent presented an update on the plan, which the business group unanimously endorsed.

27. One of these was the loss of instructional aides. The *Plan for Student Learning* resulted in a reduction in instructional aide positions and a redirection of those personnel dollars toward professional development for teachers.

5 Policy Dynamics—Schools and Accountability Policies

1. In practice, few school charters have been revoked on the basis of student performance. In California, charter schools are required to define a set of outcomes that their students will meet and how these outcomes will be measured. However, assessing schools on outcomes that are often ambiguous and difficult to measure has proven more difficult in practice (Wells et al., 2002). Moreover, as I documented in my discussion of the state policy context, California's statewide testing program began in 1998. Thus, even if we assume that standardized tests are an appropriate measure of student performance in charter schools, for the first five years of charter school reform in California there was no way to assess how charter schools performed relative to other schools.

2. CAP was begun in the mid-1980s and tested students in grades three, six, eight, and twelve; the last administration occurred in 1991 when the California Department of Education was able to find the funds to test eighth graders.

3. Initially the testing program was challenged by religious conservatives. Subsequently, the California Teachers Association and the California School Boards Association also joined these efforts (Gunnison and Lucas, 1994).

4. Author's calculations using California Department of Education data.

5. A small subculture at the school advocated a more performance-oriented approach to standards-based teaching. If we understand teachers' conceptions of teaching as falling on a continuum between developmental/content standards/performance standards, most teachers would be somewhere in the middle and advocate for the use of developmental teaching methods to teach content standards. Other teachers supported performance standards.

6. This topic was the subject of an ongoing debate that started largely in the undercurrents of school life (during lunch, between meetings). With a shift in school leadership, the debate moved to more public forums and the staff began a more sustained conversation about what "developmental learning" meant and how it should look at the school.

7. See also Downey, von Hippel, and Hughes' (2008) distinction between student achievement (standardized test scores at one point in time), learning (the amount that students learn in an academic year), and impact (the difference between students' in-school learning and the amount they would have learned if they had not attended school). Downey, von Hippel, and Hughes' analysis suggests that while achievement is highly correlated with school socioeconomic characteristics, learning and impact are not.

8. One teacher referenced one-way accountability when she commented, "you want my test scores to be great, do you mind giving me a book in order to have these kids read?"

9. In 1998–1999, 28 percent of the Geary Unified School District's students were English-language learners.

6 The Relationship Between Policy Talk and Implementation

1. Hess (2001) proposes a similar framework. Hess distinguishes between regulatory accountability—which combines elements of bureaucratic accountability and performance accountability as described by Garn and Cobb (2001)—and

market accountability. See also Kirst (1990), which draws on and elaborates a framework proposed by Levin (1974).

2. The question did not ask principals to specify whether or not the school improvement plan was required by the state or district. As a result, these responses cannot be reliably classified as internal or external accountability. However, they do provide another source of information about how schools assess their progress, and the results can be compared to that of other questions.

3. Standard errors available from the author on request.

4. Interestingly, on most questions, the standard deviations for the charter school principals' responses tended to be higher than those of the conventional public school principals which suggests that there was greater variability in the responses of charter school principals. The exceptions to this pattern were the standard deviations for the questions asking the principals to assess their own and their teachers' influence on performance standards, which is consistent with the overall pattern of greater internal accountability in charter schools.

5. Indeed, it could be argued that the large sample sizes are in part responsible for the statistical significance of the findings.

REFERENCES

"40% of Public School Pupils in U.S. Are in Areas Where Law Requires Segregation." (May 18, 1954). *New York Times*, 21.

Abramson, L. (October 2, 2006). "Remaking the New Orleans School System." *NPR*.

Amsler, M. (1992). Charter Schools, *Policy Briefs*. San Francisco, CA: Far West Laboratory for Educational Research and Development.

Anyon, J. (1997). *Ghetto Schooling*. New York: Teachers College Press.

Arizona Department of Education. (1995). *Arizona Charter Schools: Charter Schools Handbook*. Phoenix, AZ: Author.

———. (2002). *Accountability in Arizona's Charter Schools*. Phoenix: Author.

———. (2003). Arizona Charter Schools Questions and Answers. Phoenix: Author.

Arum, R. (2000). "Schools and Communities: Ecological and Institutional Dimensions." *Annual Review of Sociology*, 26(1), 395–418.

Asimov, N. (May 12, 1992). "Bold Blueprint for Teaching in Primary Schools." *Los Angeles Times*, A1.

———. (August 31, 1994). "Controversial Test OKd by Assembly." *San Francisco Chronicle*, A15.

Baker, P. C. and Green, B. D. (2006). "Urban Legends, Desegregation and School Finance: Did Kansas City Really Prove That Money Doesn't Matter?" *Michigan Journal of Race and Law*, 12(1), 57–106.

Barnes, H. (n.d.). Waldorf Education . . . an Introduction. Association of Waldorf Schools of North America. Retrieved May 30, 2000, http://awsna.org/waldorf/hb_intro.htm.

Beales, J. R. and Wahl, M. (1995). "Private Vouchers in San Antonio." In T. M. Moe (Ed.), *Private vouchers* (41–73). Stanford, CA: Hoover Institution Press.

Berliner, D. and Biddle, B. (1995). *The Manufactured Crisis: Myths, Fraud and the Attack on American Public Schools*. Reading, MA: Addison Wesley.

Berman, P. and Clugston, R. (1988). "A Tale of Two States: The Business Community and Education Reform in California and Minnesota." In M. Levine and R. Trachtman (Eds.), *American Business and the Public School: Case Studies of Corporate Involvement in Public Education* (121–149). New York and London: Teachers College Press.

Berman Weiler Associates. (1988). *Restructuring California Education*. San Francisco: Author.

Bidwell, C. (1965). "The School as a Formal Organization. In J. G. March" (Ed.), *Handbook of Organizations* (972–1022). Chicago: Rand McNally College Publishing Company.

Bowles, S. and Gintis, H. (1976). *Schooling in Capitalist America*. New York: Basic Books.

Bulkley, K. (October 1, 2001). "Educational Performance and Charter School Authorizers: The Accountability Bind." *Education Policy Analysis Archives*, 9(37).

Bulkley, K. and Fisler, J. (2002). *A Review of the Research on Charter Schools* (CPRE Web Paper Series WP-01): Consortium for Policy Research in Education.

Bush, G. W. (2001). *No Child Left Behind*. Washington, DC: Government Printing Office.

Byers, P., Dillard, C., Easton, F., Henry, M., McDermott, R., Oberman, I., and Uhrmacher, B. (1996). *Waldorf Education in an Inner City Public School: The Urban Waldorf School of Milwaukee*. Spring Valley, NY: Parker Courtney Press.

Calif. Educ. Code §§ 47600–47664 (2006).

California Department of Education. (1997). "Although No Standardized Test Meets High Standards, Eastin Makes Reluctant Recommendation to State Board" (Press Release, October 31). Sacramento: Author.

———. (1999). *Request for Applications: Public Charter Schools Grant Program*. Sacramento: Author.

———. (2000). *1999 Base Year Academic Performance Index (API)*. Sacramento: Author.

California State Board of Education. (1993). *Charter School Questions Update*. Sacramento: California Department of Education.

Chubb, J. E. and Moe, T. M. (1990). *Politics, Markets and America's Schools*. Washington, DC: Brookings Institution.

Ciotti, P. (1998). *Money and School Performance: Lessons from the Kansas City Desegregation Experiment*. Washington, DC: Cato Institute.

Clouder, C. and Rawson, M. (1998). *Waldorf Education*. Hudson, NY: Anthroposophic Press.

Coburn, C. E. (2001). "Collective Sensemaking about Reading: How Teachers Mediate Reading Policy in Their Professional Communities." *Educational Evaluation and Policy Analysis*, 23(2), 145–170.

Cohen, M. D., March, J. G., and Olsen, J. P. (1972). "A Garbage Can Model of Organizational Choice." *Administrative Science Quarterly*, 17(1), 1–25.

Coleman, J. S., Schneider, B., Plank, S., Schiller, K. S., Shouse, R., and Wang, H. (1997). *Redesigning American Education*. Boulder, CO: Westview Press.

Colo Rev. Stat. §22–30. 5.101 (2006).

Colvin, R. L. (April 5, 1995a). "State Test Finds Students Lagging." *Los Angeles Times*, A1.

———. (September 13, 1995b). "State Report Urges Return to Basics in Teaching Reading." *Los Angeles Times*, A1.

———. (November 10, 1996). "Appointments Seen as Blow to Math Reforms." *Los Angeles Times*, A3.

———. (May 19, 1997a). "Third Time May Be the Charm for State Tests." *Los Angeles Times*, A3.

———. (November 1, 1997b). "Eastin Reluctantly Picks Statewide Test Publisher." *Los Angeles Times*, A21.

————. (November 15, 1997c). "Publisher Chosen for State Exams." *Los Angeles Times*, A21.

Connor, K. and Melendez, M. (1994). *Education Reform Briefing Book*. Sacramento, CA: Senate Publications.

Cook, E. L. (1993, January 12). Despite Applause, Some See Lack of Concern in Symington's Plans. *Arizona Daily Star*.

Cookson, P. W. (1994). *School Choice: The Struggle for the Soul of American Education*. New Haven: Yale University Press.

————. (1999). "Privatization and Educational Equity: Can Markets Create a Just School System." *Current Issues in Comparative Education*, 1(2), 57–64.

Cronbach, L. (1995). "July 1994 Letter to William Dawson, Acting Superintendent of Public Instruction." In *A Valedictory: Reflections on 60 Years in Educational Testing* (18–19). Washington, DC: National Research Council.

Cuban, L. (1995). "The Hidden Variable: How Organizations Influence Teacher Responses to Secondary Science Curriculum Reform." *Theory Into Practice*, 34(1), 4–11.

————. (2000). "Why Is It So Hard to Get 'Good' Schools." In L. Cuban and D. Shipps (Eds.), *Reconstructing the Common Good in Education*. Stanford, CA: Stanford University Press.

Dale, A. and DeSchryver, D. (Eds.) (1997). *The Charter School Workbook: Your Roadmap to the Charter School Movement*. Washington, DC: The Center for Education Reform.

Datnow, A., Hubbard, L., and Mehan, H. (2002). *Extending Educational Reform: From One School to Many*. New York: Routledge.

Delpit, L. (1995). *Other People's Children*. New York: The New Press.

Developmental Primary Task Force. (1992). Developmental Primary Task Force Report. Geary City: Geary Unified School District.

Downey, D. B., von Hippel, P. T., and Hughes, M. (2008). "Are 'Failing' Schools Really Failing? Using Seasonal Comparison to Evaluate School Effectiveness." *Sociology of Education*, 81(3), 242–270.

Dvorak, J. A. (1992, November 7). Carnahan vows to hit tough issues head-on. *Kansas City Star*, A1.

Edmunds, L. F. (1975). *Rudolf Steiner's Gift to Education: The Waldorf Schools*. London: Rudolf Steiner Press.

Education at a Crossroads. Hearing before the Subcommittee on Oversight and Investigations of the Committee on Education and the Workforce, 105th Cong., 2nd Sess. (1998).

Educational Enterprise Corporation. (1997). Inspiration School Charter. Geary City: Author.

Eisner, E. W. (1992). "Educational Reform and the Ecology of Schooling." *Teachers College Press*, 93(4), 610–627.

Elementary Grades Task Force. (1992). *It's Elementary*. Sacramento: State Superintendent of Public Instruction.

————. (2000). *Elementary Makes the Grade!* Sacramento: California Department of Education.

Elmore, R. (1990). "Introduction: On Changing the Structure of Public Schools." In R. Elmore (ed.) *Restructuring Schools: The Next Generation of Educational Reform* (1-28). San Francisco: Jossey Bass

Elmore, R. F. (1991). Review of *Politics, Markets, and America's Schools* by John E. Chubb; Terry M. Moe. *Journal of Policy Analysis and Management*, 10(4), 687–695.

———. (2004). *School Reform from the Inside Out: Policy, Practice, and Performance.* Cambridge, MA: Harvard Educational Press.

Elmore, R. and Associates. (1990). *Restructuring Schools: The Next Generation of Educational Reform.* San Francisco: Jossey Bass.

Entwhistle, D. R., Alexander, K. L., and Olson, L. S. (1997). *Children, Schools and Inequality.* Boulder: Westview Press.

Feigenbaum, H. B. and Henig, J. R. (1997). "Privatization and Political Theory." *Journal of International Affairs*, 50(2), 338–355.

———. (1994). "The Political Underpinnings of Privatization: A Typology." *World Politics*, 46(January), 185–208.

Finn, C. E., Manno, B. V., and Vanourek, G. (2000). *Charter Schools in Action: Renewing Public Education.* Princeton: Princeton University Press.

Firestone, W. A., Bader, B. D., Massel, D., and Rosenblum, S. (1992). "Recent Trends in State Educational Reform: Assessment and Prospects." *Teachers College Record*, 94(2), 254–277.

Fischer, H. (January 9, 1993). "Coalition Seeks to Get 15 Initiatives on Ballot." *Arizona Daily Star.*

Fla. Stat. Title XLVII §1002.33 (2006).

Freeman, D. and Freeman, Y. (1988). *Sheltered English Instruction* (ERIC Digest ED301070). Washington, DC: ERIC Clearinghouse on Languages and Linguistics. Retrieved July 2008, http://www.ericdigests.org/pre-9210/english.htm.

Fusarelli, L. (2001). "The Political Construction of Accountability: Where Rhetoric Meets Reality." *Education and Urban Society*, 33(2), 157–169.

Gallagher, C. (2000). "A Seat at the Table." *Phi Delta Kappan*, 81(7): 502–507.

Gardner, L. (1997). *Navigating Through the Standards Maze, Making Charters Work: Strategies for Charter School Developers.* Sacramento: Charter School Development Center.

———. (2001). *Designed to Align: The Latest Updates on the State Standards and Assessments.* Sacramento: Charter School Development Center.

Garn, G. (1999). "Solving the Policy Implementation Problem: The Case of Arizona Charter Schools." *Education Policy Analysis Archives*, 7(26).

Garn, G. and Cobb, C. (2001). "A Framework for Understanding Charter School Accountability." *Education and Urban Society*, 33(2), 113–129.

Geary Public Schools Task Force. (1978). *Moving Forward: New Directions for the Geary Unified School District.* Geary City: Author.

Geary Unified School District. (1992). *Shared Decision-Making Task Force Report.* Geary City: Author.

———. (2000). *Shared Decision-Making Handbook* (Draft). Geary City: Author.

Gerber, E. R. (1998). *Interest Group Influence in the California Initiative Process.* San Francisco: Public Policy Institute of California.

Gewertz, C. (November 1, 2005). "New Orleans Board Backs Charters as Governor Calls for Stepped-up State Role." *Education Week.*

Glass, G. V. (2008). *Fertilizers, Pills and Magnetic Strips: The Fate of Public Education in America.* Charlotte, NC: Information Age Publishing.

Glass, G. V. and Matthews, D. A. (1991). "Are Data Enough?" *Educational Researcher*, 20(3), 24–27.

Gotanda, N. (1991). "A Critique of Our Constitution as Colorblind." *Stanford Law Review*, 44(1), 1–66.

Grant, G. and Murray, C. (1999). *Teaching in America: The Slow Revolution.* Cambridge, MA: Harvard University Press.

Greene, M. (1995). *Releasing the Imagination: Essays on Education, the Arts, and Social Change.* San Francisco: Jossey-Bass.

Gunnison, R. B. and Lucas, G. (1994, June 18). "What's in the CLAS That Infuriates Its Critics?" *Los Angeles Times*, A1.

Gusfield, J. R. (1981). *The Culture of Public Problems: Drinking, Driving and the Symbolic Order.* Chicago: University of Chicago Press.

Hannan, M. T. and Freeman, J. (1989). *Organizational Ecology.* Cambridge, MA: Harvard University Press.

Hannaway, J. (1993). "Political Pressure and Decentralization in Institutional Organizations: The Case of School Districts." *Sociology of Education*, 66, 147–163.

Hart, G. K. (November 4, 1993). "Dubious Proposition was a Wake-up Call." *Los Angeles Times*, B7.

Hart, G. K. and Burr, S. (1996). "The Story of California's Charter School Legislation." *Phi Delta Kappan*, 78(1), 37–40.

Hartley, M. (1999). "A Voice from the State Legislature: Don't Do What Arizona Did." In R. Maranto, S. Millman, F. Hess, and A. Gresham (Eds.), *School Choice in the Real World: Lessons from Arizona Charter Schools* (198–211). Boulder, CO: Westview Press.

Hassell, B. (1999). *The Charter School Challenge: Avoiding the Pitfalls, Fulfilling the Promise.* Washington, DC: Brookings Institution Press.

Hearts and Hands Community School. (1993). *Hearts and Hands Community School Charter.* Geary City: Author.

———. (1998). *Hearts and Hands Community School Charter.* Geary City: Author.

Heise, M., Colburn, K. D., and Lamberti, J. F. (1995). "Private Vouchers in Indianapolis: The Golden Rule Program." In T. M. Moe (Ed.), *Private Vouchers* (110–119). Stanford, CA: Hoover Institution Press.

Helfand, D. (December 10, 1998). "Education Board Expected to OK Phonics Rules." *Los Angeles Times*, A1.

Henig, J. (1989–1990). "Privatization in the United States: Theory and Practice." *Political Science Quarterly*, 104(4), 649–670.

———. (1994). *Rethinking School Choice: The Limits of the Market Metaphor.* Princeton, NY: Princeton University Press.

Hess, F. M. (2001). "Whaddya Mean You Want to Close My School: The Politics of Regulatory Accountability in Charter Schooling." *Education and Urban Society*, 33(2), 141–156.

Hill, P., Lake, R. J., and Cielo, M. B. (2002). *Charter Schools and Accountability in Public Education.* Washington, DC: Brookings Institution Press.

Hilltop Charter School. (1998). School Charter. Geary City: Author.

Honig, B. (1989). *The New California Schools* (Vol. VII, No. 1). Sacramento: California State Department of Education.

Horsley, L. (February 19, 1995). "Progress in Case Leaves Questions." *Kansas City Star*, A1.

Ingersoll, R. (2001). "Teacher Turnover and Teacher Shortages: An Organizational Analysis." *American Educational Research Journal*, 38(3), 499–534.

Inspirational School (1997). *Inspiration School School Charter*. Geary City: Educational Enterprise Corporation.

Jacob, B. (2001). "Implementing Standards: The California Mathematics Textbook Debacle." *Phi Delta Kappan*, 83, 264–272.

Johnson, S. M. (1990). *Teachers at Work: Achieving Success in Our Schools*. New York: Basic Books.

Johnson, S. M., and Landman, J. (2000). "Sometimes Bureaucracy Has Its Charms: The Working Conditions of Teachers in Deregulated Schools." *Teachers College Record*, 102(1), 85–124.

Jensen, T. (1991a). *A Modest Proposal*. Geary City: Author.

———. (1991b). *Memorandum*. Geary City: Author.

Katznelson, I. (2005). *When Affirmative Action Was White*. New York: W. W. Norton and Company.

Keegan, L. G. (1999). "The Empowerment of Market-based Reform." In R. Maranto, S. Millman, F. Hess, and A. Gresham (Eds.), *School Choice in the Real World: Lessons from Arizona Charter Schools* (189–197). Boulder, CO: Westview Press.

Kerchner, C. T. and Menefee-Libey, D. (2003). "Accountability at the Improv: Brief Sketches of School Reform in Los Angeles." In J. G. Cibulka and W. Lowe (Eds.), *A Race against Time: The Crisis in Urban Schooling* (3–22). Westport, CT: Praeger.

Kimble, J. (2007). "Insuring Inequality: The Role of the Federal Housing Administration in the Urban Ghettoization of African Americans." *Law and Social Inquiry*, 32(2), 399–434.

Kingsley, J. W. (1993). *Charter Schools*. Sacramento: California Department of Education.

Kirst, M. (1990). *Accountability: Implications for State and Local Policymakers*. Washington, DC: Office of Educational Research and Improvement.

Kirst, M. W. (1992). "The State Role in School Restructuring." In C. E. Finn and T. Rebarber (Eds.), *Education Reform in the '90s* (77–105). New York: Macmillan Publishing Company.

———. (2002). "Swing State." *Education Next*, 2(2), 44–49.

LaPierre, D. B. (1987). "Voluntary Interdistrict School Desegregation in St. Louis: The Special Master's Tale." *Wisconsin Law Review*, 1987(6), 971–1040.

Lemann, N. (1997). "The Reading Wars in California." *The Atlantic*, 280(5), 128–134. March, J. G., and Olsen, J. P. (1986). *Rediscovering Institutions: The Organizational Basis of Politics*. New York: Free Press.

Levin, H. M. (1974). "A Conceptual Framework for Accountability." *School Review*, 82(3), 363–391.

Lewis, A. (2003). *Race in the School Yard*. New Brunswick: Rutgers University Press.

Lipsitz, G. (1998). *The Possessive Investment in Whiteness: How White People Profit from Identity Politics*. Philadelphia: Temple University Press.

Little Hoover Commission. (1996). *The Charter Movement: Education Reform School by School*. Sacramento: Author.

Loeb, S., Darling-Hammond, L., and Luczak, J. (2005). "How Teaching Conditions Predict Teacher Turnover in California Schools." *Peabody Journal of Education*, 80(3), 44–70.

Lopez, A., Wells, A. S., and Holme, J. J. (2002). "Creating Charter School Communities: Identity Building, Diversity and Selectivity." In A. S. Wells (Ed.), *When Charter School Policy Fails: The Problems of Accountability and Equity* (129–158). New York: Teachers College Press.

Lowe, R. and Whipp, J. (2002). "Examining the Milwaukee Parental Choice Program: Options or Opportunities?" *Educational Researcher*, 31(1), 33–39.

Lubienski, C. (2003). "Innovation in Education Markets: Theory and Evidence on the Impact of Competition and Choice in Charter Schools." *American Educational Research Journal*, 40(2), 395–443.

MacGuire, K. (1990). "Business Involvement in the 1990s." In D. E. Mitchell and M. E. Goertz (Eds.), *Education Politics for the New Century* (107–117). London: Falmer Press.

March, J. G. and Olsen, J. P. (1986). *Rediscovering Institutions: The Organizational Basis of Politics*. New York: Free Press.

Marks, H. M. and Louis, K. S. (1997). "Does Teacher Empowerment Affect the Classroom: The Implications of Teacher Empowerment for Instructional Practice and Student Academic Performance." *Educational Evaluation and Policy Analysis*, 19(3), 245–275.

Martinez, V., Godwin, K., and Kemerer, F. R. (1995). "Private Vouchers in San Antonio: The CEO program." In T. M. Moe (Ed.), *Private Vouchers* (74–99). Stanford, CA: Hoover Institution Press.

McDermott, R. and Varenne, H. (1995). "Culture as Disability." *Anthropology and Education Quarterly*, 26, 324–348.

McDonnell, L. M. (1997). *The Politics of State Testing: Implementing New Student Assessments* (CSE technical report 424). Los Angeles: National Center for Research on Evaluation, Standards, and Student Testing (CRESST).

Mealy, N. (1997). "Going Public: Schools Weigh the Waldorf Alternative." *California Schools* (Winter), 34.

Mehan, H. B. (1997). "The Discourse of the Illegal Immigration Debate: A Case Study in the Politics of Representation." *Discourse and Society*, 8(2), 249–271.

Meissner, S. (July 28, 1992). "Rep. Pickens Assails Plan for School Voucher System." *Arizona Daily Star*.

Mendel, E. (September 1, 1997). "California to Spend a Lot More on Schools, but..." *San Diego Union Tribune*, A4.

Merl, J. (December 16, 1992). "Test Scores Slip for Students after an Era of Gains." *Los Angeles Times*, A1.

———. (August 3, 1994). "Problems Undercut Debut of CLAS Tests, Panel ays." *Los Angeles Times*, A1.

Merl, J. and Ingram, C. (September 28, 1994). "Wilson Ends Controversial Student Testing Program with Veto." *Los Angeles Times*, A1.

Meyer, J. (1977). "The Effects of Education as an Institution." *American Journal of Sociology*, 83(1), 55–77.

Meyer, J. W., Scott, W. R., Strang, D., and Creighton, A. L. (1988). "Bureaucratization Without Centralization: Changes in the Organizational System of U.S. Public Education." In L. G. Zucker (Ed.), *Institutional Patterns and Organizations*. Cambridge, MA: Ballinger Publishing Company.

Michigan Department of Education (2005). Michigan Public School Academies (Charter Schools) *Questions and Answers*. Lansing, MI: Author.

Mich. Rev. School Code, Act 451 of 1976 (2006).

Mitchell, D. (1986). State education policy in California. *Peabody Journal of Education, 63*(4), 90–99.

Moe, T. M. (1991). *School Reform in Arizona: An Assessment of the Final Report of the Governor's Task Force on Educational Reform*. Phoenix: Goldwater Institute.

———. (1995). "Private Vouchers." In T. M. Moe (Ed.), *Private vouchers* (1–40). Stanford, CA: Hoover Institution Press.

"Moment of choice." (January 5, 2000). *Wall Street Journal*, A22.

Morain, D. (1993, October 10). "Voucher Concept Has Come a Long Way." *Los Angeles Times*, A3, A36.

———. (April 16, 1998). "Making of a Ballot Initiative." *Los Angeles Times*, A1.

Moran, P. W. (2005). "Too Little, Too Late: The Illusive Goal of School Desegregation in Kansas City, Missouri, and the Role of the Federal Government." *Teachers College Record*, 107(9), 1933–1955.

Morantz, A. (1996). "Money and Choice in Kansas City: Major Investments with Modest Returns." In G. Orfield and S. Eaton (Eds.), *Dismantling Desegregation: The Quiet Reversal of Brown v. Board of Education* (241–264). New York: Free Press.

Mueller, P. (1998). "Teacher Authority and Influence in Schools: Exploring the Dynamics of Professional and Community Power Relations in Local School Governance in Chicago." Unpublished Doctoral Dissertation: Harvard University Graduate School of Education.

Mulholland, L. and Amsler, M. (1992). *Charter Schools* (Policy Briefs 19). San Francisco: Far West Regional Laboratories.

Murphy, J. (1992). "Restructuring America's Schools: An Overview." In C. E. Finn and T. Rebarber (Eds.), *Education Reform in the '90s*. New York: Macmillan Publishing Company.

Nathan, J. (1996). *Charter Schools: Creating Hope and Opportunity for American Education*. San Francisco: Jossey-Bass.

National Center for Education Statistics. (2000). SASS & PSS Questionnaires, 1999–2000. Washington, DC: United States Department of Education.

National Commission on Excellence in Education. (1983). *A Nation at Risk*. Washington, DC: Government Printing Office.

National Conference of State Legislators. (n.d.). *Publicly Funded School Voucher Programs*. Retrieved August 30, 2008, from http://www.ncsl.org/programs/educ/schoolchoicevoucherprog.htm.

Newmann, F. M. and Associates. (1996). *Authentic Achievement: Restructuring Schools for Intellectual Quality*. San Franscisco: Jossey-Bass.

Newmann, F. M., King, M. B., and Rigdon, M. (1997). "Accountability and School Performance: Implications from Restructuring Schools." *Harvard Educational Review*, 67(1), 41–74.

No Child Left Behind. (2002). Public Law, 107–110.

Olsen, L., Chang, H., Salazar, D. D. L. R., Leong, C., Perez, Z. M., McClain, G., and Raffel, L. (1994). *The Unfinished Journey: Restructuring Schools in a Diverse Society*. San Francisco: California Tomorrow.

Pfeffer, J. and Salancik, G. R. (1978). *The External Control of Organizations: A Resource Dependence Perspective*. New York: Harper and Row.

Pierre, J. (1995). "The Marketization of the State: Citizens, Consumers, and the Emergence of the Public Market." In B. G. Peters and D. J. Savoie (Eds.), *Governance in a Changing Environment* (55–81). Montreal: McGill University Press.

Powers, J. M. (2004). "High Stakes Accountability and Equity: Using Evidence from California's Public Schools Accountability Act to Address the Issues in *Williams v. State of California*." *American Educational Research Journal*, 41(4): 763–795.

———. (March 3, 2004). "Increasing Equity and Increasing School Performance—Conflicting or Compatible Goals?: Addressing the Issues in *Williams v. State of California*." *Education Policy Analysis Archives*, 12(10).

Powers, J. M. and Cookson, P. W. (August 1999). "To School, to Market: Visions of the Market and the Reconstruction of American Education." Paper presented at the American Sociological Association Annual Meeting, Chicago, IL.

Powers, J. M. and Cookson, P. W. J. (1999). "The Politics of School Choice Research: Fact, Fiction and Statistics." *Educational Policy*, 13(1), 104–122.

Premack, E. (1997). *California Charter Law Changes from 1996 Legislative Session*. Sacramento: CSU Institute for Education Reform.

———. (1998). *California's Revised Charter School's Act: Draft #2*. Sacramento: CSU Institute for Education Reform.

Premack, E. and Diamond, L. (1994). *Charter School Implementation Challenges*. Berkeley: B. W. Associates.

Price, H. B. (December 8, 1999). Urban Education: A Radical Plan. *Education Week*, 29, 44.

Rao, H. (1998). "Caveat Emptor: The Construction of Nonprofit Consumer Watchdog Organizations." *American Journal of Sociology*, 103(4), 912–961.

Rasell, E. and Rothstein, R. (1993). *School Choice: Examining the Evidence*. Washington, DC: Economic Policy Institute.

Ravich, D. (February 26, 1993). "Honig Legacy Outlives Conviction." *Los Angeles Times*, B7.

Raywid, M. A. (1990). "Rethinking School Governance." In R. F. Elmore (Ed.), *Restructuring Schools* (152–205). San Francisco: Jossey-Bass.

Research Team. (1996). Hearts and Hands Community School Research Report. San Francisco: Author.

Richter, P. (April 19, 1991). "Bush Details Sweeping Plan to 'Reinvent' U.S. Education." *Los Angeles Times*, A1.

Robelen, E. W. (November 22, 2005). "LA Lawmakers OK Plan to Give State Control of Most New Orleans Schools." *Education Week*.

Rosenholtz, S. (1989). *Teachers' Workplace: The Social Organization of Schools*. New York: Longman.

RPP International. (1997). *A Study of Charter Schools: First-Year Report*. Washington, DC: Office of Educational Research and Improvement, Department of Education.

RPP International. (1998). *A National Study of Charter Schools: Second-Year Report*. Washington, DC: Office of Educational Research and Improvement, Department of Education.

————. (1999). *The State of Charter Schools, Third-Year Report: National Study of Charter Schools*. Washington, DC: Office of Educational Research and Improvement, Department of Education.

————. (2000). *The State of Charter Schools: 2000*. Washington, DC: Office of Educational Research and Improvement, Department of Education.

Ruenzel, D. (June 20, 20001). "The Spirit of Waldorf Education." *Education Week*.

Sarason, S. (1972). *The Culture of the School and the Problem of Change*. Boston, MA: Allyn and Bacon.

Scott, W. R. and Meyer, J. (1991). "The Organization of Societal Sectors." In W. W. Powell and P. J. DiMaggio (Eds.), *The New Institutionalism in Organizational Analysis* (108–140). Chicago: University of Chicago Press.

Selznick, P. (1948). "Foundations of a Theory of Organization." *American Sociological Review*, 13, 25–35.

Shen, J. (1997). "Teacher Retention and Attrition in Public Schools: Evidence from Sass91." *The Journal of Educational Research*, 91(2), 81–90.

————. (2001). "Teacher and Principal Empowerment: National, Longitudinal, and Comparative Perspectives." *Educational Horizons*, 79(3), 124–129.

Simpson, C. H. and Rosenholtz, S. J. (1986). "Classroom Structure and the Social Construction of Ability." In J. G. Richardson (Ed.), *Handbook of Theory and Research for the Sociology of Education*. New York: Greenwood Press.

Simon, M. (May 5, 1998). "School Bill A Big Win for TechNet." *San Francisco Chronicle*, A15.

Slayton, J. (2002). "Public Funds for California Charter Schools: Where Local Context and Savvy Meet Formula." In A. S. Wells (Ed.), *Where Charter School Policy Fails: The Problems of Accountability and Equity* (77–101). New York: Teachers College Press.

Smith, K. B. and Meier, K. J. (1995). *The Case Against School Choice: Politics, Markets and Fools*. Armonk, NY: M.E. Sharpe.

Stambach, A. and Becker, N. C. (2006). Finding the Old in the New: On Race and Class in the US Charter School Debates. *Race, Ethnicity and Education*, 9(2), 159–182.

Starr, P. (1989). "The Meaning of Privatization." In A. Kahn and S. Kamerman (Eds.), *Privatization and the Welfare State* (15–48). Princeton, NJ: Princeton University Press.

Stein, Loren. (July 11, 1995). "Reading, Writing, and Phonics Coming Back to California Schools." *Christian Science Monitor*.

Stinchcombe, A. L. (1965). "Social Structure and Organizations." In J. G. March (Ed.), *Handbook of Organizations* (972–1022). Chicago: Rand McNally College Publishing Company.

Stossell, J. (2006). "Stupid in America: How Lack of Choice Cheats Our Kids Out of a Good Education." *20/20*. Retrieved August 24, 2008, http://abcnews.go.com/2020/Stossel/story?id=2383857&page=1.

Swidler, A. (1986). "Culture in Action: Symbols and Strategies." *American Sociological Review*, 51, 273–286.

Syverson, M. A. (n.d). *California Learning Record*. El Cajon: Center for Language in Learning.

Talbert, J. E., McLaughlin, M. W., and Rowan, B. (1993). "Understanding Context Effects on Secondary School Teaching." *Teachers College Record*, 95(1), 45–67.

Tex. Stat. Educ. Code §12.001 (2006).

Timar, T. B. (1990). "The Politics of School Restructuring." In D. E. Mitchell and M. E. Goertz (Eds.), *Education Politics for the New Century* (55–74). London: Falmer Press.

Timar, T. B. and Kirp, D. L. (1988). *Managing Educational Excellence*. New York: Falmer Press.

Timmons-Brown, S. and Hess, F. (1999). "Why Arizona Embarked on School Reform (and Nevada did not)." In R. Maranto, S. Millman, F. Hess, and A. Gresham (Eds.), *School Choice in the Real World: Lessons from Arizona Charter Schools* (115–128). Boulder, CO: Westview Press.

Toch, T. (1991). *In the Name of Excellence*. Oxford: Oxford University Press.

Tuckman, B. W. ([1968]2001). "Developmental Sequence in Small Groups." *Group Facilitation*, (3), 66–81.

Tyack, D. (1990). "Restructuring in Historical Perspective: Tinkering Toward Utopia." *Teachers College Record*, 92(2), 170–191.

Tyack, D. and Cuban, L. (1995). *Tinkering Toward Utopia: A Century of Public School Reform*. Cambridge, MA: Harvard University Press.

Uhrmacher, P. B. (1995). "Uncommon Schooling: A Historical Look at Rudolf Steiner, Anthroposophy, and Waldorf Education." *Curriculum Inquiry*, 25(4), 381–406.

Varenne, H. and McDermott, R. (1998). *Successful Failure: The School America Builds*. Boulder: Westview Press.

Weick, K. E. (1976). "Educational Organizations as Loosely Coupled Systems." *Administrative Science Quarterly*, 21, 1–19.

Wells, A. S. and Crain, R. (1997). *Stepping Over the Color Line*. New Haven: Yale University Press.

Wells, A. S. and Oakes, J. (1998). "Tracking, Detracking, and the Politics of Educational Reform: A Sociological Perspective." In C. A. Torres and T. R. Mitchell (Eds.), *The Sociology of Education: Emerging Perspectives*. Albany: State University of New York Press.

Wells, A. S., Artiles, L., Carnochan, S., Cooper, C. W., Grutzik, C., Holme, J. J., et al. (1998). *Beyond the Rhetoric of Charter School Reform: A Study of Ten California School Districts*. Los Angeles: UCLA.

Wells, A. S., Vasuveda, A., Holme, J. J., and Cooper, C. W. (2002). "The Politics of Accountability: California School Districts and Charter School Reform." In A. S. Wells (Ed.), *Where Charter School Policy Fails: The Problems of Accountability and Equity* (29–53). New York: Teachers College Press.

West, P. (October 14, 1992). "School-Desegregation Plans at Iissue in Missouri Races." *Education Week*.

Wong, K. K. and Shen, F. X. (2002). "Politics of State-Led Reform in Education: Market Competition and Electoral Dynamics." *Educational Policy*, 16(1), 161–193.

Woo, E. (May 26, 1988). "Business Group Presents Plan to Overhaul, Bolster Public Schools." *Los Angeles Times*, 26.

INDEX